Charles Spencer March Phillipps



# JURISPRUDENCE

Elibron Classics
www.elibron.com

Elibron Classics series.



ISBN 0-543-97850-8 (paperback)
ISBN 0-543-97849-4 (hardcover)

This Elibron Classics book contains the complete text of the edition published in 1863 by John Murray, London.

# JURISPRUDENCE

## I. Definition of Jurisprudence

The word Jurisprudence will be used throughout the present Treatise to signify the science which teaches us to analyse and classify the rules of Justice. Justice is meant the due observance of Rights, and a Right is said to exist whenever one human being is morally entitled, in the opinion of the person speaking, to prevent or to compel, for his own benefit, the commission of a certain act by another. An act done or omitted in contradiction to an existing Right is a Wrong, and the habit of committing Wrongs is termed Injustice.

These definitions ought to be sufficient for the purpose of the present work, but no one who is acquainted with any branch of Moral Science will be surprised that I do not consider them likely to prove so. The Moralist, unlike the Physicist, is compelled to work with instruments which have been blunted by common use. His terms of art are already well known to his readers, some in a loose and popular and some in a narrow and technical, but all in some sense or other which is not precisely that, whatever it may be, in which he intends to use them. He will therefore perpetually fail to convey his true meaning, unless he can prevail upon the student to remember that words which he has been using all his life in one sense are now being used and reasoned upon in another. No mere positive statement is likely to be sufficient for this purpose. It is only by minutely specifying the distinctions between the various meanings which the word in question bears commonly and the particular meaning which it is to bear now, that the familiar sound can be prevented from bringing with it the familiar association.

It must moreover be remembered that every writer upon moral subjects, or upon subjects connected with Morality, is bound under peculiarly heavy penalties to make himself clearly understood. If he fails to do so, he runs the risk of being considered, not merely as a man who has undertaken to teach what he knows nothing about, but as a man who is endeavouring to teach what will injure and degrade human society. In the present work I shall frequently find it necessary to inquire how far certain acts, which all men justly regard as disgraceful and immoral, belong to that class of immoral acts which it is the duty of human Legislation to prohibit. It does not require the example of the great Spanish Casuists to show how easily and how fatally such speculations may be misunderstood. I therefore think it unnecessary to apologize for doing all that I can to make misunderstanding impossible.

I must first point out that, in defining Jurisprudence as the science which teaches us to analyse and classify the rules of Justice, I mean distinctly to exclude the idea that Jurisprudence teaches us, or can possibly teach us, what the rules of Justice *are.* Justice itself is an instinct, not a science. Its first principles must be taught by the conscience, not by the intellect, and they are often most thoroughly felt and comprehended by men utterly incapable of tracing their remote consequences, or of applying them to any intricate combination of facts. The virtuous simplicity of an honest bigot like Clarkson, or of a religious visionary like Sharpe, rejects with abhorrence the sophistry which has deluded the practised acumen of Jurists like Eldon and Stowell. Jurisprudence, in short, is to Justice what Language is to Thought. The scientific philologist may only talk grammatical nonsense, and true eloquence or poetry has sometimes been expressed in the rude dialect of peasants or barbarians.

What I consider to be the true principles of Justice will appear hereafter. But it would, in the mean time, be a great mistake to suppose that a perfectly scientific system of Jurisprudence may not be constructed upon the basis of any Jural principles whatever. There is no Custom or Statute so arbitrary, no Code so absurd or so atrocious, as not to allow full play to the ingenuity of the Jurist in developing its true objects and in reconciling its casual inconsistencies. The intellectual process by which a system is deduced from a principle no more depends upon the moral rectitude of the principle, than the skill with which the mariner trims his sails depends upon the direction of the wind. In fact it may be plausibly maintained that, as the science of the engineer is most conspicuous when he has to accommodate his road or his canal to the difficulties of a mountainous district, so the science of the Legislator is most conspicuous when he has to construct his system upon the harsh or absurd enactments of an uncivilized age Gaius and Tribonian displayed eminent skill and precision in working out the regulations of domestic Slavery, and there are few more beautiful specimens of judicial ingenuity than the series of decisions in which the English Courts of Equity have interwoven the barbarous feudal Law of Succession with the admirable Roman theory of Personal Obligation.

Every human accomplishment may be used either for good or for evil purposes, and consequently no human science is in its nature either moral or immoral. The teacher of a science cannot therefore be blamed for the manner of its application, and ought not to pretend that it is incapable of misapplication. I should have thought it waste of time to point out the absurdity of a principle which would make fencing-masters responsible for the practice of duelling, if English society had not already suffered so much from a similar error. The professors of Political Economy have demonstrated the unwelcome truth, that cases often arise in which a community must choose between the indulgence of benevolent feeling and the attainment of the highest possible material prosperity. Which ought to be preferred, they leave to every man's conscience. The consequence is that Political Economy has been pronounced a diabolical study, which teaches that wealth is the sole end of life and that selfishness is the sole means of wealth. Such is the effect of an over confident reliance upon common sense and common candour.

The distinction between the intellectual science and the moral principle, between the machine and the material, being now clearly understood, I proceed to distinguish the science of Jurisprudence, properly so called, from certain other sciences with which it is closely connected. There are in particular two great intellectual regions of which Jurisprudence ought to be considered as forming a common province, but with each of which it is sometimes spoken of as wholly commensurate. Both mistakes have, in my opinion, arisen from the loose and inaccurate meaning which is apt to be attributed to the word Rights. That word is very commonly interpreted either as correlative to the word Duties, or as synonymous with the word Remedies. The former fallacy has led to the confusion between Jurisprudence and Morality, the latter to the confusion between Jurisprudence and Legislation.

## II. Jurisprudence and Morality

Morality is the science which teaches us to analyse the rules of Right. The word Right, when used indefinitely in the singular number, signifies the observance of Duty, and a Duty is said to exist whenever a human being is morally bound, in the opinion of the person speaking, to do or not to do a particular act. An act done or omitted in contradiction to a Duty is said to be Wrong, and the habit of doing Wrong is termed Immorality.

It is manifest from these definitions that the science of Morality comprises that of Jurisprudence. The man who thinks that he is morally entitled to make me do a certain act, can scarcely help thinking that I am morally bound to do it. In other words, every Right has a correlative Duty and all Injustice is Wrong. But it is equally manifest that Morality comprises many rules with which Jurisprudence has no concern, and that there are many Duties which have no correlative Rights. These unilateral Duties are distinguished by the Casuists as Aptitudes. Their observance is termed Virtue, and the science which teaches us to define the rules of Virtue is known by the name of Casuistry. An act done or omitted in contradiction to an Aptitude is termed a Sin, and the habit of committing Sins is denominated Vice.

In order to perceive how closely the sciences of Casuistry and Jurisprudence are interwoven with each other, yet how clearly and accurately they may be distinguished, we have only to compare the definition of Rights with that of Duties. A Right is the relation which exists between two human beings, one of whom is morally justified in controlling, for his own benefit, the volition of the other. It is therefore a relation consisting of two distinct elements, an Authority and an Interest. In the absence of either, a Right cannot be said to exist. If I am morally bound, but not justly compellable, to do a certain act for the benefit of another, the relation between us confers no Right upon him, because he has an Interest without any Authority. If I am morally justified in compelling, but not for my own benefit, the performance of a certain act by another, the relation between us confers no Right upon me, because I have an Authority without any Interest.

Now a Duty is the situation of a human being who is morally bound to act in a certain manner. It may be of such a nature that some other person is entitled to insist upon its fulfilment for his own benefit, and in this case it clearly confers upon that person a correlative Right. It may be of such a nature that no human being can possibly compel, or can expect the slightest benefit from, its fulfilment, and in this case it is clearly nothing more than an Aptitude or precept of Conscience. But there is a large intermediate class. There are Duties whose fulfilment no man is morally entitled to compel, yet which cannot be fulfilled by one man without conferring a benefit upon some other. There are also Duties whose fulfilment can confer no benefit upon any man but the agent, yet whose breach all men are, in certain cases, morally entitled to prevent. In other words, there are Beneficial Duties which create an Interest without an Authority, and Compulsory Duties which create an Authority without an Interest. In both these cases there is the appearance, but not the reality, of a correlative Right.

In the whole history of Jural thought, there is nothing more remarkable than the inveterate confusion which has been permitted to exist between Rights and Beneficial Duties. It is perhaps most conspicuous in the attempts which have been made to define the degree of Good Faith required in transactions between one human being and another. The inability of the most eminent Jurists, both English and foreign, to explain this very simple question must, to any man of plain sense, appear perfectly marvellous. They acknowledge that there are many cases of unconscientious dealing which no Court of Justice can reasonably censure. But the obvious test, which distinguishes what every man ought to be compelled to do from what every man of scrupulous probity holds himself bound to do, never seems to strike them. They are satisfied to leave the definition of Fraud a mere question of degree, and to tell us, in a cloudy plenitude of phrase, that moral rectitude ought to be strictly enforced, except when it happens to be very difficult or very inconvenient to enforce it.

The true distinction is one which, in the ordinary affairs of life, no man of sense and honour has any difficulty in applying. It consists in the simple principle, that the measure of my Rights is not what Conscience binds you to do for me, but what it allows me to require from you. There are cases in which I am bound in honour to offer what you are bound in honour not to accept. An honourable Contractor will not refuse to perform an improvident bargain, but an honourable Contractee will not insist upon its performance. There are other cases in which I am bound to offer what you are at liberty to accept, but what you cannot justifiably demand. Dives is guilty of a Sin if he refuses to relieve Lazarus, but Lazarus is guilty of a Crime if he extorts relief from Dives. Moral Duty and moral Authority must correspond, in order to constitute a Right.

The distinction between Rights and Compulsory Duties, though practically less important, is theoretically more difficult. That there are Duties which confer no correlative Right, yet whose fulfilment may justifiably be compelled, will scarcely be disputed. The common dogma, that the Right of compulsory Legislation rests simply upon the Right of Self-defence, does not cover the whole truth. No moralist can safely deny that cases may be put, in which the stronger and wiser man would clearly be bound in conscience to protect the weaker against his own folly. It would be impossible to maintain that the control exercised over an Infant or a Lunatic is limited, or ought to be limited, by the extent to which other persons are likely to suffer from his indiscretion. And few Englishmen are dissatisfied with the Laws which make it penal to attempt suicide, to inflict wanton torture upon irrational animals, or to imitate the hateful caprices of Oriental sensuality.

But to all these instances of interference the same principle applies. They are grounded upon Philanthropy, not upon Justice. Their object is the welfare of the person whose action is controlled, not that of the person by whom the control is exercised. The Chancellor, when arranging how an Infant shall be educated or how his property shall be invested, acts in a character altogether different from that in which he decides how far an Infant is competent to bind himself by Contract or his heirs by Will. The policeman who forcibly prevents an outcast from jumping into the Thames interferes with an authority altogether different from that by which he forcibly prevents one passenger from assaulting another. With such cases the science of Jurisprudence has nothing to do. The lawgiver who prohibits a particular act, not because it is unjust to an individual or hurtful to the community, but because it is pernicious to the agent himself, may or may not be acting rightly and wisely, but he is certainly not acting upon the principles of Right as between man and man.

The question, whether a given act has been prohibited for the benefit of the agent or for that of society, must of course depend upon the actual intention of the Legislature, and is therefore a question of fact. Many instances might be given, in which very similar restraints have been enacted from very different motives. The Conventicle Acts of Charles II., for example, may be considered to have formed a part of English Jurisprudence, because they were dictated by the belief, however absurd, that the public exercise of the Presbyterian religion was inconsistent with the peace and safety of the realm. But the Ordinances of Louis XIV against heresy formed no part of French Jurisprudence. They were simply the act of a despot, who thought it his duty to force his subjects, for their own future welfare, into his own Church. So the Maine Temperance Law belongs to American Jurisprudence, because it proceeds upon the assumptions, however extravagant, that every man who drinks spirits is destroying his health and intellect and that every man who destroys his health and intellect commits an offence against Society. But the Laws of the New England Puritans against maypoles and love-locks stood upon a different principle. They arose from the conviction that such vanities were displeasing to God, and therefore ought not to be tolerated by man.

## III. Jurisprudence and Legislation

The word Legislation, when used as the name of an intellectual study and not of an external act, signifies the science which teaches us to define and classify the rules of Legality. Legality is the observance of Law, and by Law is meant any permanent rule of action, prescribed, with the intention of compelling obedience or of punishing disobedience, by one human being to another. An act done in contradiction to the rules of Law is said to be Illegal, and the power of preventing or punishing an illegal act, by appealing to an authority appointed by the Law for that purpose, is termed a Legal Remedy.

Here again it is obvious that the science of Jurisprudence is wholly contained within that of Legislation, but that the science of Legislation contains much which does not properly belong to that of Jurisprudence. Every system of Law is, or professes to be, founded upon some theory or other of Justice, and therefore Jurisprudence may be considered as the real or ostensible basis of all Legislation. But there are some indispensable portions of every legal structure which do not and cannot rest upon this foundation. Every such structure must necessarily contain, not merely Jural Law or rules for ascertaining the mutual Rights of its subjects, but Remedial Law or rules for protecting the practical enjoyment of those Rights. In fact, the Remedial is perhaps more absolutely indispensable than the Jural element. A Legislator may often leave questions of Right to the discretion of the magistrate, but he cannot, without authorizing perpetual fraud and oppression, leave forms of Remedy to the discretion of the suitor. Remedial Law is therefore a most important part of the science of Legislation, but it does not properly belong to that of Jurisprudence.

Take for example that vast and complicated system which is termed the Law of Procedure. That law is indeed a science in itself, and a science of the highest importance. To what tribunal the suitor is to apply, in what form he must state his case, by what mode of trial the issue is to be decided, by what process the sentence is to be executed, are questions of the utmost consequence to every member of the community. But they are questions which depend upon practical expediency, not upon abstract justice, and which must be solved, not by deductive reasoning from general principles, but by actual experiment. Nor can their solution be either uniform or permanent. The essential rules of Justice are the same now and for ever. But the rules by which Justice is executed are right when they succeed in their object, and wrong when they fail in it. And it is obvious that the same forms of procedure which are found faultless in the Courts of one age or nation, might become shamefully oppressive in those of another.

Closely connected with the Law of Procedure is the Law of Evidence. Every question of Right must be decided by the application of Principles to Facts, and there are many cases in which, from the imperfection of human testimony and judgment, the Facts cannot be clearly ascertained. This is of course particularly likely to happen in questions of Right which more or less depend upon the mental situation of the parties to a given transaction, and therefore, in order to simplify such questions as much as possible, most Legislatures have laid down certain arbitrary rules upon the subject of moral Evidence, whose object is to substitute reasonable Probability for unsatisfactory Proof. This is usually effected by fixing certain definite Presumptions where the moral fact to be proved is Motive, and by requiring certain definite Forms where the moral fact to be proved is Intention. The Laws which presume Maturity at a certain age, and Dereliction after a certain interval, are examples of the first kind. The Laws which require certain Contracts to be proved by written evidence, and certain Gifts to be attested by one or more witnesses, are examples of the second. But it is obvious that all such regulations are founded upon calculations of Expediency, and consequently that the Law of Evidence does not properly belong to the science of Jurisprudence.

The same reasoning may be applied to the great science of Constitutional Law. It is an instrument, not an object. The whole machinery of Legislation, the prerogatives of the Crown, the privileges of Parliament, the distribution of the Franchise, the forms of an Election, the ceremonies of an Enactment, are nothing but means to an end. They no more belong to the science of Jurisprudence than the art of shipbuilding belongs to the science of Navigation. The contrary doctrine, though long and loudly maintained, has been wholly due to political violence or to pedantic prejudice. It seems to have been originally invented by the theologians of the Caroline school. It was eagerly taken up, though in a very different sense, by those Parisian philosophers of the last century who, with characteristic attachment to theory and indifference to consequences, taught that political power is one of the inalienable Rights of man. It was copied from them by the English Radicals and Chartists of the last generation, and was, upon one memorable occasion, sanctioned by the rash declaration of certain eminent Conservative statesmen, that the Elective Franchise ought to be regarded as the property of the Elector.

The French, misled by that puerile love of superficial precision which is perhaps their worst intellectual fault, are still, with a few illustrious exceptions, unable to perceive that Political Government is purely an experimental Science. With all their dialectical skill, they have not in general arrived at the simple conclusion, that accurate reasoning upon imperfect premises must infallibly lead to inaccurate results. They are so far from appreciating the instinctive sagacity with which an English statesman makes allowance for disturbing influences whose nature he does not pretend fully to understand, that they are accustomed to deride as illogical the nation which deigns to recognise such informal elements of calculation. The consequence is, that their ordinary treatment of such subjects has hitherto been, not only practically worthless, but childishly absurd. Everyone knows the contemptuous impatience which seizes upon the educated English mind, when a French publicist commences a pamphlet upon Representative Institutions by an attempt to *poser les principes.* Such theories, to men accustomed to the practical discussions of the English Press, appear about as valuable as medieval treatises upon Hydrostatics, commencing with the dogma that Nature abhors a vacuum.

In this country the delusion may now be considered as extinct. We have learnt to look upon political institutions, not as eternal truths or as unchangeable necessities, but as indices constructed to represent, with as much precision and as little trouble as possible, the existing political influences which actually constitute the virtual will of the community. We have learnt to see that, as a perfect style is simply the true reflection of the writer's thought, so a perfect Constitution is simply the true reflection of the national volition. We therefore judge such systems entirely by their practical results. We dislike Despotism, not because it contradicts the natural Rights of man, but because it generally leads to bad Legislation and to bad Government. We dislike Democracy for precisely the same reason. Indeed, we have sometimes carried this principle too far. In our impatience of the pedantry which represents political freedom as an end, we have sometimes been tempted to forget its inestimable value as a means; a means, not only of securing national prosperity, but of forming and ripening national character.

## IV. Jurisprudence and Interpretation

But a fourth important Moral Science still remains to be distinguished; a science which, although created by Jurisprudence and confirmed by Legislation, cannot strictly be said to form a necessary part of either. Jurisprudence is the science of Justice, and Legislation is the science of Law. Justice determines what men's Legal Rights ought to be, and Law what they are. But suppose that both Justice and Law confer upon every human being, or upon every human being not disabled by special circumstances, authority to modify his own Rights by his own intentional act. In this case it is clear that a new element of inquiry has been introduced. In order to define the Rights of a given individual it may now be necessary to ascertain, not only the physical facts of the case, but the mental intention of the person or persons to whom they owe their existence. In some cases it may be possible to do this by direct evidence. But when no such evidence can be produced, or where that which is produced cannot be relied upon, it becomes necessary to infer the nature of the intention from the circumstances of the external act. In other words, it becomes necessary to Interpret the transaction.

Now the Literal Interpretation of intentional transactions cannot be considered as a Science. The intention naturally inferrible from a given act is, properly speaking, a mere question of fact. We have to inquire, first by what external signs the agent did in point of fact express his meaning, and secondly what meaning such signs are in point of fact usually understood to express. But it is evident that this mode of Interpretation will carry us but a little way. It will enable us to conjecture the intention which actually existed in the mind of the agent when he did the act. But the fulfilment of every transaction is liable to be interrupted by numerous accidents, many of which are such as the parties could not possibly foresee. Whenever this happens, the principle of Literal Interpretation altogether fails us. That which was actually meant to take place has become impossible. That which the parties would have wished if they had foreseen the event has not been expressed. The whole transaction must therefore, if it is to be literally interpreted, be considered as a nullity.

This conclusion, a conclusion which would introduce perpetual disappointment and uncertainty into every conceivable transaction between man and man, can only be escaped by adopting the principle of Logical as distinguished from Literal Interpretation. We begin of course by ascertaining what the agent has done or said, and by inferring from it what he actually intended. This is, or ought to be, a question for the decision of a Jury. We then proceed to consider whether there are no general principles of Probability which enable us to conjecture what intention he would, if he had foreseen the events which have happened, have formed and expressed. If so, we have succeeded in laying down a Canon of Logical Interpretation; a Canon liable no doubt to be overruled by the declared intention of the parties concerned in any particular transaction which may come within it, but still sufficient to rescue us from uncertainty where no such intention can be shown. And by collecting and classifying a sufficient number of such Canons, a Science of Logical Interpretation may be, and has been, gradually constructed.

It is deeply to be regretted that the English Courts have not distinctly recognised the principle of Logical Interpretation. Had they ventured to do so, a system of rules upon the subject could have been extracted from their recorded decisions, whose admirable wisdom the intellect of the whole world might be defied to surpass. But the practical value of their ingenuity has been in a great measure destroyed by their timid reluctance to rely upon it. They have never acknowledged the plain distinction, that Interpretation consists, first in finding out what a given person actually meant, and secondly in inferring what he would have meant if he had known what was going to happen. They therefore shrink alike from the practical absurdity of confining themselves to the former question, and from the theoretical boldness of admitting the necessity of the latter. And the result has been a large class of precedents, in which the Magistrate first clearly explains the Logical Interpretation of the instrument before him, and then proceeds, with more or less success, to sift its whole phraseology in the hope of finding some hint which may enable him to extract the same result from its Literal Interpretation.

The inability of the English Reporters to comprehend the same distinction has been a source of the greatest possible inconvenience to the student, if not to the public. A surprisingly large proportion of our judicial precedents will be found to consist of cases in which the only question before the Court was, whether any meaning could be discovered in a certain quantity of nonsensical jargon. That our Law of Procedure should consider such questions as worth the attention of a dignified Magistrate may well excite astonishment. If, when John a Nokes picks a pocket, we set a Jury to guess at his intention, why should we not do the same when John a Stiles leaves an unintelligible will? But, be this as it may, it is strange that so many experienced Lawyers should have failed to perceive the entire unimportance, as a precedent, of the construction annexed to a form of words which will probably never be used again, or the inexpediency of encumbering our Reports with discussions about as interesting to the Jurist as the evidence which may have established the fact that a certain vagabond upon a certain night robbed a certain hen-roost.

The investigation of this subtle and difficult science is a task highly important to the practical Legislator, and profoundly interesting to the philosophical Jurist. But still it cannot be said that the theory of Logical Interpretation belongs to the science of Jurisprudence. In practice, it is true, the one is the auxiliary, and the highly useful if not indispensable auxiliary, of the other. But in principle their foundations are altogether distinct, and each is complete in itself. In order to lay down the rules of Justice we do not require to ascertain facts. We take the facts of each case for granted. And the rules of Interpretation are only serviceable for the purpose of enabling us to substitute general probability for undiscoverable fact. The rules of Justice may therefore be distinctly and fully discussed without any assistance from, or any knowledge of, those of Interpretation. The two sciences, in short, stand to each other in precisely the same relation as Optics and Astronomy. It is the office of the subordinate to collect and verify the materials, which it is that of the superior science to analyse and classify.

It would certainly appear that there can scarcely be two subjects of inquiry more easily distinguishable than the questions, what a man is permitted to do and what he has actually done. But the first Lawyer who is asked what he means by the Law of Testation, or by the Law of Contract, will show by his answer that he has not learnt to distinguish them, or rather that he has diligently and successfully learnt to confound them. Nor ought we to be surprised at this. I believe, strange as the assertion may appear, that there is no Legal treatise in existence which points out that the Law of Validity and the Law of Interpretation, rest upon distinct principles, and ought to be considered as distinct subjects of thought. If they are sometimes separately discussed, they are quite as often found blended in the same sentence. It is scarcely necessary to specify the celebrated school of Jurisprudence to whose incapability of logical analysis we owe this state of intellectual confusion. There never existed but one system of Legal philosophy, at once shallow enough to adopt such an arrangement and authoritative enough to procure its adoption by the rest of the world.

## V. Necessity of Analysis

I have now defined what I mean, and what I do not mean, by the word Jurisprudence, and I proceed to explain the use which I intend to make of the definition. I have long been of opinion that the study of that science is, or might easily be made, one of the most interesting and delightful to which the human mind can apply itself. It is founded upon principles which every man instinctively understands, and it deals with facts most of which are to every man practically familiar. Experiment, so far as experiment has had any chance of being fairly tried, seems to confirm this conclusion. Every doubtful question of Right which comes before the public in a form at once practical and intelligible is found to excite the keenest interest in every society of educated men. Was Scott justified in denying the authorship of Waverley? was Phillips justified in defending Courvoisier? was Garibaldi justified in his descent upon Sicily? These questions, and such as these, have everywhere been standing subjects of discussion. No poem or romance ever attracted more interest than the controversial passages of Lord Macaulay's History. And, above all, the only untechnical Introduction to English Law has been for more than a century one of the most popular books in the language, although it is the work of a dull and shallow sophist, who never used an idea which he had not borrowed and who never borrowed an idea which he did not spoil.

And yet, notwithstanding all these powers of pleasing on the one side and all this readiness to be pleased on the other, we find that the study of Jurisprudence is universally acknowledged to be the most difficult and repulsive in existence. We are assured by all who have thoroughly mastered the science, not only that its deeper recesses are singularly intricate and obscure, but that its outer approaches are so rugged as to repel all but the most active and resolute intellects. Above all, we hear with astonishment the ignominious admission of the most acute and enlightened Jurists, that it is morally impossible to arrange in strict logical succession the principles and conclusions of the great science of Jurisprudence. Surely, if all this has hitherto been so, it must be owing to some peculiar and artificial cause. Surely it is inconceivable that the science whose basis is Conscience and Reason, and whose materials are the common relations of human life, should be the only one which is incapable of being reduced to a clear and coherent system. It seems a strange assertion that the properties of numbers, or the proportions of lines and angles, are a subject of inquiry so much less abstruse than the rules of common sense and common honesty.

I do not hesitate to declare my own conviction that the peculiar difficulties of the study of Jurisprudence are entirely owing to the perverse ingenuity with which its principles have been disarranged. In saying this I allude, not to the technical barbarisms which formerly scared the English student, but to the metaphysical subtleties which have been inherited from a far higher source. I believe that, if accurate thought upon the subject of Jurisprudence is a matter of any importance, the complete reconstruction of the whole elementary part of the science is an absolute necessity. I should make this declaration with much greater diffidence, if I did not feel sure that every rational jurist is already convinced of its truth. I am confident that no intelligent student ever makes himself master of Blackstone's Commentaries without becoming thoroughly dissatisfied with those principles of analysis which have hitherto been universally adopted. And I am satisfied that the adoption of these principles has been entirely owing to excessive deference for a remote and semi-civilised age; an age whose practical sagacity in legislation was no doubt always admirable but whose attempts at philosophical speculation have been found as inadequate a receptacle for modern thought as a classical galley would be for the armament of an English frigate.

It appears to me that the whole complicated confusion of thought in watch the science of Jurisprudence is enveloped may be traced to a single root. The object of all moral science is the application of Principle to Fact. For this purpose it is exceedingly convenient, if not absolutely necessary, to invent technical names for those particular combinations of Fact with which the Moralist is most commonly required to deal, the signification of the terms adopted being of course previously defined with the utmost precision of which language is capable. From the abuse of this indispensable practice has arisen that most dangerous and fatal intellectual vice which is known as Pedantry. The reasoner is apt to forget that his definitions are not necessary truths, hut phrases invented to save trouble. He begins to reason upon them as if they were substantive realities instead of artificial formulas. He allows himself to mistake the scaffolding which his own hands have set up for the everlasting materials which the will of Providence has created for his use. In a word, he separates Fact from Principle by interposing Definition.

There cannot be a livelier illustration of this familiar blunder than the clever tale in which a great living fabulist has ridiculed the pedantic abuse of statistical calculation. Its principal character is a philosopher who prides himself upon his exclusive devotion to what he expressively terms Hard Facts. But no sooner do we make acquaintance with Mr. Thomas Gradgrind than we discover that he is represented, whether intentionally or otherwise, as not knowing what a Fact is. His reasoning is that of the foolish woman in another of the same author's fictions, who protests that she never will acknowledge a Fact which goes against her conscience. He falls into one absurdity after another by steadily confining his attention to those Facts which he finds himself able to explain and classify. He is incapable of perceiving that the evil consequences of an unhappy childhood, or of an unhappy marriage, are Facts as hard as if their causes could be expressed in a numerical table. We find, in short, that Mr. Gradgrind's whole character is that of a visionary theorist, and that, when he talks of a Hard Fact, he only means an Intelligible Definition.

The worst effect of this pedantic habit of substituting phrases for things, when adopted by Jurists and Legislators, has of course been its practical injustice. Those who are curious to ascertain the extent to which it has furnished an excuse for wilful tyranny, may consult the arguments by which the old Spanish Publicists maintained the exclusive right of their countrymen to the navigation of the Atlantic. The doctrine of the Scottish Law concerning the mutual rights of the Celtic chiefs and their clansmen is perhaps as strong an instance as could be cited of the involuntary errors which it has caused. The feudal customs afforded no technical name for the kind of title claimed by the Highland peasantry, and its existence, in spite of clear understanding and immemorial usage, was therefore utterly denied. That the formidable authority thus vested in the chiefs was wisely and unselfishly used, and that its exercise has saved the Grampian glens from an Irish famine, has been confidently asserted and may be true. But this is no excuse for the Laws which deprived a nation of its home, because they could not find a phrase to designate its tenure.

Our present concern, however, is not with the practical injustice which Pedantry has caused, but with the confused circuity of thought which it has infused into the science of Jurisprudence. The waste of intellectual power which has thus been occasioned is in itself a very serious misfortune to mankind. Many acute and able Jurists might be mentioned, whose minds have been so narrowed by the inveterate practice of Technicalism that they have become incapable of comprehending the effect of the simplest fact until they have called it by some scientific nickname. We find them perpetually discussing, not the just and reasonable consequences of a given transaction, but its proper conventional denomination as a *quasi* Delict or a *quasi* Contract. We are told that the Augustan Civilians were divided into adverse factions by the controversy, whether an Exchange does or does not fall within the definition of a Sale. And we find an eminent English magistrate declaring himself unable to conceive how the country could be governed without the assumption of some title recognised by the forms of Constitutional Law.

The whole elementary study of Jurisprudence has been thoroughly perverted and disorganized by this habit of technical circumlocution, but one of its evil consequences deserves to be specially distinguished. I mean the principle of classifying legal rules by their effects and not by their elements. Instead of the natural and simple inquiry, what will be the legal result of a given combination of facts, the Civilians are perpetually examining what combinations of fact will produce a given legal result. By this method of analysis they have introduced an element of confusion into the whole science, from which scarcely any legal work, I might almost say scarcely any legal mind, has hitherto extricated itself. Its effect upon Jurisprudence has been precisely that which would be produced upon Natural History by classing animals according to their habits instead of their anatomy, or upon Medical Science by classing diseases according to their symptoms instead of their causes. It is no wonder that, while Jurists thus reject the first principles of Logic, the logical arrangement of their science should be pronounced impracticable.

## VI. Possibility of Analysis

I intend to try, by the present Treatise, the experiment of presenting the Science of Jurisprudence to the student in its natural shape and order. For this purpose I shall first inquire from what inevitable circumstances the necessity for such a science has arisen. These circumstances, whatever they may be, will constitute the natural elements of the Science, and by the various combinations of which they may be capable the Science itself, in its simplest and most elementary form, will be composed. The natural and everlasting foundation being thus laid, it will become comparatively easy to comprehend the effect of the various artificial superstructures which the will of man has erected or may erect upon it. To investigate the details, or even to sketch the outlines, of human Legislation is of course no part of my plan, but I shall endeavour to indicate the general principles by which it is connected with, and through which it may be said to form a part of, the universal science of Jurisprudence. I believe that the result of this conception, if adequately worked out, will be a clear and comprehensive view of that great system of problems whose solution is the object of Law. Every question of Right which can possibly arise between two human beings would be stated in its proper succession and connection, and a method of analysis would thus be provided by which any conceivable system of Law might at once be arranged in precise and perfect logical order.

Those writers who pronounce such an arrangement to be impossible do not comprehend the true distinction between moral and mathematical science. That distinction consists in the fact, that human beings possess faculties by which they can demonstrate physical, but none by which they can demonstrate moral Truth. In other words, the problems of Morality can only be approximately solved by the human intellect. We often differ upon their precise decision, and even when we all agree we can never be sure that our opinion is perfectly correct. But surely it does not follow that the problems of Morality are incapable of being presented in as logical a form as those of Geometry. Surely the plan of the labyrinth need not be unsymmetrical, because we are incapable of finding the clue. We do not argue that the tops of inaccessible mountains, or the beds of unfathomable oceans, must be less perfect in their geological formation than the rest of the Earth, and why are we to conclude that a series of questions proposed by Providence to mankind must be illogical because they are supposed to be unanswerable?

To what extent the problems of Jurisprudence are really incapable of a definite and indisputable solution, is a subject which will be considered in its proper order. For the present we will assume that they are wholly so. But even if insoluble, they certainly are not unintelligible. We may be unable to determine the answers, but we cannot pretend that we do not understand the questions. They are those which naturally arise from the physical and moral conditions of human existence. What those conditions are, we are sufficiently informed by experience. It only remains to try whether we are able to analyse and classify them. If so, the difficulty is at an end. We see what human life actually is, and we know what questions of Right it suggests. Those questions constitute the Science of Jurisprudence. The elements of Jurisprudence are therefore the facts of human life, and, if we can arrange the facts of human life in their proper logical order, we shall ascertain the only true and perfect analysis of that great Science whose object it is to define and classify their moral consequences.

It is precisely because the problems of Jurisprudence are clear and immutable, while their solutions must always be more or less variable and doubtful, that a thorough comprehension of the former ought always to precede any inquiry into the latter. The late Dr. Arnold, with admirable good sense and sagacity, has advised all historical students to make themselves thoroughly acquainted with Physical, before they pay any attention to Political Geography. Let them clearly keep in mind the bearings and the distances, the coasts and the rivers, the watersheds and the mountain-ranges, and they will find it easy to remember the position of towns and the demarcation of frontiers. First ascertain the anatomical structure, and then you will readily understand the adjustment of the drapery. The same excellent advice cannot be too strongly pressed upon the student of Jurisprudence. The confusion of the Historian who takes towns and frontiers for geographical landmarks, will be trifling when compared to that of the Jurist who takes Statutes and Customs for Jural principles.

I firmly believe that the intolerable aridity usually attributed to legal study is entirely due to the infatuation with which the student usually persists in exploring the details of his science before he comprehends its outlines. It is his purpose to make himself master of the solutions which have been proposed by a certain Legislature for a certain series of moral problems which every civilized community finds it necessary to solve. Common sense seems to suggest that his first step ought to be the inquiry, what these problems are and how their solution becomes necessary. If you wish to understand the working of a machine, you first find out what it is meant to do and what assistance each of its parts is meant to contribute. But I am acquainted with no writer who offers any such preliminary information to the student of Jurisprudence. What the Law actually is, and how it became what it is, he may easily find most ably discussed. But from such discussions he will derive about as much instruction as a strategist might do from an architectural description of the cities on his line of march.

What every Jurist has first to do is to make himself master, not of the Law itself, which may be pernicious and must be imperfect, but of that great system of Jural problems which forms the framework of all Law, and which, as it arises out of the conditions of human existence, must retain its importance while the human race survives. Let him once clearly perceive how these questions have become necessary and how they are connected with each other, and he will have little difficulty in understanding and criticizing the various solutions of which they are capable. Let him once thoroughly comprehend what is *to be* done, and the inquiry how it *has been* done will become an easy one. He will find that, when the nature and circumstances of the question are familiar, the most absurd or complicated answers become intelligible and even interesting. He will learn to reject with disdain the unscientific fallacy which pleads absurd Legislation as an excuse for illogical analysis. He will become conscious, in short, of having acquired a method of study which no system of Law can possibly baffle, because it is founded, not upon the arbitrary decisions of human opinion, but upon the unchanging necessities of human nature.

## VII. Method of Analysis

The first stone of the structure must be one which the great Jurists of antiquity have wholly omitted. Every intellectual composition consists, or ought to consist, in a definite answer to some definite question. Even with narratives, if clear and precise, this is always the case. How Achilles came to quarrel with Agamemnon, how the English nation came to expel the Stuarts, how Mr. Waverley came to marry Miss Bradwardine, are questions which embrace the whole compass of the immortal works in which they are answered. But the ancient definitions of Jurisprudence do not contain this element of Unity. Jurisprudence, they tell us, is the science of human Rights. And what are Rights? Rights, is the answer, are either Personal or Real. But, is the natural objection, has the word Rights no definite meaning in itself? Have Personal Rights and Real Rights no common characteristic? If not, why do you call them by a common name and include them in a common Science? For anything that you have shown us to the contrary, the science of Personal Rights may be as distinct from that of Real Rights as the science of Chemistry from that of Geometry.

No distinction can be intelligibly drawn where no connection has been established. The division between Real and Personal Rights, or between what I should prefer to term General and Special Obligations, is in itself both logically correct and practically important, but it ought to be preceded by their common definition. Seius is bound not to build upon one field, because it is already appropriated by Titius. He is bound not to build upon another, because he has expressly covenanted with Titius to that effect. Here are two Rights, wholly different in many of their consequences, but having this result in common, that there is in both cases a particular act which Titius is entitled to restrain Seius from doing. The universal element thus existing in every conceivable Right forms the link by which the whole science of Jurisprudence is united and identified. That universal element is the moral justification of one human being in controlling for his own benefit the volition of another. It is therefore by inquiring whether a given question does or does not relate to the existence of such a justification, that we ascertain whether it does or does not form part of the science of Jurisprudence. And we thus conclude the final purpose of that science to be the classification of the various answers which are capable of being given to the general question. In what cases is one human being morally entitled to control for his own benefit the volition of another?

The first division of this subject I shall denominate Natural Jurisprudence, because it relates exclusively to the mutual Rights of human beings existing in the state of Nature. The phrase is one whose use, I am well aware, requires some boldness and may he thought to require some apology. It has been the theme of much sentimental absurdity and the butt of much silly ridicule, but it is in my opinion capable of being defined with precision and used with convenience. I need scarcely say that I reject, as peremptorily as the shallowest scoffer at the dreams of Monboddo, the conditions of vertebral elongation and of herbivorous nudity. But I acknowledge myself to be one of those theorists who are unable to consider Justice and Injustice as the creatures of human Law. I believe that questions of Right might easily arise, and might be satisfactorily decided, between human beings co-existing without any artificial social connection. And I am therefore unwilling to dispense with a phrase by which the Status of such human beings is intelligibly expressed.

The next division will be that of Civil Jurisprudence. It is obvious that the faculties naturally possessed by mankind are sufficient to account for the formation of those great associations of human beings which are termed Political States or Communities, and consequently that the questions of Right which arise from their existence might be intelligibly discussed under the head of Natural Jurisprudence. But such an arrangement, if not theoretically incorrect, would practically be altogether absurd. It is a fact that the distribution of the human race into independent societies has long been complete. It is also a fact that the original circumstances of that distribution are historically unknown and theoretically disputable. Our only rational course is therefore to consider Civil Society simply as an existing phenomenon, and to deduce its Jural consequences, not from the nature of its possible origin, but from that of its actual organization. By reasoning otherwise we should be closing our eyes against facts as they are, in order to speculate upon them as they may have been.

At this point the present Work will stop. But in doing so it will only have achieved half its intended purpose. An immense field for juridical speculation, familiar to the practical Lawyer though hitherto unaccountably neglected by the philosophical Jurist, will still lie before us. It is an undoubted fact, that no human society has ever been known to exist without the establishment of innumerable artificial Usages among the persons composing it. Some of these Usages arise from the natural though imperfect development, others from the mischievous or unnecessary perversion, of the human intellect. But all of them are, as existing facts, more or less important to the communities among whom they exist, and none of them can be traced to any origin more definite than the imperceptible progress of cultivation or the imperceptible growth of delusion. They ought therefore to be considered as accidental phenomena, by whose existence the natural relations of a certain portion of the human race have to a certain degree been altered. And in the inquiry, how far this alteration extends, would consist the science of what may be termed Conventional Jurisprudence.

It is evident that a complete investigation of Conventional Jurisprudence as it now exists, or ought to exist, among mankind, would require little less than a connected history of human progress and human error. But it would not in my opinion, be difficult to lay down certain general principles by which all the Conventional usages which are known to have existed, or which can be conceived as existing, among mankind, might be accurately divided into classes, and to illustrate each class by the example of some particular Usage familiar to every modern Lawyer. Such a classification would embrace the subjects of Moral and Religious Usage with their development in Ecclesiastical Jurisprudence, of Commercial Usage with its consequences of

Bankruptcy and Partnership, of Feudal Usage with the peculiarities of English Real Property Law. It would also comprise a variety of incidental but not less important subjects, such as Scientific Usage with Locomotive and Maritime Jurisprudence, Pecuniary Usage with the Jurisprudence of Debts and Legacies, Testimonial or Documentary Usage with the rules relating to Title Deeds and Negociable Securities.

The great object of the system of analysis which I have now briefly described is to reduce the whole science of Jurisprudence to a single expression, by adopting the human individual as the Unit, the determination of whose Status is its final object and from whose various situations the entire series of its problems must arise. We begin by taking the simple fact of his existence and by combining that fact with the subsequent consequences of his volition and with the antecedent peculiarities of his character. We then proceed to consider the effect of these natural circumstances when combined with the fact, whether considered as natural or as artificial, of his Allegiance to a Political community. And we may possibly hereafter conclude by further combining the results of Natural and Civil with those of Conventional Society. I say with the utmost confidence that the human imagination may safely be defied to conceive any possible opposition of interests between two human beings whose causes and consequences may not, according to these principles of analysis, be classified with mathematical precision.

## VIII. Roman Method

If these principles of analysis are correct, they are applicable, not only to the investigation of one supreme and universal Science of Jurisprudence, but to the construction of any required system of Municipal Law. The great difference between the two undertakings will of course be, that the local or national Usages which would form special exceptions to the general Theory must pervade and override the whole of the particular Code. But, subject to this qualification, the method which is most clear and natural to the speculative Philosopher will prove equally so to the practical Legislator. He will commence by solving those questions of Right which have arisen between his subjects simply as fellow creatures, and in doing this he will carefully deduce the consequences of those conditions of existence which are common to the whole community, before he interferes with such as are peculiar to any portion of it. And he will conclude by defining the extent to which he intends the rights of the individual Citizen to be overruled by the paramount interests of the State.

Such a method of Legislation would be very different from that which we have inherited from the great Roman Civilians. Of those famous masters of Jurisprudence no Jurist ought ever to speak but with sincere respect. It is impossible to overrate their liberal wisdom or their technical dexterity and ingenuity. But the skill of the mechanic is one thing and the science of the architect is another. The Imperial Jurisconsults deliberately gave their minds to the construction of a great intellectual system, which they intended to serve as a receptacle for the comprehension and classification of Jural Truth so long as mankind should exist. In this attempt, accomplished as in many respects they were, I do not hesitate to affirm that they have failed, and that, if their failure does not deserve to be termed ignominious, it is only because the philosophical deficiencies of their age made it inevitable. In my opinion, and I believe in the opinion of every one else who understands the subject, we owe them a method of analysis as illogical and inconvenient as ever was applied to any human science.

It is possible that, in forming my judgment upon this subject, I may to a certain extent have been misled by the compilations of the Byzantine Legislators. Very little acuteness is required to perceive that the Institute of Justinian is a collection of most valuable materials, arranged by most unskilful hands. Its actual distribution is so chaotic as to be beneath criticism, but it undoubtedly contains the elements of a complete and coherent system. That system I presume to have been the genuine production of the great Antonine Civilians, and by its value I appreciate their merit as philosophical Jurists. Further research might perhaps show that this presumption is too absolute, and it is subject to this possibility that I must be understood to give my opinion. It certainly appears to me that the best Roman theory of Jurisprudence, though far superior to what the pedantic stupidity of Tribonian and his colleagues could comprehend, is radically pervaded by all those peculiar intellectual errors which I have already specified as fatal to Jural analysis.

The entire omission of Conventional Jurisprudence is undoubtedly the chief defect of the Civilian method of analysis. For that defect, indeed, the great inventors of the system are scarcely responsible. The social and moral uniformity of the ancient civilized world appears to have been such, that its Legislators had less occasion than those of many single modern States to consider the local or sectional peculiarities of their subjects. But for the Civilians of modern Europe there is no such excuse. They have before their eyes a world inhabited by an almost infinite variety of races and nations, all resembling each other in their natural characteristics, and all differing from each other in their artificial habits. Under such circumstances it is pitiable to find so many philosophical Jurists rejecting the obvious elements of general uniformity and special peculiarity, and clinging to the antiquated delusion that all the complicated relations of civilized society can really be stowed away in those two paltry receptacles known as the Law of Persons and the Law of Things.

Two great intellectual faults, though rather deserving the name of bad habits than of false principles, appear to have prevailed among the best Roman Jurisconsults. The first is an aversion for broad and comprehensive principles and maxims, and a consequent habit of premature division and subdivision. No sooner do they mention the Law of Persons, or of Obligation than they begin, without laying down a single general rule upon the subject, to explain that all Persons are either Freemen or Slaves, and all Obligations either Civil or Praetorian. It never seems to strike them that every word must have some meaning, and every fact some effect, of its own, and that this primary meaning or effect must be distinctly defined before the modifications of which it is capable can be understood. The consequence of this error is the want of unity which pervades all the relics of Roman Law. Admirable as they are in themselves, they often resemble the contents of a museum rather than the materials of a building.

The other peculiar defect of which I speak is that confusion of Definition with Fact which I have already designated as Pedantry. The Roman Jurists seem to believe that the word Servitude or Contract is, like the word Oxygen or Triangle, the name of a combination of facts possessing certain properties, not by the opinion of Man, but by the necessity of Nature. This fault has always been a common one among men of science, but there are two particulars in which the pedantry of the Roman Forum has been singularly unfortunate. In the first place, no pedantry was ever more inexcusable in itself. Its disciples quibbled, not upon the words of Statutes which they were legally bound to carry into literal execution, but upon the doctrines and definitions of private Jurisconsults like themselves, from which they were at liberty to dissent. In the second place, no pedantry was ever more hurtful in its consequences. The technical phrases of the Roman Law have always been a storehouse of ready-made pretexts for international oppression. It would have been difficult, even for a Spanish Publicist, to claim the whole continent of America upon grounds of natural Justice, but it was easy to contend that the man who landed upon an uninhabited coast did an act which might possibly be included within the Roman definition of Occupancy.

We are assured by the best authorities that it would be difficult to overrate the influence of Roman Jurisprudence upon almost every department of modern thought. I shall not undertake either to confirm or to contradict this assertion. But, assuming it to be true, I do not hesitate to declare my opinion that it would have been well for mankind if Roman Jurisprudence had never existed. The practical skill with which the great Imperial Jurists solved problems and laid down rules is only available for the purposes of one particular science. But their arbitrary and pedantic method of analysis might be imitated, and we are to suppose has actually been imitated, by the professors of every existing intellectual pursuit. To me it appears highly probable that modern thinkers would have blundered, whether ancient thinkers had blundered before them or not. But if we really owe to the Roman Civilians all the absurd complication of thought which has been common to their age and to our own, there can be no doubt that the preservation of their labours has been an immense misfortune to the human intellect.

## IX. The English Methods

The few English Jurists who have endeavoured to reduce the science of Jurisprudence, or any of its more considerable branches, into a systematic form, have thought themselves safe in following the principles of distribution adopted by the Roman Codes. The consequence is, that there is scarcely an English law-book capable of being understood when read from beginning to end by a person unacquainted with its subject. I have now before me one of the ablest and most accurate compendia used by the Profession, whose author, having copied the method of the Civilians, finds himself compelled to discuss in his first Book the question whether one copartner can bind another by a Bill of Exchange, while deferring until his third Book the information what a Bill of Exchange may be. Blackstone, it is true, has with unwonted originality substituted the distinction of Rights and Wrongs for that of Rights and Actions. But by doing so he has only avoided a logical blunder at the expense of a practical absurdity. For, since every Right must have its correlative Wrong and every Wrong its correlative Right, his arrangement would, if accurately worked out, make the one half of his treatise a precise repetition of the other.

I know no reading more humiliating to an English Jurist than that of the exaggerated praises which have been lavished upon Blackstone's Commentaries. That the work has been of great practical service to students of the Common Law, cannot of course be doubted. But that it should ever have been admired as a model of analysis, or as a philosophical explanation of first principles, is a striking proof how very slight a pretence to perspicuity was sufficient to delight the bewildered disciples of Coke upon Littleton. To the scientific Jurist its superficial precision will probably appear about as admirable as a museum neatly arranged by a tasteful upholsterer might do to a scientific Naturalist. Whoever is of a different opinion will do well to test it by taking up a volume of legal Reports, and by trying to distribute the principles of Law there laid down under their proper heads according to Blackstone's system. Such an attempt will soon show that the commentator has taken a most effectual means of clearness and brevity, by simply omitting all those parts of his subject which he did not know how to classify.

I am far from intending to depreciate the many admirable legal treatises which have been written by English authors. Nowhere will the student find questions of practical Law discussed with greater learning and sagacity. The blame which these writers have incurred, if it can be called blame, is that of having thought too highly of their predecessors and too humbly of themselves. They are no more responsible for the faults of the system which they have found established, than an artist for the architectural defects of the palace which he adorns with his works. But the same great fault will be found in all their writings. They are wholly without Unity of Design. Take for instance the best Treatise upon English Testamentary Law. It contains a series of very able Essays, wholly unconnected with each other. There are fragments from the Law of Validity and of Interpretation, of Property and of Obligation, of Evidence and of Personal Status, all excellent in themselves and all thrown together at random. In fact, there is usually as little logical sequence between the chapters of an English text-book as between the cases in an English volume of Reports.

Nothing can, in my opinion, be more absurd and unjust than the lamentations which we constantly hear concerning the scientific inferiority of English to foreign Jurists. The present difference between them is, that the latter adopt a wrong system and the former none at all. Of these two errors I deliberately prefer the second. Ignorance is bad, but delusion is worse. The elaborate misarrangement of the Code Napoleon is little less illogical, and much less likely to be rectified, than the unsophisticated chaos of the Statutes at Large. Nor do I admit that the dissimilarity is so discreditable to the English legal intellect as it is usually considered. I believe its true explanation to be, that English Jurists are generally dissatisfied, and foreign Jurists generally satisfied, with the Roman principles of analysis. The natural consequence is that those principles are almost wholly neglected here, while they are deeply studied abroad. Upon this point I think that the advantage is with us. We may not have discovered what is right, but we have detected what is wrong. If we have not found out a solution of our own, we have at least the merit of not believing in that of Justinian.

The author of such a work as the present will scarcely be suspected of looking down, as Bentham expresses it, with contempt upon Theory from the pinnacle of Practice. A scientific Jurist may perhaps be superior to the best practical Lawyer, but a good practical Lawyer is surely superior to an unscientific Jurist. Screwing truth out of rogues in a witness box, for the purpose of hammering it into fools in a jury box, is by no means the highest possible exercise of the human intellect. It is an art in which a very ordinary man may excel and a very able man fail; an art whose greatest masters have been found quite unable to take the lead in an assembly of educated gentlemen. But it is an art whose successful exercise is quite as useful, and deserves quite as much credit, as the elaborate composition of false Logic and false Metaphysics. The English Barrister seldom pretends to be a philosopher, but he has usually the merit of doing thoroughly what he professes to do, which is more than can be said for many of the theorists who are accustomed to regard him as so greatly their inferior.

The same remark applies to the technical performances of the English Legal school. Their work is never planned upon a largo scale, but it is usually perfect in itself. Ulpian tried to write like a philosopher and Coke was content to write like a Lawyer, but it must be remembered that Coke was a most profound Lawyer and that Ulpian was a very indifferent philosopher. Good Law is better than bad Metaphysics. The truth is that justice has never yet been done to the extraordinary aptitude of the English mind, or of the English language, for legal investigation and discussion. The bigoted Optimism, so common in England fifty years ago, found its expression in the well-known platitude, that the Common Law is the perfection of human wisdom. The equally bigoted Radicalism which soon after arose made it an article of faith, that all English Jurisprudence is a mere contrivance to ensnare clients for the benefit of Lawyers. The vaunts of Blackstone found their natural re-action in the gibes of Bentham. But with the single exception of Lord Macaulay, whose perfect intellect never failed to appreciate intellectual excellence, I remember no unprofessional writer who has given any indication that the legal arguments of the English Bench and Bar, considered merely as dialectical exercitations, had ever struck him as worthy of admiration.

It has lately been publicly asserted, upon what ought to be good authority, that the scientific element in English Legal study is perceptibly declining. All who regret the existence of the deficiency ought to rejoice at its increase. That it will continue until it becomes intolerable, and that when it becomes intolerable it will speedily disappear, no one who knows anything of the English character can doubt. The improvement will take place, as all English improvements now take place, upon strict economical principles. The time will come when the great landed and monied classes will begin to realize the immense practical importance of a perfect legislative and judicial system, and will consider the best means of providing one. From that time the demand for legal science will rapidly create the supply. It will be easy to make it understood, that a thorough acquaintance with abstract Jurisprudence is likely to be a short path to competence and a sure path to honour. And the consequence of such an understanding will probably be the growth of a school of Jurisconsults as superior to the great Antonine Civilians as the Antonine Civilians to their ablest modern disciples.

## X. Theory of Natural Justice

I have now explained the principles upon which I intend to analyse the Science of Jurisprudence, or in other words to classify the questions capable of arising upon the mutual Rights of mankind. In doing this, I have done all that is strictly necessary for the purposes of the present Treatise. It would be quite possible, without laying down a single positive rule, to arrange all the problems of human Right in logical order, and to show by what successive combinations of Fact they are raised, and in what manner the solution of one depends upon that of another. But it will scarcely be expected that I should content myself with so uninviting a task. A man who has constructed a machine naturally longs to see it at work, even though he has no materials to employ it upon. It so happens that this is not precisely my case. There are certain moral principles which have been the subjects of exaggerated speculation among the theorists of a former generation, and of what I consider unreasonable scorn among the critics of the present. I am of opinion that the application to these principles of the Analysis which I have explained will be a useful experiment, because it will test both the moral merit of the principles and the logical merit of the analysis, and this experiment I intend to try.

I believe that there exist certain general rules of Justice which now are, which always have been and which always will be, instinctively recognized by the human conscience. I further believe that these rules are such as to be capable of being applied by the human intellect to every possible combination of facts upon which a question of Right can arise between any two human beings, and that by such reasoning the abstract Rights of one human being as against another may, under any conceivable circumstances, be logically defined. In other words, I believe in the existence and in the utility of that moral principle which is commonly termed Natural Justice. That there is, among the Moralists of the present day, a strong reaction against this opinion, every educated man is aware. Another and a wiser age may possibly think as lightly of the shallow ingenuity by which that reaction has been effected, as of the shallow sentimentalism by which it was provoked. In the meantime there will be no difficulty in showing that the doctrine of Natural Justice, whether true or false, is not unworthy of candid consideration.

It will probably be generally admitted that, as a matter of fact, every human being is born with a certain mental faculty, commonly termed Conscience, which makes him capable of deriving pleasure or pain from what he considers the moral character of a given human act. I do not mean that this fact can be ascertained by dissection. Its existence must be judged by its results. Nor do I assert that such results can be discerned in the conduct or the language of every human being. The possession of a conscience is not, like the possession of a liver, a necessary condition of physical life. In many men, and in some few races of men, the natural faculty may have been left dormant until it has become apparently extinct. But this is no reason for denying its original existence. It is said that the use of Fire is the only exclusively human attribute whose exercise no human being has yet been found to have forgotten. It is certain that there are tribes of savages whose language is wholly inarticulate. And yet no physiologist denies that every human being is naturally endowed with the faculty of speech.

But, assuming that every man has a Conscience, it does not of course follow that there is any resemblance between the moral judgment of one man and that of another. Every man has a palate, but it would be impossible to specify any particular flavour, or combination of flavours, which is universally liked or disliked by mankind. May not Morality, like eating, be a mere question of taste? and, as one man's meat is said to be another's poison, may not one man's Duty be another's Sin? Undoubtedly there are grounds upon which such an opinion may be plausibly supported. The differences of human judgment upon questions of Right and Wrong are acknowledged to be endless. The wisest Jurists are divided, not only upon the mere subtle and recondite questions of Jurisprudence, but upon the precise definition of many of its leading principles. The wisest Casuists are unable to agree in the solution of some of the most familiar cases of Conscience. Even in the ordinary affairs of life, one honest and sensible man is often found to admire the same conduct which another condemns. Surely, it will naturally be said, there can be but one inference from such admissions as these.

The fallacy of this argument does not lie very deep. It consists in the mistaken assumption that, where ultimate results differ, no common element can exist. Such a conclusion will not bear a moment's examination. It is easy to cite a disputed principle of Legislation as a conclusive proof that there are no such things as rules of Natural Justice. But it would be equally easy to prove, by a similar process, that there are no such things as Acts of Parliament. If the application of a Statute is sometimes rendered doubtful by a peculiar combination of circumstances, why may not the same thing happen in the case of a moral maxim? Or why should not the true principle upon which punishment is to be apportioned, or property to be taxed, be as disputable as the question, which of two given enactments is to govern a given case? There is no rule, physical or moral, whose consequences can never be doubtful. And that two men with consciences should dispute the moral character of a complicated transaction, is as natural as that two men with eyes should dispute the physical character of a distant object.

But these really doubtful points are comparatively both rare and harmless. The more scandalous instances of moral obliquity almost always arise from a mistaken view, not of Principle, but of Fact. The ordinary cases, in which either the acts or the motives of the persons concerned are the subject of dispute, need scarcely be mentioned. But what seem questions of Principle will often be found to arise, not between those who appeal in common to Natural Right, but between those who assert and those who deny the fact, that Natural Right has been specially superseded by a higher authority. One enthusiast declares Self-defence to be a sin. Another maintains that Celibacy is a virtue. Others think they have a mission to assassinate unpatriotic princes, to kidnap Jewish babies, to flagellate heterodox Clergymen. They none of them deny the general rule, but they allege the revealed Will of God to be that it should in certain cases be disregarded. Such exceptions are simply moral miracles, and are no more inconsistent with the existence of a universal standard of moral Right, than physical miracles are inconsistent with the physical Laws of Nature. The Romanist believes, and the Calvinist disbelieves, that, under certain solemn circumstances, certain articles of food undergo a Divine transformation. But surely it would be absurd to infer from this, that the physical senses of the Romanist differ from those of the Calvinist.

Of the Moral Axioms which I intend to assume as the First Principles of Natural Justice, I need say very little. They will be found to be very few in number and very simple in character. I shall be particularly careful to assume nothing which is capable of being deduced from any proposition already assumed, because I believe that the chief cause of the discredit into which the science of Natural Jurisprudence has fallen is the unnecessary extent to which assumption has been substituted for deduction in ascertaining its principles. Nothing has ever struck me as more unaccountable than the manner in which some very able Utilitarian writers have taken for granted that, according to the theory which they dispute, the nicest and most intricate questions of Right are to be decided by mere intuition. It is no wonder that Justice is treated as matter of experiment, if the only alternative is to treat it as matter of guesswork.

## XI. Historical Theory

The study of Legal Antiquity has led some able writers of our own time to doubt the possibility of constructing any uniform system of Law by deduction from the natural instincts of mankind. Their researches have tended to the conclusion that the moral sense, which in some shape or other every human being may be supposed to possess, varies indefinitely in various climates, races and degrees of civilization. It may fairly, they seem to think, be contended that a man's conscience is an acquired habit or power, like his skill in riding or shooting, and not, like his eyesight or his digestion, a natural faculty. If this be the case, the superiority of Natural Justice over arbitrary Law undoubtedly vanishes. The one can no more be reduced to a permanent system than the other. The moral maxim is the expression of transient opinion, as the practical dogma is the expression of transient necessity. Both have been alike undiscovered, and will be alike forgotten. The principles of Right, which we consider eternal, might have been as unintelligible to our ancestors as astronomy or electricity, and may appear as absurd to our posterity as the geography of Strabo appears to ourselves.

There can be no doubt that, upon such a question as this, we must judge of our relation to the future by the relation of the past to us. The earliest records of antiquity represent the human race as living a vagrant pastoral life in separate families, each family consisting of the Patriarch himself, his wives and concubines, his lineal descendants with their wives and concubines, and his slaves or voluntary followers and dependents. Recognized Law there was absolutely none. The mutual Rights of the members of a family were regulated by the discretion of the Chieftain, and the mutual Rights of distinct families were not regulated at all. The earliest artificial Communities, whether locomotive as Tribes or stationary as Cities, may be supposed to have been constituted by the union, whether voluntary or casual, of groups of patriarchal families. Such a compact would probably regulate the Rights of the families concerned as against each other, but it could not be expected to make any difference in the Rights of the members of a family as between themselves. A primitive State was a league of Patriarchs, not a community of individuals, and the Magistrate had no more jurisdiction between a son and his father, than the Amphictyonic Council between a Spartan citizen and his Ephor.

If we insist upon considering such a state of Law as

fairly representing the primitive idea of Natural Justice, it is certain that the ancient races of mankind were morally altogether different from ourselves. We can no more comprehend what they thought and felt than a Negro can comprehend the physical constitution of an Esquimaux. But surely there is no necessity for any such assumption. We have every reason to believe that primeval Law was the product, not of opinion or of theory, but of pressing necessity. In a barbarous or semi-barbarous state of society the claims of the Community are so overwhelming as to extinguish the Rights of the Individual. A few families of shepherds or farmers, prowling through a wilderness or perched upon a mountain citadel, have no time to think about the Rights of man or the rules of Justice. Mutual protection is the purpose for which they are living together, and social action, or rather social existence, is the sole object of their institutions. Their Laws are more like the regulations of an army than the Jurisprudence of a civilised State. Individual discontent is not to be wantonly provoked, but the efficiency of the whole as a machine is the final purpose to which everything else must give way.

Many harsh and barbarous usages were thus, in primitive times, unavoidably necessary. Many others were rendered occasionally necessary by the violent and lawless habits of the races who adopted them. Rules for a crew of buccaneers cannot be framed upon principles of enlightened equity, and Pothier or Savigny, if he had been a Spartan citizen, could scarcely have given his countrymen better advice than Lycurgus gave them. Much absurd and sanguinary Legislation also arose, not from distorted ideas of Natural Justice. but from false assumptions of Fact or false opinions of Expediency. The Phoenicians offered human sacrifices, not because they thought homicide generally right, but because they worshipped a deity whose wrath could be averted by no other means. The Spartans scourged their children before the altar of Diana, not because they thought it a usage commendable in itself, but because they believed it likely to make brave soldiers. A scientific Jurist who was foolish enough to worship Moloch, or to believe that torture inspires courage, would probably have made provision for the same practices. When fair allowance has been made for the operation of all these disturbing influences, there will perhaps remain little reason for expecting to find, among the primeval races of mankind, ideas of natural Right different from our own.

This conclusion is not wholly unsupported by evidence. The oldest historical record in the world is evidently the production of an age in which, although modern Jurisprudence was unknown, modern ideas of Right and Wrong were quite intelligible. The Book of Genesis places before us the Patriarchal system in its sternest simplicity. The father has full power to expel his son from the family, to confiscate his property, to sell him into slavery, to take away his life. But it does not follow that the sons have no Rights as between themselves, Rights defeasible no doubt by the paternal authority but in the meantime fully recognized by private conscience and by public opinion. We find one brother punished for the murder of another, not by the discretion of the Chieftain as for an offence against the Family, but by the interposition of the Deity as for an atrocious moral crime. We find one brother selling the produce of his industry to another without the knowledge of their common father, and finally successful in enforcing a most oppressive bargain. The Hebrew writer would probably have denied the jurisdiction of any earthly magistrate to interfere with the Patriarchal prerogative of Adam or of Isaac. But surely it cannot be maintained that he thought Abel had no rights as against Gain, or Jacob none as against Esau.

It may perhaps be suspected that the exclusively Historical theory of Jurisprudence is partly due to the reaction provoked by the opinions of that shallow though ingenious sect of Jurists which is represented in the English language by Blackstone's Commentaries. Nothing, it must be allowed, can well be more justly offensive to a profound and patient student of Antiquity, than the manner in which these writers dealt with the origin and progress of social institutions. Without an attempt to ascertain the actual facts, they confidently assumed that what they thought natural and right must necessarily have taken place. They simply considered what proceedings would be probable and reasonable among a party of modern Europeans shipwrecked upon an uninhabited coast, and they proceeded to ascribe the result to the primitive tribes who are supposed to have colonised the plateaux of Central Asia. The style in which Black stone, writing purely from his own imagination or from that of the foreign theorists whom he copied, describes the development of the Law of Property among mankind, is perhaps the most astonishing specimen upon record of complacent presumption.

It is difficult to speak too highly of the Historical method of investigation as applicable to the study of Jurisprudence, or of the merit and learning of some writers by whom it has recently been employed. But there is one error which they may be thought to have unconsciously copied from the pseudo-Historical theorists whom they have demolished. Both schools seem to assume that Primitive Law and Natural Law are synonymous. The one takes for granted that the Law which they choose to think Natural must necessarily have been Primitive, the other that the Law which they have ascertained to be Primitive must necessarily be Natural. Neither seems to consider that by a State of Nature we mean, if we have any distinct meaning at all, that state in which the natural faculties of human beings are most fully developed; that for this purpose two conditions are necessary, the means of self-development and the absence of external restraint; and that, the further we go back into antiquity, the less intellectually enlightened and the more rigidly disciplined are the races among whom we find ourselves.

## XII. Pseudo Historical Theory

The doctrine that primitive Morality is fairly represented by primitive Law has been greatly assisted by the dreams, for they are unworthy to be styled theories, of those worshippers of the Past who affect to sympathize with both. The fanciful pictures of barbarian virtue and simplicity so familiar to our childhood can scarcely, by any sane degree of credulity, be accepted as true, but they may easily be accepted as true portraits of barbarian feeling and belief. Modern readers are unlikely to agree with the opinions of Cato, but they are not unlikely to believe that such opinions were commonly held by the Romans of the earlier Republic. But, whatever may have been the real or pretended prejudices of a few dull and arrogant minds, there can be little doubt that the harsh usages of uncivilized society are in general a necessity and not a choice. They may often be borne without visible discontent, for patriotic self-sacrifice, in a small State surrounded with enemies, is developed to a degree which members of a powerful and secure Community can scarcely imagine; to a degree, indeed, which often makes it quite as much a vice as a virtue. But the more we examine the history of such States, the more we shall become convinced that their peculiar Laws are a burthen which is never likely to be endured except when it cannot safely be shaken off.

Take as an example the institutions of the ancient Spartan Republic, perhaps the most thoroughly brutalizing and demoralizing ever systematically enforced by a society of human beings. No reasonable man will assume that Lycurgus embodied his conceptions of Natural Right in the Laws of Sparta. A task was set him, with which Natural Right had no more to do than with the regulations of a monastery or of a prison. He had to draw up rules of discipline for a clan of savage Dorian warriors, surrounded by deadly enemies and supported by rebellious serfs. He was never asked for his opinion upon the best plan for the formation of a free, happy, civilized nation. What the Spartans were they intended to continue. Peace with their neighbours and justice to their Helots were out of the question. They were fully determined to exist, if they existed at all, as a dynasty of predatory slave masters, and they applied to their wisest politician for advice upon the most effectual means of obtaining this result.

Lycurgus did his work, not like the enlightened philosopher which he may or may not have been, but like a practical Statesman. He clearly saw that a nation which was to exist by foreign and domestic robbery, must exist for nothing else. He therefore sacrificed everything to this single end. The social life of the Spartans was to be that of a besieged garrison. Every citizen ate and drank, slept and took exercise, not at his own pleasure, but under strict gymnastic discipline. No man was trusted to choose his own wife, or to educate his own children. No man was allowed to engage in any intellectual pursuit, to cultivate any useful or ornamental arts, to visit foreign countries, to imitate foreign customs or inventions. Such an existence has sometimes been endured by a society of enthusiastic volunteers, but has never, before or since, been made compulsory upon an entire nation. The life of a Puritan backwoodsman in Massachusetts, with all its peril and all its privation, was infinitely less intolerable. That of the medieval orders of monastic chivalry, in their earliest and most ascetic days, is probably the nearest approach to Spartan austerity which any Teutonic race has witnessed.

There can be no doubt that the Legislator fully achieved his purpose. The Spartans became, and for many generations continued, a nation of almost invincible soldiers; a nation of such soldiers as fought at Inkerman or went down in the Birkenhead, They did not merely succeed in keeping their slaves prostrate and their enemies at bay. They became the supreme State of the Hellenic Confederacy, and maintained their supremacy until the advance of civilization began to make intellectual cultivation necessary to military success. But we know at what a price they purchased their triumphs. We know that they were a race, such as it would be unmerited praise to class with the comparatively noble savages who overthrew the Roman Empire. They were not merely rude and ignorant, rapacious and ferocious. Their vices were those, not simply of barbarians, but of servile or mercenary barbarians. They bore much more resemblance to the soldiers of Alva than to the warriors of Alaric. It might be difficult to point out another nation, which has combined lasting and brilliant political success with such utter intellectual barrenness and such thorough moral depravity.

The strange delusion, that the Spartan discipline was intended by its inventor as a school of moral perfection, is certainly not due either to the hypocrisy of the Spartans themselves or to the sympathy of their contemporaries. The Funeral Oration of Pericles sufficiently shows how heartily the cultivated Athenian rejoiced in his superiority. What the Spartans thought of their own institutions can scarcely be ascertained, for it is probable that few of them knew how to think, and it is certain that none of them knew how to write, upon that or any other subject. Yet it is not difficult to conjecture that they were bitterly impatient of the slavery which they endured. The brutal yet childish violence of the Spartan character is precisely what may be observed in men whose daily existence has been harassed by a constant sense of benumbing oppression. It closely resembles what Gibbon has recorded of the savage anchorites who followed Athanasius and Cyril from the Thebaid, and it is not wholly unlike what the present generation has witnessed in certain Russian generals and ambassadors trained at the Court of the Emperor Nicholas. But, be this as it may, there is no proof that the Spartans themselves ever professed that admiration for the Laws of Lycurgus which is affected by sentimentalists like Plutarch or Thomas Day. They never pretended to be a college of Stoic philosophers, trained to virtue by ascetic self-denial. They probably knew perfectly well that they were a gang of banditti, compelled by constant peril to undergo a discipline which made their lives utterly wretched.

## XIII. Utilitarian Theory

Many Moralists are of opinion that such reasoning as this may be carried a great way further. If the existence of primitive Custom proves nothing but its temporary necessity, why should the existence of modern Opinion be held to prove anything more? May not our sense of Wrong be mere anxiety to prevent what we have found hurtful? and may not the English belief that it is disgraceful to commit Forgery prove as evanescent as the Spartan belief that it is disgraceful to dislike black broth? This brings us to the celebrated doctrine, that General Utility is the ultimate Test of Moral Right. That doctrine has been maintained by men whose names ought never to be mentioned without respect. It owes its origin to the celebrated Bentham, whose services to Jural Science it would be difficult to overrate. The late Lord Macaulay, whom no Englishman will for many years be able to mention without a passing phrase of sorrow and admiration, has left us an elaborate speech in its support; a speech which, brilliant and ingenious as it is, can scarcely be pronounced worthy of his great name. And the late Mr. Austin, whom no Jurist ever surpassed in depth and subtlety of thought, has gone so far as to declare the theory of an intuitive Moral Sense to be a pernicious jargon.

The Utilitarian Theory, in its simplest and as I think its most logical form, may be briefly stated as follows. Jurisprudence is an empirical, not a deductive Science. It rests upon no immutable principles. Its rules are to be determined by careful experiment and observation, and by nothing else. It exists for the greatest happiness of the greatest number of human beings, and by the greatest happiness of the greatest number it must be strictly regulated.

It is, in short, just such a system as the ordinary police regulations of a town or district. Property has been found a convenient institution and so have street lamps, therefore both must for the present be protected. Breach of Contract has been found an inconvenient practice and so has riding upon the pavement, therefore both must for the present be forbidden. Marriage and railroads, Inheritance and sewers, Testation and turnpike gates, are all to be maintained so long as we find them useful. I am not one of those who hold such opinions to have an immoral tendency. The merit of unselfish devotion may be the same, whether its object is the Will of God or the welfare of Man. But it certainly appears to me that the human Conscience does, in point of fact, present phenomena which the principle of Utility does not explain.

That the interest of a Community must as a general rule be preferred to that of its individual members, cannot reasonably be denied. Every citizen of a State may fairly be considered to have surrendered his individual Rights so far as is necessary for the common safety or prosperity, and therefore no citizen has a right to complain if his Rights are, in a case where it is really necessary, set aside by the State to which he belongs. If, for instance, John Cade really believed that it was necessary for the welfare of the English nation to make alphabetical instruction an indictable offence, undoubtedly he was morally justified in doing so. The Ostracism of the Athenians, the Patria Potestas of the Romans, the Suttee of the Hindoos, were very absurd and very atrocious customs, but they would not have been atrocious if they had not been absurd. Had such institutions really been indispensable for the general welfare, they might, however horrible in their nature, have been lawfully established. That a brave and good man owes all he has to his country, is a maxim which Englishmen have always acknowledged and have seldom disobeyed.

It may therefore be conceded that the Utilitarian principle is perfectly satisfactory so far as it goes. It may further be conceded that it goes far enough for all the purposes of civilized Legislation. It is quite sufficient in a country like England, where no Right can exist which Society is not interested to enforce, and no Wrong be inflicted which Society is not interested to prevent. Its true deficiency is, that it affords no rule for doing Justice between individuals where there is no Society which has any concern in the matter. It can give no answer to the question, why two trappers in the wilderness, or two shipwrecked mariners upon a desert island, are not to rob or murder each other if they feel inclined to do so. Such questions are therefore treated by the Utilitarian Moralists with convenient disdain, as fanciful speculations upon an extravagant hypothesis. A state of existence in which one man is not injured by a crime committed against another is to them a fantastic dream, only fit to amuse a lunatic of genius like Rousseau or at least an extraordinary and exceptional accident, whose moral consequences it is not worth while to discuss.

It must be acknowledged that the theories of the great French philanthropist, upon what he chose to consider the state of Nature, were such as his critics may well be excused for treating with some degree of levity. Yet their own error is perhaps the less pardonable of the two. To a Frenchman of the last century, life unrestrained by conventional usage was a Utopian dream. To an Englishman of the present day it is a familiar reality. We know, by the experience of others if not by our own, that all human beings do not live in streets full of shops, with police offices at their corners. We know how an exile from civilization acts and feels when he is compelled to exercise his own judgment, without a chance of responsibility to any human authority, in resisting claims or revenging injuries. We have no right to confound such authentic narratives with traditions about the Aryan immigration, or with fanciful pictures of the human animal in the Hunting state. We have proof that every honest man feels himself bound to respect the Rights of others although General Utility is out of the question, and we ought not to be satisfied with any system of Moral Philosophy which does not account for such scruples.

Above all, the Utilitarian theory supplies no principle by which the mutual Rights of independent States can be satisfactorily determined. It may be pronounced with some confidence that the oppression of one individual by another cannot possibly be for the general benefit of their fellow citizens. But it can by no means be laid down that the oppression of one State by another may not be for the general benefit of the human race. Who will venture to foretell whether it is for the greatest happiness of mankind, that the Southern States of the North American Union should succeed or fail in their Secession? Even looking at the past, who will decide whether the happiness of mankind has upon the whole gained or lost by what most Moralists consider the great crimes of History? Who will strike the balance between the good and the evil caused by the Roman conquest of Gaul, the Norman conquest of Ireland, the Spanish conquest of America, the English conquest of India? Yet surely every conscientious mind must feel that the Rights of nation against nation are even more sacred than those of man against man. Surely there must be something false in an ethical rule which does not enable us to condemn the partition of Poland or the French invasion of Spain.

## XIV. Quasi-Utilitarian Theory

But the principle of Utility is very often explained in a manner which, as it appears to me, destroys its peculiar character without removing its peculiar difficulties. Most of the Utilitarian Moralists, while they assert that General Utility is the test of Right and Wrong, refuse to admit the inference that Right or Wrong is a mere experimental question. They hold that an act is good or evil, not according to the nature of its actual consequences, but according to the nature of the consequences which it is the obvious tendency of similar acts to produce; just as Naturalists decide the character of an animal, not from the accidental eccentricities of the individual, but from the ordinary habits of the race. Suppose, for instance, that Friday murders Robinson Crusoe. It is not impossible that the benefit to the murderer may prove greater than the suffering of the victim, it is highly probable that no difference may be felt by any other human being, and yet it is quite certain that the act is an atrocious crime. No rational mind can fail to perceive that the general tendency of unprovoked Homicide is to make human existence utterly miserable, and this obvious truth is sufficient to show that unprovoked Homicide is contrary to the Will of Providence.

If this is all, the Utilitarian principle becomes a mere metaphysical theory. It simply admits and explains the fact, that there are certain acts which the human conscience instinctively enjoins or forbids. By this concession everything which I require is conceded. The only practical question in dispute is, whether Justice depends upon actual experiment or upon general principles. If there be any invariable rule of Right, upon that rule I will undertake to construct a system of Natural Jurisprudence. Whether the instinctive feeling by which alone such a rule can be established is termed a perception of Justice or of Utility, is to me a matter of profound indifference, although for my own use I prefer a word of two syllables whose meaning is generally understood, to a word of four syllables whose meaning may easily be mistaken. Nor should I have said anything more upon the subject, but for the disdainful asperity with which some very able Utilitarian writers denounce the sentimentalism which is content to talk of a Moral Sense without analysing its nature. Their contempt for a habit which I acknowledge to have been my own has induced me to examine their system, and it certainly appears to me both practically unimportant and theoretically imperfect.

The only practical advantage which I have ever heard

ascribed to this guasi-Utilitarian theory, is one which I should have thought not worth disputing had it been alleged by less respectable authority. It seems to have been thought that a Right founded upon general Utility may lawfully be waived or released, but that a Right founded upon eternal Justice must necessarily be enforced to the utmost. If, it is said, the English nation had thought themselves entitled to tax their American colonies upon principles of Utility only, they would have desisted from the attempt when they found it likely to prove injurious. But the King claimed a natural prerogative over his colonial subjects, and that prerogative he thought himself bound at all hazards to enforce. Surely no Moralist ever maintained a doctrine so monstrous as the unlawfulness of abandoning a lawful Right. Admitting, what no Jurist in his senses will admit, that one man can possibly have a natural Right to tax another, why may he not relinquish that Right at his pleasure? The example is unhappily as inconclusive as the argument. Can any man believe that the American War of Independence was really caused by nothing but an erroneous intellectual theory? Or is there any imaginable alphabetical combination which the passions of an angry people cannot convert into a pretext for tyranny?

Considering the question as one of theory, I cannot admit the position, that the general tendency of every unjust and immoral act is pernicious to mankind. I think that there are acts which every good man must condemn, yet whose general tendency is doubtful if not beneficial. And there is obviously one important class of crimes, whose justification logically follows from the Utilitarian doctrine. If general Utility is the test of Right, it follows that no action which is generally useful can be wrong. It must therefore be laid down, that suffering or death may lawfully be inflicted upon an innocent individual, whenever the interest of the community requires it. The unscrupulous counsel of the wicked High Priest becomes at once a moral axiom. There are no doubt many instances in which such a sacrifice is dictated by Duty, and some in which it may be demanded without injustice. But cases may be produced from History, in which individuals have been deliberately put to death for the benefit of nations to whom they owed no allegiance, but to whom their existence was the cause of obvious peril. Surely no man will deny, either that such crimes may easily occur, or that when they occur they are worthy of severe condemnation.

Three centuries ago England was struggling for existence against a great Catholic Empire. The English Sovereign was childless, and the heir presumptive to the Crown was a foreign Princess and a bigoted Romanist. It happened that this unfortunate Lady was a prisoner, or rather a treacherously detained guest, within the English dominions. The English Government deliberately put her to death. The ineffable folly which has represented her as an angelic martyr, and the patriotic gratitude which attaches to the memory of her murderers, have done something to extenuate the abhorrence which such an act ought to excite. It was an act which every impartial moralist must consider as an execrable national crime. But it is impossible to deny that it effected a great national deliverance. Had Mary Stuart survived Elizabeth Tudor, the inevitable consequence would have been a desperate civil war combined with a Spanish invasion. The probability is that, under such circumstances, England would have lost her independence. With her would have fallen the hopes of European freedom. The murder of the Scottish Queen removed at once this terrible risk. Yet surely no man will justify that murder, or will maintain that it forms a precedent which ought in such cases to be followed.

## XV. Positive and Natural Law

Every system of civilised Jurisprudence will be found to resolve itself into two elements; rules deduced by the reason of the magistrate from the general principles of Natural Justice, and rules dogmatically fixed, whether by immemorial Custom or by express Legislation, for the purpose of national policy or of judicial convenience. The distinction is universally recognised, but there are two opposite points of view from which it may be contemplated. The practical Lawyer naturally considers the rigid formula, which he dares not disobey, as the original substance of Jurisprudence, and the flexible maxim, which he may venture to use his own discretion in applying, as the adventitious modification. He therefore designates the former as Law properly so called, and distinguishes the latter by the subordinate title of Equity. The speculative Jurist, commencing with theory and not with practice, is as naturally led to regard the everlasting principle as the essential rule and the temporary or local enactment as the casual exception. The arbitrary element in Jurisprudence he distinguishes as Positive Law. The rational element he denominates Natural Law, and considers it as the unchangeable foundation of all Legislative Science.

The speculative Jurist may be philosophically right, but there can be little doubt that he is historically wrong. His analysis certainly does not reverse the process by which national systems of Jurisprudence are actually constructed. Positive Law can be shown to have existed in an age when Natural Law, as a definite science, was altogether unknown. All primeval Jurisprudence of which we know anything appears to have consisted entirely of dogmatical Statutes, inexorable to any extreme of fraud or hardship, impenetrable to every consideration of natural Equity. The Satirists who ridicule the subtle refinements of modern Justice would be strangely surprised by the ceremony of a Roman Sale or Settlement in the days of republican simplicity. They would witness a scene like a very unintelligible pantomime, and they would be informed that, if a single unmeaning phrase or absurd gesticulation chanced to be omitted, the most solemn promises or the most palpable bad faith would not be allowed to bind the parties concerned.

It may not perhaps be difficult to account for this inflexible and irrational tenacity. There is no reason to suppose that the primitive races of mankind differed from ourselves in their ideas of honesty or humanity. The rude equity of a Syrian Patriarch, or of a Greek Themist, may possibly have been as fair and reasonable as that of an English Justice of the Peace. But there is an infinite difference between the instinctive shrewdness of a sensible arbitrator and the comprehensive wisdom of an accomplished Jurist. Many minds, singularly acute in detecting isolated truths, are utterly incapable of laying down or applying a general principle. Every reader remembers Scott's witty sketch of the country gentleman who was unable to comprehend the claims of the national Revenue, except as impersonated in the various gangers of his acquaintance. The same inveterate propensity to dwell upon minute details has damaged the professional reputation of magistrates, very different in authority and intellect from the Laird of Ellangowan. No English Lawyer can fail to recollect an instance in which inexhaustible learning, unerring sagacity, the most patient industry, the most conscientious integrity, failed, in the absence of comprehensive powers of generalization, to make a great Chancellor or an enlightened Legislator.

These considerations will go far to account for the cumbrous rigidity of the primitive Codes and Customs. So long as Justice was left to the unrestrained discretion of the Prince or the Priest, it was probably a simple process. But the first dawn of intelligence must have shown that the worst system of Law is preferable to the irresponsible tyranny of a Caste, and it might well be expected that the earliest Positive Law would have little connection with reason or morality. Reason and morality, indeed, are always the same. But experience proves that there is no more difficult task than to define in words a moral rule which every one comprehends by instinct. No honourable man, no virtuous woman, is ever at a loss to decide what conscience requires to be done, and yet, when the Casuists attempted to draw up a Code for the direction of Conscience, all their subtle skill could not preserve it from the fatal ridicule of Pascal. The duties which a man owes to his fellows are of course far more capable of being reduced to rule than those which he owes to himself. But still their investigation requires an accuracy of thought and a flexibility of language which are the growth of an age very different from that of Moses or of Menu.

Two metaphysical facts, Intention and Motive, pervade the whole science of Natural Law. What the parties meant, and how they were induced to mean it, are questions which a modern Jurist holds essential to the investigation of every transaction between man and man. But they are questions which Archaic Jurisprudence might be expected, and will be found, entirely to exclude. The skill with which a practised man of the world learns to decipher the intention in the act is as incomprehensible to a semi-barbarian as the skill of a backwoodsman in following a trail might be to a European Lawyer. The Doli Mali Exceptio of the Roman Prætor, the warnings against fraud or collusion which constantly qualify the rules laid down by English Courts of Justice, would probably have been wholly unintelligible to Alfred or Numa. The Lawgivers of antiquity would have derided the presumptuous dream that Law can bind the human will or prevent a bad man from entertaining bad intentions. That they insisted upon publicity in order to guard against fraud, and upon intricate formality in order to insure deliberation, is indeed highly probable. But directly to prohibit fraud, or directly to require deliberation, would have struck them as absurd. It never occurred to them that they could ascertain the existence of any but visible facts, and this explains their minute attention to external ceremony.

# XVI. Progress of Positive Law

As the establishment of Positive Law was probably due to the intolerable uncertainty of lawless arbitration, so the introduction of Natural Law appears to have been due to the intolerable rigour of primitive Legislation. In Jurisprudence, as in all the other sciences which regulate ordinary life, the early progress of the human mind resembled that of a ship beating to windward, which heads first one way and then the other and never goes about until her actual course becomes dangerous or inconvenient. The arbitrary discretion of the Judge was controlled by the enactment of a few inflexible rules. The harshness of the Customary or Statute Law was modified by the evasions of the Judge. It may perhaps be thought that the natural expedient would have been the rectification of Positive Law by the same authority which created it. But in the primitive ages of the world this seems seldom or never to have been attempted. Law once established, by whatever means, had in those days a mysterious power over the minds and consciences of men, and many of the ancient Codes are said to have borne strange and barbarous traces of the jealous abhorrence with which innovation was discouraged.

Perhaps the utmost rigour of Archaic Legislation did not display the primitive slavery to Form, or the primitive indifference to Justice, so forcibly as the earliest expedient by which it was evaded; just as the recklessness of a duellist may be said to be more clearly proved by the trifling apology which he is willing to accept, than by the trifling offence which he is eager to avenge. That expedient consisted in the Magistrate's deliberate assumption of a false state of facts, supported by his deliberate refusal to admit evidence to the contrary; a proceeding now well known as a Legal Fiction, but for which the conservative scruples of antiquity might well have been expected to find a much harsher name. But no such consequence occurred. The English Statute of Entails, the Roman and Hindoo Law of

Agnatic Succession, were thus virtually set aside with general acquiescence. It may almost be suspected that the ancient races regarded an inconvenient law rather as a living tyrant, whom they dared not disobey but whom they were glad to deceive, than as an abstract Rule, which might be abolished but which ought meantime to be respected.

Only the simple cunning of a rude and early age was likely to invent, or to tolerate the invention of, a Legal Fiction. The next expedient contrived to ameliorate without directly abrogating Positive Law, though by no means strictly legitimate, was far more ingenious and scientific in its character. It consisted in annexing a moral or conscientious obligation to the strict Legal Right, and in holding that the latter, though its existence could not be denied, must be exercised subject to the former. A substantially valid but informal Will might not prevent the Testator's property from devolving upon his heir-at-Law, but the heir-at-Law was held bound to execute the Testator's intention. A Contract procured by Fraud might be sufficient to create a Legal Right of Action against the Contractor, but the Gontractee was held restrainable from actually suing upon it. The system which thus artfully extracted the kernel, without breaking the shell, of a morally unjust claim, became known to Jurists by the technical name of Equity.

In the Roman Forum, where the Moral Obligation was imposed by the same Magistrate who had to decide the Legal Right, the superinduction of Equity upon Law was affected with little difficulty or disturbance. But in England, owing to a combination of peculiar circumstances, the administration of Equity was committed to, or rather usurped by, a Court constituted for certain special purposes and having no jurisdiction to entertain the ordinary Legal Actions. The consequences have been very singular, and were for a long time very inconvenient. During two or three centuries there were perpetual conflicts between the rival systems, the Courts of Equity often prohibiting an appeal to the Law and the Courts of Law often endeavouring to prevent the interference of Equity. This state of things has long been at an end, but its traces continue perceptible in every part of English Equity. Its subtleties constantly remind the student of the times when a Chancellor had to consider, not whether it was just to give or to refuse Relief, but whether he dared or feared to assume Jurisdiction. In fact, the English line of demarcation between Law and Equity resembles one of those ancient frontiers whose limits have been fixed, not by mutual convenience, but by the predatory warfare of hostile tribes, and those Jurists who pretend to explain its irregularity upon any consistent principle might as reasonably endeavour to delineate the Welsh or Scottish Marches by the rules of scientific mensuration.

But it is scarcely necessary to point out that the modification of Positive Law by the discretion of the Magistrate does not infer the cultivation, or even the existence, of Natural Law as a systematic science. Great practical sagacity may be shown in evading the injustice of primitive Legislation, by Magistrates wholly unacquainted with the theory of Jurisprudence. The mere instinct of Right is often sufficient to make a conscientious Judge wish for the discretionary power of dispensing with a particular Law in particular cases. It does not follow that, when he has got such a discretion, he knows how to use it upon any consistent principle. Still less does it follow that the altered rule which he wishes to enforce is part of any general system of Jurisprudence. It is only when we find judicial discretion used to carry out the conclusions of a definite and uniform system of ideal Justice, that we can pronounce the study of Natural Law to have fairly commenced. There is an infinite difference between impatience of actual Wrong and comprehension of abstract Right.

# XVII. Origin of Natural Law

It seems reasonable to assume that the creation of Positive Law left untouched, so far as it did not expressly take away, the arbitrary discretion of the Judge or ruler. The earliest attempt to define the principles upon which that discretion was to be exercised, and to reduce them into a systematic form, may therefore be considered as the origin of Natural Law. It is not until civilization is very far advanced, that we can discern any clear trace of such an attempt. Legal Fictions were clearly mere pretexts for escaping from the operation of particular Legal rules which had been found inconvenient. So far from proving that the principles of Natural Justice were beginning to be understood, their scrupulous adherence to Form and their utter disregard of Fact may be considered as strong proof to the contrary. Nor, in most cases, does the modification of Positive Law thus introduced appear to have been less arbitrary or more flexible than the original rule.

The Equity of the Roman Prætors had a very curious origin. It was founded upon, or rather suggested by, a sort of supplementary Code framed by the early Roman Lawyers and consisting in a collection of such elements of Positive Law as were common to all Italian States. This Code was termed the Jus Gentium or Law of Nations, as distinguished from the Jus Civile or domestic Roman Law, and was used in administering justice between foreigners residing in the Roman dominions. At its commencement it was probably regarded with contempt as an institution peculiar to an inferior race, but in process of time it became the object of mysterious reverence. The opinion began to prevail that these universal usages were the relics of an antique Code which had existed throughout the world in some age of primitive perfection, and the Jus Gentium acquired the honourable title of Jus Naturale or Natural Law. The Prætors applied it to modify the Jus Civile, and the Jurisconsults began to supply its deficiencies by rules drawn from their own conception of Natural Justice. At this point of time the Science of Natural Jurisprudence may be said to make its first appearance in the history of mankind. A system of Prætorian Equity was by such means gradually composed, which was consolidated into a distinct Code by the Perpetual Edict of Hadrian, and was finally, together with the Jus Civile, fused into one system of Imperial Law by the Legislation of Justinian.

The Equity of the English Chancellors originally consisted of certain doctrines imported ready made from the Imperial Law, or rather from the Imperial Law as modified by the Papal Canonists. These doctrines were originally laid down by men who had deeply and successfully studied the science of Jurisprudence. But it must not be inferred from this, that the science of Jurisprudence was understood by English Priests under the Plantagenets and Tudors. The Civil Law in the hands of Wolsey differed from the Civil Law in the hands of Gains or Papinian, as a log of timber differs from a living tree. It might be set erect, but it had no principle of growth. The Churchmen of the fifteenth and sixteenth centuries regarded the Institute and the Pandects simply as a Code of Positive Law. They were unwilling to shackle their power over Conscience by publishing precedents to which they might be expected to conform, and indeed there is every reason to believe that the great majority of their Decrees were mere circumstantial Awards. But if any of their decisions upon doubtful points of application had been preserved, we should probably have found them full of the same scholastic quibbles which abound in the medieval interpretations of the Statutes and the Feudal Customs.

The truth is that it was not until after the Restoration, perhaps not until after the Revolution, that any English Judge attempted to build up anything like a system of Natural Law. Up to that time, the judgment of an English Court was either an arbitrary guess at Justice, or a verbal criticism upon some dogma of Positive Law. Every Jurist knows that at the commencement of the eighteenth century there was, properly speaking, no Commercial Law whatever in England. All the nice and complicated questions which arose upon mercantile transactions were treated by the Judges as questions of Usage, to be decided as matter of fact by a Jury. In other words, they were left to the discretion of twelve casual arbitrators, who gave no reasons and incurred no responsibility. When a more scientific method of determining legal points arose, it was long regarded, both by Lawyers and by Laymen, with dislike and suspicion. It is not yet a century since an anonymous politician, whose elaborate rhetoric is now admired as little as it deserves, denounced the greatest magistrate of the age for deciding causes upon principles of common sense. It is not half a century since a very different authority, the illustrious Bentham, sneered at one of the most scientific departments of English Jurisprudence for preferring flexible Justice to dogmatic uniformity.

In this respect, the Courts of Equity were by no means superior to the Courts of Common Law. They started from a higher level, but they do not appear to have ascended more rapidly. Lord Nottingham, who became Chancellor in 1673, has the credit of the first attempt to mould English Equity into a science, and Lord Nottingham can scarcely be considered as a more enlightened Judge than Chief Justices Hale and Holt, one of whom preceded and the other shortly follower him. Lord Hardwicke, who held the Great Seal from 1787 to 1756, was the next Chancellor who materially improved the system; and Lord Hardwicke was decidedly inferior as a Jurist to Lord Mansfield, who was Chief Justice from 1756 to 1789. Indeed, had the Equity Judges, a hundred years ago, been really superior to their colleagues, it is probable that the Courts of Common Law would now be little more than criminal tribunals. There can be no doubt that, if Lord Mansfield had presided in the Court of Chancery, the admirable Commercial Code which he constructed would have been introduced into that Court, that every merchant in the realm would have applauded so useful an innovation, and that the whole regulation of British trade would have become a branch of Equity.

The improvements of that great Judge may be said to have fairly established the science of Natural Jurisprudence in England. Since his time it has attracted constantly increasing attention, and we may now boast that from no nation has it received more valuable contributions. But these contributions have assumed a shape singularly characteristic of the national intellect. They consist, not of theoretical disquisitions, but of Reports of Cases actually decided in the Courts, comprising a clear statement of the facts and an accurate copy of the decision. Most of these records turn, as might be expected, upon points of Positive Law only interesting to an English Lawyer. But a large proportion are such as any Jurist, of any nation, may study with profit and. delight. General principles ought not to be neglected, but every reasonable theorist will admit that thorough comprehension of general principles is only to be obtained by ample experience of particular examples. In this respect the advantages of the English student are probably unsurpassed. He may not have access to any speculative authority comparable to the great Roman, French and German Civilian. But even the celebrated Response Prudentum, the Lexicon of the Imperial Jurisconsults, must have been, as a treasury of practical Jurisprudence, far inferior both in minuteness and in authority to the English Reports.

## XVIII. Limit of Natural Law

It is obvious that every system of practical Legislation must and ought to include a very considerable proportion of Positive Law. The office of the Magistrate is simply to do justice between the parties in every particular case which comes before him, and he has no authority to lay down any of those arbitrary rules which, however necessary for the public convenience, cannot be enforced without occasional private hardship. He cannot fix the number of witnesses which shall be necessary to the validity of a Will, or the number of years which shall complete a title by Prescription. To do this is the office of the Legislator. But it is not an office with which the science of Jurisprudence has necessarily any concern. The questions which require this sort of peremptory solution are usually mere questions of Fact or of Form. In the phrase of English Jurists, they are questions for the Jury and not for the Judge. In such cases the object of the fixed rule is simply to avoid the frequent necessity of deciding a doubtful question of fact upon vague conjecture, and to take away the consequent opportunity for undiscovered perjury and fraud. The whole subject properly belongs to the Law of Evidence, and is therefore a branch of Remedial and not of Jural Legislation.

But there are two great provinces of Law which ought, so far as circumstances allow, to be left to the discretionary judgment of the Magistrate. All Jural Law is founded upon Natural Justice, and all that part of Remedial Law which relates to Procedure is founded upon Practical Expediency. Now it is obviously impossible to foresee, or to define by verbal rules, the endless variety of circumstances upon which the Justice or the Expediency of a case may depend. How far it is practicable to dispense with verbal rules in defining the Law of Procedure, is a question with which we have at present nothing to do. But no legal student can doubt that the Principles of Natural Justice can be far more effectually established by precedent than by enactment. A series of examples, each specifying the Legal result of a given combination of facts, is the only instrument by which an enlightened system of practical Jurisprudence ever was or ever will be constructed. It is only through the infinite variety of Fact that the infinite flexibility of Principle can be developed. Human invention and human language are utterly inadequate for the purpose.

The few though unfortunate attempts of this kind

which are to be found in the English Statute book are not to be ascribed to the presumption of the English Legislature. They are due to a principle, or rather a practice, which appears to be peculiar to the English Bench; the powerful yet indefinite authority of Judicial Precedent. It is clear that no English Judge can be legally censured for deciding a point of Law according to his own *bonâ-fide* opinion, so long as the exercise of that opinion is not expressly prohibited by Act of Parliament. But the traditions of the Legal Profession require every Judge to pay considerable deference to the recorded opinions of his colleagues and predecessors. In what cases that deference obliges him to do what he thinks injustice, or justifies him in doing it, is entirely a question for his own discretion. He may say, if he pleases, that he feels himself compelled to overrule the decisions which have been cited before him. He may say, if he pleases, that he considers the point as settled by Precedent, and therefore to be decided without reference to his own opinion.

Upon the expediency of this practice no one who is not a professional Lawyer ought to pronounce a confident opinion. It may be that the temporary convenience of the suitor outweighs, and ought to outweigh, the injury done to the science. But that this injury is serious and lasting, no one acquainted with the history of English Jurisprudence can doubt. An absurd decision is pronounced by some legal pedant of the sixteenth century. It is followed with reluctance by one or two of his immediate successors. It is then evaded, upon various subtle pretexts, in a succession of cases which clearly come within its principle. At length a resolute Judge boldly declares that it is not Law. But his declaration comes too late. His successor, a deeply learned and timidly cautious Lawyer, expresses serious doubts whether the current of authority is not too strong to be resisted, except by the interference of the Legislature. The question soon after presents itself for decision, and the opinion of the doubter is solemnly confirmed. Then comes a Declaratory Act, laying down a verbal rule For the purpose of defining a Jural principle, and the whole tedious process ends in the substitution of one bad law for another. This is the history of many a class of cases which has been the perplexity of English Jurists and Judges, and the intolerable burthen of English Reporters.

There is no difficulty in defining the true principle by which the weight of Judicial Precedent ought to be determined. Every Judge is of course morally bound, and ought to be legally compellable, to respect as Law the recorded opinion of any Court which has jurisdiction to reverse his own decisions upon appeal. Every Judge is likewise morally bound to ascertain the opinion, and to consider the reasons, of his colleagues and predecessors. But no Judge ought to be considered as morally bound to decide a question of Law contrary to his own ultimate opinion of the Justice of the case, except when he is legally compellable to do so. If two Magistrates have been successively intrusted by the Legislature with the same authority, upon what principle is A bound to imitate the errors of B. because B. chanced to live and to blunder a hundred years ago? Precedents should be followed either upon sincere conviction or upon legal compulsion, not upon the conventional ground of professional etiquette.

It may well be doubted whether the traditions of the English Bench will ever undergo such a change as this. But if there is anything by which such a change can be effected, it is the systematic study of a scientific theory of Jurisprudence. The whole prodigious power of a general principle, fully recognized and thoroughly understood, is required to extricate the human intellect from the toils of mistaken Precedent. That power is one by which the English legal mind is commonly believed to be far from easily moved. The truth perhaps may be, that it is one whose application to the English legal mind has been far from fairly tried. Let Englishmen once clearly comprehend the practical value of the machine, and they will soon prove themselves able to appreciate its scientific construction. When they have effected this, they may begin to look forward to the gradual formation of the most perfect system of Law whose existence the imperfection of the human intellect will permit. Such a system would consist in a Code of fixed Rules, founded upon rational calculations of general expediency; and combined with a Collection of Judicial Precedents, constantly improved by the additions and alterations of a succession of accomplished Jurists.

# BOOK I
# NATURAL JURISPRUDENCE

The question to be discussed in the present Book is the following: In what cases do the natural conditions of human existence confer upon one human being the moral Right of controlling for his own benefit the volition of another? It is evident that this question presupposes a certain combination of physical facts. It cannot possibly arise, except when two human beings are in such a situation that one of them has the physical power of causing pain or pleasure to the other. In other words, the existence of the science of Jurisprudence requires the Coexistence of two or more human beings; and therefore it is by defining the questions of Right which may arise from this fact, or from the circumstances which necessarily accompany it, that every explanation of that science ought to commence. The first question therefore is, Does one human being naturally possess, or can he by the exercise of his or their natural faculties acquire, any and what Right of Control over his fellow-creatures?

We naturally begin by considering whether certain mutual Rights may not arise from Personal Coexistence, considered as a solitary fact. But we know that human existence never is a solitary fact. The Coexistence of two human beings in empty space, if not absolutely impossible, would probably take place under conditions such as would make their mutual Rights scarcely worth discussion. It is, at all events, a physical certainty that all the human beings of whose existence we are aware are confined by gravitation to the surface of a spherical mass of granite termed the Earth, and that the greater part of this surface is clothed with certain substances whose use is found by experience to be necessary or useful for the maintenance of human life. These facts make it necessary to inquire how far the mutual Rights arising from the Coexistence of Persons may possibly be altered by the existence of Things.

But the subject of Natural Jurisprudence is not yet exhausted. We have hitherto assumed, in speaking of the exercise of the natural faculties, that the natural faculties of all human beings are the same. But we know that this is not the fact. We know that there is at least one great physical distinction by which the whole human race is divided into two classes, each having faculties peculiar to itself. We also know that Nature has established many moral and physical disabilities or disparities, and many moral and physical connections or relations, by some or one of which almost every human being is more or less distinguished from the average of mankind. Sex, age, mental and bodily peculiarities, the ties of consanguinity and the characteristics of Race, combine to constitute the Status, or natural position among mankind, of every human being. And therefore the inquiry, to what extent such abnormal circumstances ought to modify the natural Rights of the normal or typical human individual, is necessary to complete the subject of Natural Jurisprudence.

In this manner we take the natural circumstances of human life in their natural order of succession. We begin by supposing the existence of two or more human beings, possessing such faculties only as are common to all mankind. We then examine the questions of Right which arise from that fact, whether taken singly or combined with the existence of the material Creation. And we finally inquire what difference will be made by the existence of peculiarities which are *not* common to all mankind. The subject of Natural Jurisprudence is thus divided into three branches, and the present Book into the following three Chapters: — I. Personal Rights and Obligations. II. Real Rights and Obligations. III. Statual Rights and Obligations. In supposing the existence of two or more human beings it will of course be found convenient to distinguish them by different symbols, and I trust that I shall not be accused of levity if I select for this purpose certain familiar patronymics which, to an English reader, represent with no inadequate vivacity the Titius and Seius of the Roman Responses.

All Jurisprudence, says the illustrious Gaius, relates either to Persons, to Things or to Actions. It may be doubted whether any man ever did so much in so few words to confound any human science, as the Jurist who first invented this celebrated formula. The Law of Persons, grievously mutilated and preposterously misplaced as in the Institute it is, may possibly have been meant to comprise Statual as distinguished from Universal Jurisprudence; and so far the analysis would be correct. But with the division, of all Rights into Real Rights and Actions, or in other words into General and Special Obligations, commences the admission of the fatal principle which classifies by consequences instead of causes. From that moment all hope of a clear and logical arrangement is at an end. For since every fact which confers upon me a General Right must necessarily impose a Special Obligation upon any one who infringes that Right, and since any fact which imposes upon me a Special Obligation may incidentally confer upon the Obligee a General Right to my property, it follows that both divisions must be fully understood before either can be intelligibly explained.

The absurdity of such an arrangement has been felt and acknowledged by the best modern Jurists; but this, strange and incredible as it must appear, has not prevented them from adopting it. Their only excuse has been the gratuitous assumption that, imperfect as the Roman principle of distribution confessedly is, no other can be suggested which is not equally so; an assumption which, if it were true, would justify the inference that the study of Jurisprudence is unfit for and unworthy of a rational being. But it is utterly untrue. And not only is it untrue, but I venture to assert that it would never have occurred as true to any thoughtful mind, unless trained to look at natural Fact through the distorting medium of Legal Conception. Perhaps no spectacle is more exasperating than that of an acute intellect bewildered by

Hero-worship. It becomes easy to understand the bitterness of Hottoman, when we see thinkers like Savigny and Austin committing illogicality with their eyes open, because they will not believe that what Tribonian failed, to do can ever be done.

The Rights which I have termed General were distinguished by the Roman Jurists as Real, and the Law relating to Real Rights was termed by them the Law of Things; the word Things being applied, not only to visible objects capable of human use, but to all exclusive Privileges of whatever description. This singular terminology seems to have arisen from the idea, that the Law of Things must be considered as relating to questions of Right, not between one Person and another, but between Persons and Things. The necessary consequence of this distinction was of course the non-existence, or rather the non-recognition, of any Obligations correlative to Real Rights. For a Person might intelligibly, however incorrectly, be said to possess a Right as against an inanimate or irrational Thing; but an inanimate or irrational Thing could not be intelligibly described as bound by an Obligation to a Person. The word Obligation is therefore, throughout the Imperial Codes, exclusively used as the correlative of a Personal or Special Right.

It is scarcely worth while to point out the intense confusion of thought which such an analysis indicates. Every straightforward thinker can see for himself that all Rights are and must be Personal; that a General, if it differs in this respect from a Special Right, differs from it only in binding an indefinite number of persons; that a Thing cannot be the Object, though it may he the Subject, of a Right; and that a Personal privilege, whether Special or General, has no existence apart from that of the Person or Persons whom it binds, and cannot therefore in any intelligible sense be termed a Thing I mention the subject for the sole purpose of excusing my departure from a terminology which the best Jurists have hitherto adopted, but which I consider highly inaccurate and inexpedient. I cannot consent to understand the word Obligation as anything short of the absolute correlative of the word Right. I think it absurd to say that I have a Right to prohibit all mankind from doing a certain act, and yet that mankind are under no Obligation to respect my prohibition. And I shall therefore, whenever I find the phrase convenient, speak without scruple of General as well as of Special Obligations.

But in explaining the principles of Universal Jurisprudence I shall adopt, not the illogical division of General and Special Rights, but the natural order of thought which is suggested by the successive combinations of Fact from which questions of Right may arise between human beings. I shall also carefully abstain, from any definition either of Persons or of Things. What is a Person and what is a Thing are questions for the Physiologist. The Moralist has no concern with them. Every living human being is to him a Person and every other object of human sensation a Thing; and nothing else is either. The Roman Civilians, it is well known, defined a person as the possible Possessor, and a Thing as the possible Subject, of a Legal Right. To the juridical Antiquary the metaphysical ingenuity of the conception may no doubt be interesting, but to the philosophical Jurist it will appear perhaps the most fatal of the many pedantic refinements which Legal Science has used to prevent Reason from taking hold of Fact.

## CHAPTER I
## PERSONAL RIGHTS AND OBLIGATIONS

Does a human being naturally possess, or can he by the exercise of his or their natural faculties acquire, any and what Right of Control over his fellow-creatures? The simplest possible case in which this question can arise is that which excludes all community of Volition between the human beings whose Coexistence we have assumed, and which therefore leaves each man's Rights and Obligations dependent upon his own individual situation or conduct. In other words our first inquiry must be, Does one coexistent human being necessarily possess, or can he without his own Consent acquire, any and what Right of Control over another?

The next step is to combine the fact of Coexistence with that of Consensual Action. It is evident that, in supposing the Coexistence of two human beings, we suppose the possibility of a combination between them to exercise their natural faculties for a common purpose. Such a combination, it is true, does not presuppose the fact of mutual Consent. It may take place by mere accident, or by the will of one party without the assent of the other. But if we suppose an act to be voluntarily done or omitted by one person in obedience to the intentional inducement of another, we introduce a new element of discussion. Such an act or omission is termed Consensual, and it is obvious that its Jural effect may intelligibly be thought different from what in the absence of Consent it would have been. Our second question therefore is, Can one human being confer upon another, by the Consensual exercise of their natural faculties, any and what Right of Control which he could not have otherwise acquired?

The foundation of all Consent is an Intention entertained by one person to control the volition of another, and every voluntary act or omission is Consensual which takes place in consequence of, or which would not have taken place without, the intention of another person to make it take place. The simplest form of a Consensual transaction is therefore an act done or omitted by one person in compliance with the communicated Wish of another. Such a communication is termed a Mandate; except when it can be shown to have been made in compliance with the known antecedent Wish of the party who receives it, in which case it changes its name and becomes an Assent. But it is likewise clear that an act may be done or omitted by one person, not simply in compliance with the Wish of another, but in reliance upon the truth of some statement or representation made by another. Such a representation is termed a Promise when it is capable of being verified by the act of the person who makes it, and a Falsehood or Deception when it is not.

The present Chapter will thus be divided into the four following sections: — I. Individual Obligations.. II. Consensual Obligations. III. Promissory Obligations. IV. Deceptional Obligations.

## I. Individual Obligations

§ 1. The fundamental Axiom which forms the basis of the whole system of Natural Justice I conceive to be, that one human being has *no* right to control for his own benefit the volition of another. In the exceptions to this Axiom, therefore, the whole subject-matter of Jurisprudence may be said to consist. They are of course very numerous and occasionally very intricate, but it will be found that they are all deducible from a few exceedingly simple and obvious maxims. I believe, indeed, that it would be possible to go still further than this. I think that there is a single principle, from whose necessary consequences every such exception may be said to flow. That principle is, that no human being can justifiably do what will make the physical condition of another less comfortable than it is by Nature. It would not, in my opinion, be difficult to show that every question of Right which can possibly arise depends upon the application of the rule, that every man is entitled to enjoy whatever benefits the Will of Providence or the exercise of his natural faculties may confer upon him.

§ 2. It is not however my intention to adopt any such comprehensive axiom as the foundation of the present Work. By doing so I should be securing logical uniformity at the expense of strength, clearness and brevity. My object is to explain the natural and necessary connection between the principles of common Justice and the rules of technical

Law. It is quite unnecessary for this purpose to trouble ourselves with any metaphysical theory about the ultimate root from which the principles of common Justice may be considered to spring. I greatly prefer to take those principles as I find them generally acknowledged by the class of mankind to which I have the honour to belong. I shall therefore assume that the standard of Right and Wrong usually recognized by educated Englishmen is correct, and shall make it the basis of my reasoning. I select this standard, not only because it is that with which I am most familiar, but also because, imperfect as it probably still is, I believe it to be far the highest which has ever been adopted by any large community of human beings.

§ 3. But before I proceed I must once more remind my readers that the opinions upon Jurisprudence contained in the present work have not been inserted for the sake of their own intrinsic value. They have been used merely as a tailor uses his wicker figures, not because he thinks them worth looking at in themselves, but because he wishes to show how well his clothes are made. The merit of the present work, if it has any, is the exposition of a method of analysis which will teach any rational man to understand how the great questions of Jurisprudence arise, and how they are connected with each other. This purpose will be most clearly and briefly effected by attempting to answer as well as to state them. But every such attempt must be regarded as purely hypothetical. I have not hesitated to give my own opinions of what Law ought to be, but I have only done so in order to exemplify the true method of learning what Law is.

§ 4. That one human being, merely as such, is entitled to insist upon the performance for his own benefit of any positive service by another, has never been maintained. To say that a man owes assistance or hospitality to his fellow creatures is an inaccurate form of expression. It is to his own conscience that he owes such duties, and that he is responsible for their neglect. Selfishness and obduracy are very odious moral vices, but they are not Jural Wrongs; and the attempt to treat them as such would infallibly end in affording a ready pretext for universal tyranny and oppression. It is only by negative Obligations that one human being is naturally bound to another, and it is only by some positive act that a breach of Natural Right can be committed. The present question therefore is, what acts is one human being, merely as such, naturally entitled to prevent another from doing?

§ 5. The question, how far one human being is restrainable from inflicting Moral Suffering upon another, is one which can scarcely be discussed under the head of Natural Jurisprudence. There is no class of acts which can be defined as necessarily or naturally offensive to the moral feelings of mankind in general, and the accidental fact that a particular person feels, or chooses to pretend that he feels, moral pain at the sight of a particular act, is of course no reason for allowing him to prevent it. It is only upon the ground of antecedently established Moral Opinion that such cases can be solved. Can Brown, for example, be restrained from telling Jones a falsehood concerning Robinson? Taken as a Slander, the question depends upon the opinions of Jones. Taken as an Insult, it depends upon the opinions of Robinson. But, in the absence of definite Moral Usage, there can be no such offence as either.

§ 6. But it may safely be laid down as an Axiom of Natural Justice, that one human being has no right to commit any act of Physical Violence against another. Physical Violence is of two kinds, that which inflicts Physical Suffering and that which imposes Physical Constraint. Physical Violence comprises any act which can destroy life, disable strength, weaken health or inflict pain. Physical Constraint comprises every act which can impede the natural exercise of Volition. That no man has a right to commit any such act unless compelled by circumstances to do so, and that all such acts may lawfully be prevented, is a rule so obvious in its justice and so simple in its application that I think it unnecessary to do more than suggest it. Whatever impatience of the theory of Natural Law may at present prevail, I cannot persuade myself that it has yet become necessary to show by argument that one man is bound to give some reason for knocking down or locking up another.

§ 7. Whoever does an act which he might lawfully have been prevented from doing, may of course be lawfully compelled to remove its injurious consequences. The simple fact, that Brown has by the exercise of his volition inflicted suffering or constraint upon Jones, is therefore sufficient, in the absence of all qualifying circumstances, to create a Special Obligation between Brown and Jones. Every Delinquent is moreover liable to make compensation, not only for the injury directly inflicted by his Delict or breach of Natural Justice, but likewise for any incidental injury which the Plaintiff may, without any wilful negligence of his own, have sustained in consequence of its commission. Nor can this additional liability be repelled by proof that the Delinquent did not foresee, or even that he could not possibly have foreseen, the indirect mischief which he was doing. It may be hard that a man should forfeit a fortune by a momentary act of violence, but it would be much harder to lay the forfeiture upon the man by whom the violence was sustained. Whoever breaks the rules of Natural Justice does so at his own peril, and cannot refuse compensation because he has done more harm than he expected.

§ 8. Upon the same principle, a wrongful act which indirectly inflicts an injury on a third person will confer upon him a separate and independent right of requiring compensation for that injury, although it was neither intended nor foreseen by the wrong-doer. And the rule is the same where the ulterior injury is inflicted, not by the immediate act of the Delinquent, but by an act which he has wrongfully made necessary for the defence of another. Suppose, for instance, that Brown wantonly throws a firework at Jones, and that Jones by throwing it from him injures Robinson. There can be no doubt that Brown is responsible for the injury done to Robinson, but there is no ground for permitting Robinson to require compensation from Jones. The wrongful act of Brown was the true instrument of the mischief, and the accidental circumstance of its immediate infliction by the justifiable act of Jones can make no difference in the rights or liabilities of the parties concerned.

§ 9. We will next suppose the Wrong to have been done, not by unavoidable accident or by culpable negligence, but by wilful intention. In this case the injured party acquires the additional Right of Retaliation or Punishment. He is entitled, not only to receive full compensation for the injury which he has sustained, but likewise to inflict upon the wrong-doer the same amount of physical suffering which the wrong-doer has inflicted upon him. The liability of every human being to undergo himself whatever he wilfully causes to be undergone by another is an Axiom of Natural Justice, and perhaps of all such Axioms the most thoroughly understood and the most universally enforced. But it may be necessary to remind some scrupulous consciences that the Justice of an act is one question and its moral innocence another. It does not lie in the mouth of the aggressor to complain because others do to him as he has done to others. But no Moralist will deny that the man who requites an injury, not from a sense of necessity but from a desire for revenge, commits a sin against his own conscience.

§ 10. But, assuming a wrong-doer to be criminally punishable for the wrong which he intended to commit, does it follow that he is so for its unforeseen consequences? The English Law decides that it does, but the decision seems a questionable one. It is difficult to understand how a man who meant one thing can be justly punished for having meant another. Suppose, for instance, that Brown fires at Jones and accidentally shoots Robinson. Brown has here committed two wrongful acts, for both of which he must make reparation. He is criminally answerable for his felonious attempt, and civilly answerable for his culpable negligence. But there is neither justice nor common sense in blending the disappointed intention and the unintentional act. The attempt to shoot Jones would have been equally wrongful if Robinson had been a hundred miles off. The wound inflicted upon Robinson might have been equally wrongful if Brown had fired at a target. Two black rabbits, as Strafford reminded his judges, do not make a black hare.

§ 11. It may be doubted whether, in the absence of any artificial connection between the parties, one human being is morally entitled to inflict Punishment upon another for a criminal offence committed against a third, otherwise than through the medium of the right of Retaliation thereby conferred upon the injured party. Thus, supposing that Brown has committed an assault upon Jones, it is difficult to see how Robinson can justify himself for retaliating upon Brown the injury done to Jones, except by showing, either that he has done so by the special authority of Jones, or that there is some antecedent relation between himself and Jones which gives him an independent right to do so. But in neither of these cases can Robinson be said to acquire a separate or Individual right of control over Brown. Punishment inflicted by special authority presupposes the Consent of the agent and the injured party. And Criminal Law, properly so called, is founded upon Civil and not upon Natural Jurisprudence.

§ 12. The wilful infliction of pain or damage may therefore be justified by the Right of Retaliation. It may also be justified by the necessity of self-defence. If I attempt to do an act which another person is entitled to prevent, I thereby confer upon him the right of forcibly resisting the completion of my attempt; and, if he cannot successfully do so without inflicting damage upon my person, he is no more responsible to me for such damage than he would have been if I had expressly authorized him to inflict it. Whatever scruples some Christian sects may profess respecting the right of self-defence, considered as between the assailed party and his own conscience, it can scarcely be denied to exist as between the assailed and the assailant. The most non-combative of Quakers would probably admit that, whether the man who kills an assassin commits a sin or not, he certainly does not commit an act of which the assassin has any right to complain.

§ 13. The principles by which the right of self-defence ought to be regulated have been very variously and very unsatisfactorily stated. The Civilians make it depend upon the kind and degree of apprehension entertained by the assailed person, which they describe in terms so vague as to recal the well-known story of the witness who, when pressed to explain what he meant by a large stone, defined it as a stone equal in size to several small ones. Blackstone, in one of the very few passages where he has attempted to lay down a principle of his own, takes the punishment incurred by the crime as the measure of the resistance justified by the attempt; a doctrine upon which it is sufficient to remark that it would make me guilty of wilful murder if I were to inflict death in resisting an assault upon my life by a lunatic. And Locke, by maintaining that every attempt at wrongful violence places the parties in a state of War, seems to allow the infliction of instant death whenever one passenger is jostled by another.

§ 14. The true principle is that the limits of self-defence must be determined by the question, What was really going to take place? The assailed party has a right to use so much violence as is necessary to preserve his person from violence by the assailant, and no more. The point to be decided therefore is, not what the one feared or what the other deserved, but what the assailant would actually have effected if the assailed had used milder means of resistance. The slightest attempt at constraint will justify homicide if it cannot be otherwise resisted. The most atrocious attempt at murder will not justify a single blow after the danger is over. The bravo of former days, who went about pushing passengers off the pavement, could not complain if they withstood him sword in hand. But St. John was clearly guilty of a wrongful act in stabbing Guiscard after he had failed in his attempt to assassinate Harley.

§ 15. It now remains to consider whether one human being can, by the independent exercise of his natural faculties, impose upon another any obligation, or confer upon him any right, in addition to those which arise from the simple fact of their coexistence. The foundation of every Jural Right must necessarily, as we have already seen, be a Moral Duty; and our first inquiry must therefore be, Are there any and what means by which I can make it your duty to comply with my wish, or mine to comply with yours? The answer is obvious. I can, without any consent of yours, make it your duty to be Grateful to me, or mine to be Faithful to you. In other words, I can bind you to comply with my wish by conferring upon you a Benefit, and I can bind myself to comply with your wish by making you a Promise. The question therefore is, to what extent the Duties of Gratitude and Fidelity can be held to confer a correlative Right upon the person who will be benefited by their discharge.

§ 16. The foundation of every Beneficial Duty is necessarily a Wish entertained by one person and known to another. Such a state of facts may easily exist without any mutual Consent, since we know that one human being is often able, by the unassisted exercise of his own natural faculties, to become acquainted with the feelings and intentions of another. In such a case, any act done by the one party in compliance with the wish entertained by the other is termed a Benefit, and the acceptance of a Benefit will undoubtedly impose upon the Beneficiary the moral duty of requiting it. But it cannot be said to confer upon the Benefactor any moral right to exact a requital. On the contrary, there is no opinion in which men of honour more uniformly agree than in denouncing as base and dishonest the demand of a recompense for that which was originally offered as a gift. Ingratitude therefore, although no doubt a heinous moral sin, cannot be considered as in itself a Jural Wrong.

§ 17. The Intention of doing or of not doing a certain act, adopted by one human being and by him communicated to another, is of course insufficient to create a conscientious Duty, much less a Jural Obligation. Such a communication, if made with the knowledge that the person to whom it is made wishes the Intention to be fulfilled, becomes a Promise. Whether every man who makes a Promise is morally bound to fulfil it, need not be here discussed. It is sufficient that every man to whom a Promise is made is not morally entitled to insist upon its fulfilment. If Brown undertakes to confer a gratuitous benefit upon Jones, Brown may act dishonourably in breaking his engagement, but Jones would act no less dishonourably by attempting to enforce its performance. Nor can the circumstance, that the benefit promised by Brown to Jones was intended as a recompense for a benefit previously bestowed by Jones upon Brown, be held to alter the case. If the acceptance of a favour is not in itself sufficient to create an obligation, a Promise to requite it must be considered as gratuitous.

§ 18. A gratuitous Promise does not amount to a revocable act. It is a mere nullity. In the absence of any further communication between the parties, nothing which the Promissee may do in reliance upon it can possibly affect the Promissor. Suppose, for instance, that Brown promises to assist Jones in a certain undertaking, and that Jones, making the attempt in consequence of his belief that the Promise will be kept, sustains loss or damage by its breach. It would be most unreasonable to hold that this state of facts is sufficient to make Brown responsible to Jones. To such a demand the answer would be that Brown, not having been aware that Jones intended to act upon the faith of the Promise, was at liberty to change his mind without giving notice to Jones, and that Jones may thank his own negligence for his disappointment. Good Faith may be in all cases a moral Duty, but to make it a Jural Obligation requires the Consent of two or more persons.

## II. Consensual Obligations

§ 19. A Wish entertained by one person and communicated to another cannot be considered as a Mandate. Such a communication resembles a gratuitous Promise, and therefore imposes no responsibility upon the person by whom it is made. But if the communication is made with the intention of inducing the Mandatary to do or not to do some particular act, or even if the Mandator becomes aware that it is about to produce such an effect and does not countermand it, he must clearly be considered as having made the act or the omission his own. He therefore becomes bound to indemnify any third person whose rights may have been unavoidably infringed by the obedience of the Mandatary. But he cannot be held responsible for a wrongful act committed by the Mandatary with the intention of obeying the Mandate, but not indispensable for that purpose; nor even for his unavoidable non-performance of a Special Obligation of whose existence the Mandator was not aware when he gave the Mandate.

§ 20. As between the parties themselves, the Mandator is undoubtedly bound in Justice to indemnify the Mandatary against whatever loss or damage he may, without any fault or negligence of his own, incur by his obedience. And from this it seems to follow that, when the Mandator becomes responsible to a person injured by the Mandatary, he will be further liable to indemnify the Mandatary against his own responsibility. The contrary opinion has probably arisen from a confusion between the principle of Compensation and that of Punishment. The full amount of necessary suffering must of course be inflicted upon every one of the guilty parties, however numerous. But the equivalent due to the injured party is a fixed quantity. Its amount will be the same whether the wrong was done by one person or by a hundred, and it therefore seems reasonable that it should be borne by the party for whose gratification the act was committed.

§ 21. But the case is altered if it can be shown that the obedience of the Mandatary, although immediately and ostensibly the consequence of the Mandate, was primarily intended for his own benefit. In this case, if the act which has been done is a Wrong against a third person, the actual Agent is to be considered as the principal delinquent, and the Mandator, or rather adviser, merely as his Accomplice. If therefore Brown is induced, by the influence of Jones, to assail Robinson in revenge for an affront offered by Robinson to Jones, Brown is entitled to be exonerated from his responsibility by Jones. But if the assault, though caused by the interference of Jones, was intended as a revenge for an affront sustained by Brown himself, Jones is clearly entitled to be exonerated by Brown. Thus Richard III., not Tyrrel, is primarily responsible for the murder of Edward V., because the act is done for the benefit of the instigator though by the hand of the Agent. But Macbeth, not Lady Macbeth, is primarily responsible for the murder of Duncan, because the act is done for the benefit of the Agent though by the influence of the adviser.

§ 22. We have hitherto supposed the Mandate to be given by one person and the act to be done by another. But the same rules apply to acts jointly done by more than one agent. Every person who co-operates in the commission of a Wrong, or who in other words does any visible act without which the Wrong would or possibly might have been incomplete, will of course be bound to make compensation for the entire injury inflicted. But if it can be proved that one of two or more joint delinquents acted in obedience to the wish and for the ultimate benefit of another, that delinquent ought to be liable merely as an Accomplice. And if it should appear that all the co-delinquents acted by mutual consent for the execution of a Wish common to them all, they must upon the same principle contribute to make compensation in proportion to the benefit or gratification which each has derived from the act. In other words, the civil responsibility of every joint Wrong ought to be divided, according to the number of its visible Agents, among the persons by whose influence and for whose ultimate gratification the co-operation of each Agent took place.

§ 23. Take as an example the murder of Thomas of Canterbury. Four Barons have assassinated an Archbishop at the instigation of a King, and the question now is, not who is to be hanged for the murder, but who is to make good the blood-ransom. In order to answer it, we must ascertain the person or persons for whose benefit or gratification the act was really committed. The four Barons may be roughly estimated to have taken an equal share in the visible act, and they are therefore *primâ facie* equally liable to contribute. But they killed the Archbishop entirely to please the King. Then the King is bound to exonerate them from their liability. Or did one of them join in the act from motives of private malice? Then he must contribute one-fourth, and the King the other three-fourths. Or was one of them compelled or tempted to join by the influence of the rest? Then he is entitled to be indemnified by his co-delinquents, and they by the King.

§ 24. The effect of a Mandate for the performance of an act which would otherwise have been a Wrong as against the Mandator, will of course be the justification of the act if afterwards committed by the Mandatary. If for instance I request a dentist to draw my tooth, or a groom to take charge of my horse, it is clear that I cannot sue the dentist for an assault or the groom for a larceny. But it is equally clear that such a Mandate, being intended for the benefit of the Mandator and not for that of the Mandatary, is revocable at the pleasure of the Mandator, and that it will not justify an execution by the Mandatary after he has received notice of its revocation. And from this it follows that the Mandate, even while it exists, will only justify the performance of the Mandatary subject to whatever exceptions or qualifications the Mandator may have chosen to annex to it.

§ 25. The possibility of effective Assent implies of

course that of justifiable prevention. A declaration that I intend to permit the fulfilment of an intention which I have no right to oppose would obviously be a mere nullity. The operation of Assent is therefore confined to those cases where the act to which it is given would otherwise have been a Wrong against the person who gives it. In such a case the consequences of a gratuitous Assent will be the same as those of a Mandate. No act can be treated as a Wrong by a person who has assented to its commission, whether the motive of the Assert is the benefit of the Assentient or that of the Agent. Nor can the circumstance that the Assent was given for the benefit of the Agent prevent its revocation, or justify an act done by virtue of it after the Agent was aware that it had been revoked. To revoke a gratuitous Assent may or may not be conscientiously right, but to insist that it shall not be revoked would clearly be conscientiously wrong.

§ 26. There is no substantial difference between Assent to an act intended and Assent to an act already done, except that in the latter case the Assentient has no opportunity of revocation. A Release, which is simply a declaration that the Relessor does not intend to treat as wrongful a particular act previously committed by the Relessee, is therefore, although gratuitous, an irrevocable bar to the obligation. Whether the Relessee can honourably insist upon it may perhaps be doubted, but it is clear that the Relessor cannot honourably disregard it. The moral duty may or may not have ceased to exist, but the moral right has unquestionably been extinguished. Upon this obvious reasoning is founded the well-known distinction of the Civil Law between Obligations which generate Actions, that is to say which may be actively enforced, and those which only generate Exceptions, that is to say which can only be defensively pleaded.

§ 27. This brings us to the important question, whether the benefit of a Special Obligation is transferable by the act of the Obligee. That with the assent of the Obligor it is so, can scarcely be disputed. In this case the Transfer is simply a Conditional Release. If you will do for this person what you are already bound to do for me, I will hold you discharged. There can surely be no doubt that, if you comply with my request before it is revoked, I am bound by my undertaking. But can a Special Obligation be transferred against the will of the Obligee? In the case of a merely personal Obligation, certainly not. Not only may the task of conferring a certain benefit upon one person be much more difficult and troublesome than that of conferring it upon another, but there would in many cases be no common measure by which its fulfilment could be satisfactorily tested.

§ 28. We have hitherto supposed the case of a gratuitous or unconditional Assent. But of course an Assent may be given upon condition that the party who receives it shall, before he avails himself of it, confer some reciprocal benefit upon the Assentient, and in this case the Assent is said to be founded upon Valuable Consideration. The effect of such a transaction will be very different from that of a gratuitous Assent. If the party receiving the Assent complies with the condition, the Assent will become an irrevocable obligation, and will bind the Assentient as such. If the party receiving the Assent avails himself of it without having fulfilled the Condition, the Assentient may compel him to do so. And if the party receiving the Assent signifies his acceptance of its terms, both parties become reciprocally bound, the one by the Assent and the other by the Condition. But an Assent, although given for Valuable Consideration, is revocable until it has been accepted, and its acceptance after notice of revocation will therefore not bind the Assentient.

§ 29. A Release may be tacit as well as express. There is no substantial difference between saying that I will not enforce my right, and acting so as to make you believe that I am not going to enforce it. There can consequently be no doubt that the acquiescence of an Obligee in the non-performance of his obligation ought, if continued long enough to raise the presumption that he never means to enforce it, to be considered as a tacit Release of his claim. What period of delay, unassisted by any indication of abandonment and unexplained by any circumstances of difficulty, ought in a given case to be sufficient for this purpose, is of course a question of fact. It is therefore a question which ought, according to the English principles of Procedure, to be left to the conjecture of a Jury, if the great difficulty of deciding it had not induced all civilized Legislatures to evade the necessity by arbitrarily fixing a certain lapse of time as a Bar by Prescription.

§ 30. We are told that the question, whether the principle of Prescription arises from private Justice or from public Policy, has been long and keenly debated among the continental Civilians. A dispute among geographers, whether the surface of the Earth consists of land or of water, would deserve about as much attention. How is it possible to doubt that it is compounded of the two? Can any Moralist think it consistent with justice, that one man should be permitted to ruin another by first decoying him to incur liabilities which he cannot discharge and then insisting upon them? Or can any practical Lawyer deny the expediency of fixing, apart from all proof of fraud or negligence, a certain limit beyond which no dormant claim shall be revived? I believe that all civilized systems of Prescription will be found to contain these two elements. There is the presumptive and the final bar by lapse of time, the one being manifestly founded upon Justice and the other upon Policy.

## III. Promissory Obligations

§ 31. We have seen that a gratuitous Promise is in itself a mere nullity, and that it will not even make the Promissor responsible for any loss or damage which the Promissee may incur by acting upon the faith of its fulfilment.[1] But the case will be altered if the Promissor becomes aware that the Promissee is about to do or to omit, in consequence of the Promise, some act which he would not otherwise have done or omitted. In this case the Promissor is bound, if he does not intend to keep his Promise, to give the Promissee timely notice that he has changed his mind. And if he omits to do this, he must either fulfil his Promise or make compensation to the Promissee for whatever loss or damage may be inflicted by its breach. I am not necessarily bound to suppose that you intend to believe my words and to act upon them, but, if I stand by and knowingly permit you to do so, I become responsible for the consequences.

§ 32. As regards the liability of third persons, there is an obvious and important distinction between the breach of a binding Promise and that of a natural Right. A natural Right creates an obligation not to do a particular act, by which every human being is or may become bound to every other. A binding Promise creates an obligation to do or not to do a particular act, by which Brown is bound to Jones. The breach of such an obligation is only a Wrong as between Jones and Brown. If therefore Brown breaks his Promise to Jones, Robinson cannot require compensation from Brown for any injury, not being in itself a Wrong, which he may indirectly sustain from the breach.[2] Nor will Robinson, by inducing or assisting Brown to break his Promise, or even by wrongfully preventing him from keeping it, become responsible to Jones if he acted without notice of its existence.[3] Nothing can be clearer than that my Promise to you can make no difference to any third person who is not aware of it. The contrary opinion would enable one human being to acquire a right of property in another.

§ 33. Upon the same principle, the existence of a

---

[1] §§ 17, 18.
[2] See § 8.
[3] See § 20.

binding Promise is not in itself sufficient to invalidate a subsequent contradictory Promise by the Promissor to a third person. Thus if Brown, after promising Jones not to do a certain act, promises Robinson to do it, the second Promise is not necessarily either invalid as between Robinson and Brown or wrongful as between Jones and Robinson. It may even be contended that Robinson would not, by accepting or compelling the performance of his own Promise after receiving notice of that with Jones, become liable to make compensation to Jones. Every human being, in short, has unlimited authority to bind himself by any number of inconsistent obligations, nor can any one of his Obligees claim indefeasible priority over the rest. Upon this simple rule is founded the whole doctrine of human Freedom. I may to a certain extent make myself your servant, but I cannot disable myself from treating with the rest of mankind as a free man.

§ 34. But it may be laid down as a general principle, that every person who has notice of a Special Obligation will be bound by it in the same manner as by a natural Right. If therefore Robinson is aware that Brown has made a Promise to Jones, he will be responsible to Jones if he afterwards compels or induces Brown to break it. The principal arguments by which this conclusion has been opposed, although by no means without weight in themselves, may be said to prove too much. They are chiefly founded upon the great practical difficulty of establishing by satisfactory evidence the fact of inducement. But this is an objection which would acquit the accomplices in a crime as well as in a Breach of Promise, and that such an acquittal would be contrary to Natural Justice is universally admitted.[4] There is no reason why the inducement should be more difficult to prove in the one case than in the other, and it is strange that proof which is thought sufficient to hang a man should be thought insufficient to make him pay dam-

---

[4] See § 20.

ages.

§ 35. We have hitherto spoken of a Promise as an obligation to do or not to do a particular act. But the same principle will of course apply to an unlimited series of acts, or even to all the Promissor's future acts. One man may, to take the strongest possible case, undertake to obey in all things the will of another during their joint lives. To what extent is such a Promise valid? The answer is to be found in the principle, that one human being cannot justifiably exercise any personal Right of Control over another except so far as it is beneficial to himself. An engagement of Service is therefore valid so far as it binds the Servant to do anything which is personally useful or pleasurable to the Master, but not so far as it purports to confer upon the Master any arbitrary authority over the independent volition of the Servant. Nor, for the same reason, can an engagement of Service be made irrevocably valid at all, unless it can be shown that the assistance of the Servant is more beneficial to the Master than that of any other person whom he can procure for the purpose.

§ 36. But an engagement of Service, so long as it is permitted to continue undissolved, will clearly make the Master responsible for the manner in which his orders may be executed by the Servant. Suppose for instance that Brown, having undertaken to obey the orders of Jones, is directed by Jones to fell a tree and injures Robinson in doing so. It now rests upon Jones to show, not that the particular act by which Robinson was injured might have been omitted, but that it was not done by Brown for the purpose of felling the tree. For Jones, having acquired a certain right of control over Brown, has used it to make him fell the tree. The act is not in itself unjustifiable, and therefore Brown must either do it or make compensation to Jones for not doing it. Brown may therefore be considered as compelled by Jones to do an act whose nature he may not have foreseen when he bound himself to do it, and which he may be incompetent to do properly. Under these circumstances

Jones is surely responsible to the rest of mankind for the default of Brown.

§ 37. Compensation in case of Breach is the common element which exists in all binding Promises. But when it can be shown that a particular Breach of Promise will inflict irreparable damage upon the Promissee, a further obligation is created. In this case the Promissee will be justified in forcibly preventing a Breach of Promise, and in using whatever violence is necessary for that purpose; and the Promissor will be civilly, and supposing his attempt to be wilful and fraudulent criminally, responsible for any injury which the Promissee may sustain in resisting it. This distinction is scrupulously observed by the English Courts of Equity, whenever they are required to decree the performance, or to prohibit the breach, of an obligation. Nor does there seem to be any reason why the infliction of irreparable damage by a fraudulent or malicious Breach of Promise should not be treated as a punishable offence. In a civilized community the question may not be likely to arise, but there are regions of the Earth in which, the institution of Immovable Property being unknown, the maintenance of a whole tribe may depend upon the observance of a Treaty.

§ 38. There are of course many Promises whose Breach, admitting it to be irreparably injurious, it is impossible to prevent or even to punish. A man may undertake to do an act which proves impracticable, or an act so peculiar in its nature that there is no test by which the fact of its *bonâ-fide* performance can be ascertained. Thus when an artist agrees to paint a certain picture, or an actor to perform at a certain theatre, a compulsory execution might easily be so contrived as, without any palpable breach of faith, to be useless to the Promissee; whereas the loss which the picture-dealer or the manager has sustained by its non-performance is comparatively easy of calculation. But the English Courts of Equity rightly hold that their inability to compel the complete performance of such obligations is no reason for refusing to prevent their wilful breach, and consequently that an actor who agrees to perform exclusively at a particular theatre may be prevented from performing at any other during the period of his engagement.

§ 39. A Promise, when made in compliance with a previous Mandate or request from the Promissee to the Promissor, becomes a Pact or Convention. Such a Promise is not a mere nullity, but a revocable obligation. The Promissor has given his word with the knowledge that the Promissee wishes and expects it to be fulfilled. This will not prevent him from revoking it, but it will make him responsible for the consequences if he breaks it without having revoked it. And therefore, if the Promissee incurs any loss or damage by his reliance upon the Pact while it continues unrevoked, the Promissor will be bound to make compensation although he was not aware of the risk which the Promissee was incurring. A Promise gratuitously made will upon the same principle be converted into a Pact by the Acceptance of the Promissee, that is to say by his wish to have it fulfilled communicated to the Promissor; there being of course no substantial difference between a subsequent approbation and a previous request.

§ 40. A Promise, made with the intention of inducing the Promissee to do or not to do a certain act, becomes a Proposal. A Proposal, when first made, is clearly an imperfect act, and as such is revocable by the Proposer. Thus if Brown makes a Proposal to Jones, Jones cannot enforce it if, before he has done anything in compliance with it, Brown signifies his intention to withdraw it; since it is unreasonable that a transaction which leaves Jones at liberty should irrevocably bind Brown. But if, before the Proposer has signified to the Proposee any intention to withdraw the Proposal, the Proposee does an act in compliance with it, the Proposal becomes a Contract; and every Contract clearly imposes a certain Obligation upon the Contractor and confers a certain Right upon the Contractee. A Contract thus consists of two elements, a Promise and an Equivalent or Consideration, and in the absence of either the Obligation is incomplete.

§ 41. We are, it is true, informed by the best authority that Contract, as a subject of Legal recognition, was almost unknown to the primitive races of mankind. And even in the absence of information it would be easy to conjecture that such must have been the case. Those were times of stratagem and violence. Every foreigner was an enemy, and every man not a kinsman or a townsman was a foreigner. They were moreover times of rigid social discipline. Every community was either an army on the march or an army in garrison. No man was allowed to regulate his actions as he pleased; and the attempt to bind himself without the sanction of the patriarch or the magistrate, if not an offence, would undoubtedly have been a nullity. Under such circumstances, it is no wonder that the subject of Contract did not attract the attention of Legislators. Between the difficulty of finding somebody to contract with and that of finding something to contract about, anything like a transaction of importance must have been nearly impracticable.

§ 42. But I have already pointed out the fallacy of the inference that, if a particular branch of Jurisprudence was not recognized in a particular age, the moral instinct which is its germ did not then exist. We are not to conclude that good faith was never acknowledged as a duty, except when it was enforced as a Law. It did not require a Statute concerning Contracts to make David honour the man who swore to his neighbour and disappointed him not, nor to make Achilles despise the man who professed one intention and hid another in his heart. Nor ought we to assume that an age of warfare and rapine could see no harm in a direct breach of promise. We find, on the contrary, that the generations which admired the stratagems of Achitophel and Ulysses knew how to condemn the treachery of Joab and Pandarus. In fact it is precisely among men to whom Peace is unknown, that Truces and Treaties are likely to be held in the most scrupulous reverence.

§ 43. An undertaking by one person to be responsible

for the fulfilment of a Contract already in existence between two others is only binding when it is supported by some distinct consideration. In the contrary case it is nothing but a gratuitous Promise or Pact, and is therefore revocable if not void.[5] But one person may effectually make himself responsible to another by joining in a Contract by a third, because in this case the Contractee's compliance may have depended upon the joint liability. If therefore Brown and Robinson join in a Covenant with Jones that Brown shall or shall not do a particular act, the extent of Robinson's liability to Jones will depend solely upon the terms of the Covenant. He may merely bind himself upon Brown's failure to make compensation for non-fulfilment, in which case Brown is properly speaking the Contractor and Robinson only his Insurer. But he may, if he thinks proper, become jointly liable with Brown, in which case Jones will be entitled to require Compensation from either Brown or Robinson without regard to their mutual liabilities.

§ 44. Supposing Brown and Robinson to be jointly responsible to Jones for the fulfilment of a Contract by Brown, their liabilities as between themselves will necessarily depend upon the question, for whose ultimate benefit the Contract was intended. If the Equivalent which proceeded from Jones was enjoyed by Brown, it is clear that Robinson's undertaking, though valid as between Robinson and Jones, is gratuitous as between Robinson and Brown; and consequently that, whatever may be its nominal terms. Brown can neither enforce it himself nor permit it to be enforced for his benefit by Jones. If therefore Robinson is compelled by Jones to make Compensation for Brown's breach of Contract, he is entitled to be fully indemnified by Brown; and if Jones does any act whereby Robinson's remedy against Brown is deferred or impeded, Jones cannot afterwards require compensation from Robinson for Brown's breach of Contract. In this case, Brown is said to

---

[5] See §§ 17, 39.

be the Principal Contractor and Robinson his Surety.

§ 45. If, on the other hand, the Equivalent proceeding from Jones has been enjoyed by Robinson, the question is whether any corresponding equivalent has passed between Robinson and Brown. If so, the case is clear. Brown has contracted with both Jones and Robinson not to do the act in question, and whatever Compensation Robinson may be compellable to make to Jones for Brown's breach of Contract is part of the damage inflicted by Brown upon Robinson, and must be made good accordingly. But, in the contrary case, it is difficult to see how Robinson can refuse to indemnify Brown against his liability to Jones. Brown, it is true, has contracted with Jones not to do a certain act, but he has not contracted with Robinson. As between him and Robinson the Contract is a gratuitous Pact, which Robinson, whatever be its purport, has no moral right to enforce. The result of the whole transaction therefore is, that Brown has become responsible to Jones for the benefit of Robinson, or in other words that Brown is Robinson's Surety. The accidental fact, that the fulfilment of Robinson's Contract depends upon Brown's volition and not upon Robinson's, can make, as between Robinson and Brown, no difference whatever.

§ 46. The same principles are applicable in the case of a Joint Contract, that is to say in a case where Brown and Robinson join in covenanting with Jones that they will both or neither of them do a certain act. Here if either Brown or Robinson breaks his Contract, Jones may clearly exact full compensation from the other. But, as between Brown and Robinson, the question will be whether they were Principal and Surety or Co-Principals. If the Consideration proceeding from Jones was exclusively enjoyed by Brown, and if no counter-consideration passed between Jones and Robinson, Robinson is merely Brown's Surety; and as such is entitled to be indemnified by Brown, not only against the consequences of Brown's breach of Contract, but against those of his own. But in the contrary case both Brown and

Robinson are Principal Contractors. Each is primarily liable for his own Breaches of Contract, and therefore, if Brown breaks the Contract and Jones releases him from his liability, Jones cannot afterwards require Compensation from Robinson.

§ 47. The case hitherto supposed is that of a single or Unilateral Contract. But it often happens that a Proposee, instead of practically complying with the Proposal, contents himself with signifying to the Proposer his Acceptance of its terms. In this case a Reciprocal or Bilateral Contract is clearly concluded. The Acceptance entitles either party to insist upon the fulfilment of the terms proposed, and disables each from rescinding them without the other's consent. The Proposee, it is true, has not done any physically irrevocable act in compliance with the Proposal. But the effect of his Acceptance may be considered as morally irrevocable. His declaration and belief that he is henceforth bound to fulfil the terms proposed cannot but materially affect his subsequent conduct, and the consequent alteration in his position must be considered as an indirect compliance with the Proposal. It would therefore be contrary to Natural Justice to permit the Proposal to be rescinded without his consent.

§ 48. Finally, a Proposal may be effectually made, not to any individual in particular, but to all mankind; in which case it is convertible into a Contract by any person who complies with or accepts the terms proposed. Thus if I publicly offer a certain recompence for a specified act, or publicly undertake to perform a specified act for a certain recompence, I become bound to any one who performs the act or tenders the recompence. It is upon this ground that every man who publicly professes to exercise any art or trade for hire or profit is compellable to give his assistance in all cases where it is required, and will be responsible for the consequences if he refuses to do so. It is also upon this principle that, if I empower you to contract upon certain terms in my name, any person with whom you may conclude the Contract will become entitled to enforce it against me. A Proposal, made to the whole world and complied with or accepted by an unknown individual, is as much a Contract as a shot, fired into a crowd and taking fatal effect upon an unknown individual, is a murder.

## IV. Deeptional Obligations

§ 49. By Falsehood is meant the intentional misrepresentation of a fact. A Falsehood, although always justly condemned by honourable men as an immoral act, cannot be held to impose any Obligation upon the person who tells it, except so far as it is intended to influence the conduct of the person to whom it is told. If therefore Brown falsely asserts or denies a fact in conversation with Jones, this is not *primâ facie* sufficient to make Brown responsible for any loss or damage which Jones may by his reliance upon Brown's statement be unexpectedly induced to incur, nor even for any injury which he may be unexpectedly induced to inflict upon Robinson. But if Brown becomes aware that Jones is about, in consequence of his belief in Brown's veracity, to incur risk or to inflict injury, he will be responsible for the consequences if he neglects to inform Jones of the truth. For in this case the transaction will, if the act of Jones is consummated without Brown's interference, he a Consensual and not an Individual one since it contains the elements of an intention entertained by Jones and known to Brown, and of an act done by Brown in consequence of an interference by Jones.

§ 50. But whoever, by telling a falsehood with the knowledge that it is likely to produce that effect, induces another to do or to omit anything which he would not otherwise have done or omitted, is guilty of a Jural Fraud or Deception, and will be responsible to the deceived party for the consequences. And if the act done by the deceived party is a Wrong against another person, the Deceiver will be responsible, not only to the deceived party, but also to the person whom the deceived party has injured. But suppose that the act of the deceived party is one which, though manifestly injurious to a third person, is not a Wrong as between the sufferer and the agent. In this case it seems difficult to maintain that the Deceiver is liable to the injured person. If, for instance, Brown wilfully deceives Jones in order to prevent him from conferring a gratuitous benefit upon Robinson, there seems to be no ground upon which Robinson can require compensation from Brown. The falsehood of Brown is not a Wrong as between Robinson and Brown, and the act of Jones is not a Wrong at all.

§ 51. An act of Deception may of course be fully justified by proof that the person who committed it believed himself to be speaking the truth. It will also be fully justified by proof that it was committed for the purpose of deterring or disabling the deceived party from doing some act which the Deceiver might justifiably have prevented by force; provided of course that no unnecessary injury has been inflicted upon the deceived party. But it cannot be justified by proof that the Deceiver intended and expected its consequences to be beneficial to the deceived party. It is possible that Brown may, considering the circumstances of the case and the motives of the act, think himself morally blameless in deceiving Jones for his own good. But, if so, it must be because he acted with the intention of securing Jones against all damage or loss from the deception. The benevolence which usurps authority cannot disclaim responsibility.

§ 52. The principles which are applicable to Deception relating to facts are also applicable to Deceptional Promises. The essence of a Promise, properly so called, is of course the mutual intention of the parties. But whoever, by professing an intention which he does not really entertain, knowingly induces another to do or to omit what he would not otherwise have done or omitted, is for every practical purpose to be considered as bound by a Promise. In other words he is compellable, either to fulfil the specific expectation which he has held out to the quasi-Promissee, or to make due compensation for its non-fulfilment. And from this doctrine follows the well-known maxim of the Casuists, that every Promissor is bound in conscience to do, not what he himself intended to do when he made the Promise, but what he meant the Promissee to believe that he intended to do. The misrepresentation of an intention only differs from the misrepresentation of a fact in being necessarily capable of reparation by the Deceiver.

§ 53. This brings us to the Interpretation of Promises. Every Promise is, as we have just seen, to be taken in the sense in which the Promissor meant it to be understood by the Promissee. But suppose that the Promissor meant it to be understood in one sense, and that the Promissee actually understood it in another. It now becomes necessary to determine how the Promissee *ought* to have understood the Promise, or in other words what is its Natural Interpretation. It is possible that the language used may be taken to express, with equal plausibility, what the Promissor meant and what the Promissee understood. In this case it seems reasonable that the interpretation intended by the Promissor should be preferred, since the man who gratuitously relies upon an ambiguous Promise may fairly be required to make sure that he understands it. But, whatever may be the natural interpretation of a Promise, it is clear that the Promissor, if he becomes aware that it has been misunderstood by the Promissee, is bound at his own peril to undeceive him.

§ 54. I am of course aware that a method of arrangement which makes it necessary to explain the Interpretation of Contracts under the head of Fraud must at first sight appear far from natural. But this is because the Interpretation of Contract is a phrase which, if not inaccurate in itself, is generally altogether misunderstood. Such questions are constantly debated and decided in language which seems to assume that the subject of the dispute is the actual intention of the parties. This assumption is an evident mistake. Every such question necessarily presupposes the fact, that the intention of the parties was not the same. The subject of the dispute therefore is, not what the parties really meant, but what they might reasonably be understood to mean. In other words every Contractee, who tries to enforce his Contract in a sense which is disallowed by the Contractor, must do so, not upon the ground of mutual intention, but upon that of unintentional Misrepresentation on the part of the Contractor.

§ 55. Closely connected with the doctrine of Deceptional Promises is that of Fraudulent Concealment. One human being, merely as such, is of course no more bound to volunteer information for the benefit of another than to interfere for his physical protection or assistance. If therefore I see you riding over a precipice or steering towards a sunken rock, my neglect to warn you of your danger, however morally wicked, cannot be considered as a Jural Wrong. But it may be safely laid down that the man who volunteers information to another, or even who consents to answer the inquiries of another, does thereby impliedly bind himself to do so to the utmost of his knowledge. If for instance you ask me the way to the nearest town, and I point it out correctly, but without communicating to you my knowledge that the road has become impassable or dangerous, I make myself responsible for whatever damage or loss you may incur in consequence of the concealment. I may refuse to tell you the truth, but to tell you half the truth is to tell you an implied falsehood.

§ 56. We have hitherto confined ourselves to the case of Express Deception, that is to say Deception effected through the words or symbols which are the recognized means of communicating human thought. But Falsehood may be Tacit or Implied. It is easy to act in such a manner as to produce the inevitable impression that a certain fact does or does not exist. And therefore whoever wilfully does an act which he intends to deceive another becomes answerable for the consequences of the deception. The Jacobite foxhunter, for instance, who rode into a quarry for the purpose of inducing William III. to follow him might undoubtedly, if he had survived the experiment, have been justly pronounced guilty of a treasonable offence. There is nothing unreasonable in holding that, if I publicly and wilfully do what I know to be dangerous although it appears to be safe, I become bound to warn those whom I see following my example of the true nature of the act.

## CHAPTER II
## REAL RIGHTS AND OBLIGATIONS

We have now examined the Rights and Obligations which arise from the bare fact of human Coexistence, or which may be created by the exercise of those faculties whose accessibility the fact of human existence implies. And we next proceed to inquire, in what manner the Personal Rights and Obligations of a human being will be affected by his connection with any of the Things which compose the material Creation around him.

We all know that Property, that is to say that portion of the visible Universe which is capable of exclusive use or enjoyment by a human being, consists of two kinds of substances, closely connected with each other but altogether different in their practical character, which are termed Things Movable and Things Immovable. The surface of the Earth supports or conceals a great variety of portable articles, fit for human use or capable of being made so by human labour, but also consumable by time and destructible by violence. The same surface moreover contains within itself an imperishable principle of natural growth, by means of which it not only produces a continual succession of the movable articles already mentioned, but likewise renews and replaces its own materials when injured or removed. The existing stock and the inexhaustible reservoir are both indispensably necessary to mankind, but there may evidently be a great difference between the circumstances by which a human being can become connected with the one and with the other.

This difference principally consists in the obvious fact, that Movable Property is capable of Possession, that is to say of such corporeal contact with one human being as to make its use by any other, without inflicting personal violence upon the Possessor, physically impossible; whereas Immovable Property, although capable of Occupation or enjoyment by a particular individual, must always, excepting those minute portions required for the support of the human body, remain physically accessible to the rest of mankind. The title to a Movable Thing may therefore be by the claimant's volition combined with his Personal Rights, while the title to an Immovable Thing must depend upon principles altogether unconnected with them. But of improvement by human labour both Movable and Immovable Property are alike in great measure capable; and the principles applicable to Appropriation, or Exclusive Possession, and to Dominion, or Exclusive Occupation, are therefore much the same. The subject of Real Rights is thus divisible as follows: — I. Possessory Rights. II. Proprietary Rights. III. Occupatory Rights. IV. Dominatory Rights.

Of all the physical Facts for which the perverse ingenuity of the Roman Civilians has substituted metaphysical conceptions, perhaps none has undergone so marvellous a disguise as that of Real Possession. The complicated mysteries of its transformation have been laboriously unravelled by the illustrious Savigny, in a Treatise which some of his admirers have pronounced to be the most correct and ingenious Juridical dissertation now in existence. It is by no means improbable that this high praise may be fully deserved. But it is impossible to glance at this or any other work of that profound Jurist, without deeply regretting the necessity of the purpose for which they were chiefly designed. They all present the spectacle of one acute and powerful intellect, employed during a long life in the masterly extrication of a great science from the useless subtleties in which a number of others had wantonly entangled it.

## I. Possessory Rights

§ 57. That one human being has no right to make any part of the material creation the instrument of physical violence against another, is so clear as scarcely to be worth argument. Not only is the infliction of suffering by means of a weapon or an animal a manifest Wrong, but the same may be said of any arrangement of physical objects which is intended for the purpose of inflicting suffering upon such human beings as may come within its influence. To set mantraps, to poison wells, to encourage the breeding of noxious animals, are criminal acts which no human being can justifiably commit. But all this is the necessary consequence of the rule which forbids direct personal violence. The only true question of right arising from the existence of the material world is, not whether one man may use it to hurt another, but how far one man may obstruct its enjoyment by another.

§ 58. The rule of Natural Justice which prohibits Personal Constraint necessarily leads to the conclusion that a Person, having placed himself by his own act in physical contact with a particular Thing, acquires a Right of Possession, that is to say a Right to prevent the severance of such contact by the unauthorized act of another. The man who snatches from me the stick or the stone which I have picked up, or who pushes me off the spot of ground upon which I am standing, evidently commits an assault upon my personal freedom. It rests with him to show his justification for interfering with my right of doing what I please, not with me to establish an exclusive title to the thing or the place which he is taking from me. Every one is familiar with the right which I may acquire to a Thing, not because it is mine but because I happen to have hold of it. There can be no better example than that of a Theatre, where no man has a right of Property, but where every man has a right of Possession to the place in which he is sitting.

§ 59. The act of Wrongful Dispossession is therefore, as between the parties, a Personal Delict. The Possessor will be justified in using whatever violence may be necessary to prevent it, and the Dispossessor will be responsible for whatever damage he may do in effecting it. And when the Dispossession is completed, the Dispossessor may upon the same principle be compelled by the rightful Possessor to relinquish his wrongful possession. But the Title of a wrongful Possessor is said to be good against all the world except the rightful Possessor, by which it is meant that he is entitled to maintain it against any person who may endeavour, otherwise than by the authority of the rightful Possessor, to dispossess him. The act of Dispossession is wrongful, not because the thing taken away is mine and not, yours, but because the volition which detained it was mine and has been frustrated by you. And therefore the man who wrongfully dispossesses a wrongful Possessor can no more justify himself than the man who wilfully murders a wilful murderer.

§ 60. But can a rightful Possessor, having been dispossessed by one person, insist upon recovering Possession from another?. Assuming his title to rest upon mere Physical Possession, it is difficult to see upon what principle he is to do so. In such a case the Wrong consists, not in the fact of adverse Possession, but in the act of Dispossession. The former without the latter inflicts no injury. The man who takes an article out of my hand must restore it at my desire whether it profits me or not, just as the man who lays his hand on my shoulder must remove it at my desire whether it hurts me or not. It is enough for him that I do not choose my personal liberty to be interfered with. But the man who receives an article which has been taken from me has a right to say: How am I injuring you by detaining it? You say that your freedom has been injuriously controlled, but with that I had nothing to do. In order to make me liable you must show, not that the loss of the thing was a Wrong, but that its absence is a privation.

§ 61. The first step beyond mere Physical Possession will be found to consist in the fact, that the Possessor has derived, or may reasonably expect to derive, some physical benefit or enjoyment from the use of the thing possessed. Under such circumstances the character of the Possession is materially changed. Mere Physical Possession is nothing more than an exercise of volition, and the act of wrongful Dispossession is in such a case only the infliction of personal constraint, unaccompanied by any ulterior loss or damage. But Possession which can be shown to be beneficial to the Possessor has ceased to be a capricious exercise of personal freedom, and has become a physical convenience if not a physical necessity. And the wrongful termination of such Possession is consequently an act which must necessarily inflict, not only physical constraint, but more or less physical Privation. The title of the Beneficial must therefore be necessarily regarded as in some degree stronger than that of the mere Physical Possessor.

§ 62. Suppose for instance that a Beneficial Possessor is wrongfully dispossessed. In such a case the Dispossessor is of course compellable to replace the rightful Possessor in the same situation as if the Dispossession had never taken place. He is therefore bound, not merely to restore the thing itself, but to make full Compensation for whatever privation the rightful Possessor may have suffered, and for whatever deterioration the thing itself may have sustained, in consequence of the Dispossession. And if the thing itself cannot be found or identified, the Dispossessor must replace it by something of equal value, that is to say by something whose possession will be as beneficial to the injured person as that of the thing which he has lost. But the question whether the rightful Possessor is entitled to reject the thing itself and to require payment of its value, or in other words whether he can elect to consider the Dispossessor as a purchaser instead of a wrong-doer, is one which cannot be here discussed, because it presupposes the existence of some conventional standard by which the commercial value of the article in question can be determined.

§ 63. From this it evidently follows that, whenever one person becomes personally liable to make compensation for injury done to the property of another, the injured party likewise acquires a certain definite claim upon the property of the wrong-doer. If therefore the wrong-doer dies without satisfying this claim, the injured party will have a right to take-satisfaction out of any property to whose enjoyment the wrong-doer was at the time of his decease entitled. The relation of Debtor and Creditor, in its rudest and simplest form, is thus created between the parties. But the more complicated effects of that relation cannot yet he explained. For that purpose it becomes necessary to understand the Jural operation of those Commercial and Pecuniary Usages by which the relative values of different commodities are ascertained and a common measure provided for them all.

§ 64. As regards the liability of third persons, there is an obvious difference between the effect of a wrongful Dispossession where the Possession was beneficial and where it was not. Suppose for instance that Brown dispossesses Jones and is himself dispossessed by Robinson. It is clear that Jones, if his Possession was beneficial, here sustains an injury, not only from the act of Dispossession by Brown, but from the retention of the article by Robinson. Robinson is therefore compellable to make restitution to Jones, although he had no notice of Jones's title when he dispossessed Brown. But if Robinson, not having notice of Jones's title, makes restitution to Brown, he will not be responsible to Jones for the loss or destruction of the article by Brown. For the wrong done by Robinson terminates with his possession, and therefore he cannot be held responsible for the subsequent wrong done by Brown.

§ 65. So if Robinson, after having dispossessed Brown, receives notice of Jones's title, this will not transfer Robinson's personal responsibility from Brown to Jones. For the title of a wrongful Possessor is, as we have seen, good against all mankind except the person whom he has dispossessed.[6] Brown is therefore, as between himself and Robinson, the rightful owner of the article possessed by Robinson; and Robinson is compellable to make, and will be discharged as between himself and Jones by making, restitution to Brown. There is nothing irrational or inconsistent in this distinction between the right to recover the thing itself and the right to receive compensation from its wrongful Possessor. Robinson s Possession is wrongful as against both Jones and Brown, and, if either of them takes it from him, the other cannot complain of him for giving it up. And even if Robinson, being aware that Brown has been wrongfully dispossessed by Jones, wrongfully dispossesses Brown, he becomes a wrong-doer against both Jones and Brown, and is therefore liable to Brown as well as to Jones.

§ 66. We have hitherto supposed the simple case of wrongful but *bonâ-fide* Possession. But whoever dispossesses a Beneficial Possessor with the fraudulent intention of using the article for his own benefit commits, not merely a Wrong, but a punishable Offence well known, as Theft or Larceny. In such a case the rightful Possessor becomes entitled, not only to receive restitution and compensation, but to inflict such punishment as may be equivalent to the suffering or privation which he has endured in consequence of his loss. By an act of Larceny no Title whatever can be acquired as against either the rightful Possessor or any other person who is aware of the theft, and therefore every man is justified in rescuing articles which lie knows to have been stolen by their actual Possessor. But if he rescues them with the intention of retaining them for his own benefit, he will, as between himself and the rightful Possessor, become an accomplice in the Larceny. And the man who steals goods, not knowing them to have been previously stolen, is of

---

[6] See § 59.

course a Thief whether they really were so or not.

§ 67. We have seen that a gratuitous Release, or Assent to an act previously done, is necessarily an irrevocable act.[7] From this it follows that, when one person has wrongfully obtained possession of property from another, the Release of the rightful will confirm the title of the wrongful Possessor; and consequently that the rightful Possessor, by permitting the dispossession to continue until it becomes presumable that he intends to confirm it, will confer upon the wrongful Possessor an indefeasible title by Prescription[8]. We have also seen that a gratuitous Assent to an act not yet done is valid although revocable[9], and from this it as clearly follows that a gratuitous Transfer of Property is valid and irrevocable. For a Transfer is simply the dispossession of a Proprietor, preceded by the agreement of the parties that the property shall belong to the Dispossessor. But it also follows that every gratuitous Transfer ought, by whatever conventional solemnities the intention of the Transferor may be expressed, to be considered as imperfect, and therefore as revocable, until the Transferee's possession has actually commenced.

§ 68. But it is evident that a Transfer of Possession can only extinguish the title of the proprietor so far as it is intended and understood to do so. It is possible, for instance, to permit the use or enjoyment by one person of property belonging to another, upon such terms as to retain the entire proprietary title in the original owner and to vest nothing but a right of present possession in the actual occupant. In the case of movable articles such a transaction is termed a Loan, and in that of immovable territory a Licence. In both cases the occupant will be guilty of a Wrong if he continues to retain possession after receiving notice that his permission to do so has been revoked, or if during its continuance

---

[7] See § 26.
[8] See g 29.
[9] See § 25.

he uses the property in any manner not warranted by its original terms. But in both cases his possessory title, having been intended for his own benefit and not for that of the proprietor, is complete, while it lasts, against the rest of the world.

§ 69. This is the principle of those special or qualified Transfers, known to the English Law as Bailments, by which the rightful possession of an article is given to one person while the proprietary title remains in another. Thus if I deliver my luggage to a porter, or send my clothes to a tailor, the Transferee acquires a temporary right of possession and nothing more. His title only differs from that of a wrongful possessor in being unaccompanied by responsibility for any inconvenience which I may sustain from my dispossession. He is entitled to resist any one who attempts without my authority to take the article from him; but if it is stolen from him it is I and not he by whom the thief must be prosecuted, and if he injures it or converts it to his own use he is guilty of a Wrong. The possession of a person simply acting as the owner's Mandatary is, in short, identical with that of the owner himself.

§ 70. Upon the same principle, the beneficial possession of a movable article may be so transferred as to vest in the Transferee a temporary and qualified right of property as against the Transferor. This kind of Transfer is termed by the Roman Law Location-Conduction, and by the English Letting and Hiring. In such a case the Hirer or Conductor becomes the rightful possessor of the article during the period and for the purposes intended. But the Letter or Locator is entitled to prevent the employment of the thing hired in any manner which he has not authorized, and to require compensation from the Hirer if any damage is done to it by such employment. And when the period fixed by the Letter expires, the Hirer retaining possession of the article hired will of course become a mere wrong-doer. The practical value of the Real interest thus retained by the Letter will of course depend upon the extent to which he is empowered by the terms of the transaction to superintend the use and to ascertain the existence of the thing hired.

§ 71. The most familiar instance of a Transfer for Valuable Consideration is the transaction known to the Roman as Emption-Vendition, and to the English Law as Sale and Purchase; which consists in a conditional transfer of property by the Vendor to the Purchaser, in consideration of an equivalent to be received from the Purchaser by the Vendor. In such a case the Vendor retains only a qualified title to the thing sold until the terms of the Sale are performed, and when they are performed his ulterior possession becomes that of a mere wrong-doer. This is the doctrine of the Common Law, and there can be little doubt of its superiority, both in practical equity and in logical consistency, to that of the Civilians, who hold that a Sale is never complete until possession has been delivered to the purchaser. It is difficult to understand why possession wrongfully retained should have a different effect from possession wrongfully acquired, and it its easy to see the injustice of permitting the Purchaser's title as against third persons to be affected by the Vendor's breach of faith.

§ 72. From this it evidently follows, not only that a Purchaser who has paid his purchase-money without taking possession is the rightful owner of the thing purchased as against all the world, but that a Purchaser who has neither paid his purchase money nor taken possession may make himself so; and consequently that, if Brown fraudulently sells to Robinson property which is already sold to Jones, Jones may insist upon paying his purchase money to Robinson and receiving restitution from him, although Robinson may have paid his purchase money and taken possession of the thing sold without notice of the previous Sale to Jones. A Purchaser who takes possession without having paid his purchase money is of course a wrong-doer unless he acted with the consent of the Vendor, and even in that case it must depend upon the understanding between the parties whether he has acquired anything more than a qualified title to the property.

§ 73. But every Obligation which relates to property must necessarily be transferable at the discretion of the Obligee.[10] Suppose for instance that Brown has injured property belonging to Jones, and is consequently bound to make Compensation. Jones, as we have already seen,[11] was entitled to transfer the property in its uninjured state, and his right to do so must be considered as one of the benefits which were conferred upon him by its acquisition. If therefore we hold that Brown can deprive Jones of this right, or of its perfect and entire enjoyment, by unjustifiably damaging the transferable thing, we are permitting the wrongful act of one person to take away the natural rights of another. The only alternative to this absurd conclusion is the sound doctrine that the compensation which Brown owes to Jones must be considered as standing in the place of the value which Brown has wrongfully withdrawn from Jones's estate; and consequently that, if Jones transfers the injured property to Robinson, Robinson will thereby acquire, if such be Brown's intention, the right of requiring compensation from Brown.

§ 74. A Trust is the Obligation which exists when property is gratuitously bestowed upon one person with the intention that it shall be held for the benefit of another, and is accepted by the Trustee with notice of that intention. The simplest form of Trust is that which is created by a Transfer from Brown to Jones upon Trust for Brown himself, and which is termed a Resulting or Reverting Trust. The effect of such a transaction, as between the parties themselves, will of course he to make Jones the nominal and Brown the virtual and beneficial owner of the property, so that Jones will be bound to permit its discretionary enjoyment by Brown and will be guilty of a Wrong if he attempts to do otherwise. And the same obligation will continue binding

---

[10] See § 27.

[11] See § 67.

as between Jones and any person to whom Brown may transfer his claim.

§ 75. But, as regards third persons, there is an important difference between a Trust and a Bailment.[12] The Bailor's intention is to bestow upon the Bailee a mere right of present possession, while he himself retains the proprietary title and can therefore at his pleasure make the Bailee's possession a wrongful one. But the Trustor's intention is to vest the absolute proprietary title in the Trustee, subject only to a personal obligation for the benefit of the Trustor. Although therefore the property may be in the actual possession of the Trustor, yet the Trustee is, as against the rest of the world, to be considered as its rightful owner; because it is only by virtue of his permission in pursuance of the Trust that the Trustor is enjoying it. And therefore, if the trust property is injured or wrongfully appropriated by a third person who has no notice of the Trust, it is to the Trustee and not to the Trustor that the wrong-doer will be liable.[13]

§ 76. The English Courts of Equity rightly hold that there is in this respect a substantial difference between the effect of an incomplete Transfer and that of a Trust. If Jones retains in his possession property which belongs to Brown, no third person can acquire from Brown a valid title as against Jones. But if Jones has a claim upon property in the hands of Brown which can only be enforced through the medium of a personal obligation against Jones himself, it is clear that no man will be bound by the former who has done nothing to bind himself by the latter. If therefore Jones holds property in Trust for Brown, Brown may enforce the Trust against a purchaser or donee from Jones with notice of its existence; because whoever accepts a thing which he knows that the owner is bound to employ otherwise becomes party to a Wrong and must repair it. He

---

[12] See § 69.
[13] See § 65.

may likewise enforce the Trust against a gratuitous donee from Jones, whether with or without notice of its existence; because whoever accepts a free gift is morally bound to find out whether the owner is justified in bestowing it. But there is no ground upon which he can enforce the Trust against a purchaser from Jones without notice of its existence.

§ 77. There is, upon the same principle, a considerable difference between the title which can be conferred upon a Transferee by a Trustor, and by a Purchaser who has not taken possession. In the case of a mere Trust the right of property still remains in the Trustee, and his obligation to give up possession to the purchaser is merely personal. A transfer by the Trustor is therefore incomplete as against the Trustee until he has received notice of it; so that, if Jones holds property in Trust for Brown and Brown sells to Robinson, Jones delivering the property to Brown will not be responsible to Robinson unless he did so with notice of the Sale. But in the case of an imperfect Sale the vendor retaining possession after the purchase-money is paid becomes a mere wrong-doer. He is therefore bound not to give up possession except to the true owner, and if he does otherwise the true owner may hold him responsible.

§ 78. The rule is the same where Brown fraudulently sells his title under the Trust, first to Robinson and afterwards to Smith. In this case both Robinson and Smith are independent purchasers of a mere personal claim; and therefore Smith, if he can procure a transfer from Jones, is entitled to retain the property for his own benefit unless it can be shown that he paid his purchase-money with notice of the Sale to Robinson. But in the meantime an additional question is raised by the introduction of Smith. The property is now in the hands of one person, and the double Sale was effected by another. Which then of the two independent Purchasers has the preferable moral claim? the one who first contracted with the Trustor, or the one who first gives notice of his contract to the Trustee? In other words will

Smith, by giving notice of his claim to Jones before Robinson has done so, acquire the right to call upon Jones for a transfer although Jones receives notice of Robinson's claim before he has parted with the property?

§ 79. The English Courts of Equity have laid down the broad rule, that the title acquired by the Purchaser of a Real Obligation is incomplete until the Purchaser gives notice to the Obligor, and becomes complete when he has done so. They would therefore, in the case supposed, hold that Smith has acquired priority over Robinson by the bare fact of giving first notice to Jones, although it may be manifest that Robinson's omission to give previous notice cannot possibly have assisted to deceive Smith. In so holding they are inconsistent with themselves. For if Smith's title really becomes complete upon his giving notice to Jones, the fact of such notice ought to bind Robinson if he afterwards procures a transfer of the property from Jones. Nor can any reason be given why, if Robinson gives notice to Jones before Smith has procured a transfer, this should not restore Robinson's priority. In order to prevent this there ought to be evidence, not of a prior transaction between Smith and Jones, but of a fraud between Robinson and Smith.

§ 80. We have seen that a gratuitous Assent may be revoked, but that a gratuitous Transfer is irrevocable.[14] To which category does a gratuitous Transfer to one person in Trust for another belong? If, for instance, Brown places property in the hands of Jones for the benefit of Robinson, is this Trust revocable at Brown's pleasure or not? The true distinction seems obvious enough. If the Trust was declared with the knowledge and assent of Jones and Robinson, the transaction is equivalent to a Transfer to Robinson himself and the Trust is irrevocable. But if the Trust is communicated to Jones and not to Robinson, it must be considered as a transaction between Brown and Jones for the benefit of Robinson, and consequently as revocable by Brown with

---

[14] §§ 25, 67.

the consent of Jones. The decisions of the English Courts to the contrary seem scarcely consistent. If Brown, having declared the Trust alone, might revoke it without the consent of either Jones or Robinson, why may not Brown and Jones, having declared the Trust together, revoke it without the consent of Robinson?

§ 81. A Contract may of course relate to the transfer of property belonging to the Contractor. If I bind myself upon valuable consideration to deliver certain lands or goods to you, the undertaking is irrevocable when accepted by you and will justify you in dispossessing me. The only question is, whether it will make the property yours as against the rest of mankind. In order to give a satisfactory answer, we must recur to the distinction already noticed between a transfer by Assent and a personal Trust.[15] The same distinction is perceptible between a permission to take a thing and a promise to deliver it. In the former case the title of the Purchaser is complete when he has taken possession. In the latter its completion requires a further act by the Vendor. An executory Contract for Sale will therefore entitle the Purchaser to the thing sold as against the Vendor, but not as against a third person gaining wrongful possession, or obtaining by Purchase an actual transfer, without notice of the prior Contract.

§ 82. Now it is evident that a Proprietor may become, by his own fraud or negligence, personally bound by any number of inconsistent Contracts.[16] Suppose, for instance, that Brown contracts to sell the same property first to Jones and afterwards to Robinson, and receives the purchase-money upon both the Contracts. In this case Jones has clearly, as against Brown himself, the preferable claim, because Brown was morally justified in selling the property to Jones and not in selling it to Robinson; and therefore, if Brown refuses to fulfil either Contract, it is Jones and not

---

[15] See § 76.
[16] See § 33.

Robinson who will be entitled to dispossess him. But as between Jones and Robinson there is no moral obligation whatever; and therefore Robinson, if he can procure a transfer from Brown without notice of the Contract with Jones, will not be liable to Jones. And even if Robinson receives notice of the prior Contract after he has paid his purchase-money, this will not prevent him from afterwards accepting a transfer from Brown. But if Robinson advanced his purchase-money with notice of the prior Contract, that Contract will of course bind whatever title he may eventually acquire.

§ 83. There can be no reason why a Contract should not bind property afterwards acquired by the Contractor, provided of course that the property can be identified as the intended subject-matter of the Contract. Suppose, for instance, that Brown contracts to build a ship for Jones. The title to any ship which Brown may afterwards build will now clearly depend upon the intention of the parties. The Contract may be a merely personal one, in which case Jones will have no more claim upon the ship actually built than upon any other property acquired by Brown. It may be a prospective, sale of that particular ship, in which case Jones will acquire a right of property in the ship as her construction proceeds, and Brown, if he retains possession after she is finished and paid for, will do so as a mere trespasser. Or it may be an executory Contract for Sale, in which case Jones will acquire a Real Obligation upon the ship which will bind her in the hands of Brown himself and of all persons claiming under him except a purchaser for value without notice of the Contract.

§ 84. The title of a Beneficial Possessor does not necessarily terminate with the Possession which created it. If, after making use of a particular article, I abandon it without the intention of using it again, my Right to it is of course at an end. But if I lay it aside with the contrary intention, I retain the right to say that no man shall in the mean time make it unfit for my use, although the alteration may be such as he would have otherwise been justified in making. Thus you cannot cut down for fuel a tree under which I have been used to sleep, nor kill for food an animal which I have been used to ride or drive; unless you can show that, when I last discontinued its use, I did so with the intention of not using it again. For it is evident that whoever deprives me of something which I have been accustomed to use, and which I meant to go on using, inflicts upon me a physical Privation, and is therefore guilty, as between himself and me, of a wrongful act.

§ 85. But the title of a Beneficial Possessor does not amount, even while it continues to exist, to a Right of Property. It is a permanent, but not an exclusive Right. It confers upon the Possessor a right to say that no one else shall defeat his enjoyment, but not that no one else shall participate in it. The thing possessed is not withdrawn from the common stock, although it has become subject to a privilege for the benefit of an individual. Nor can that privilege be claimed except so far as it has been actually exercised. The horse which I have been accustomed to ride to market is mine whenever I really want him for that purpose, but I cannot lawfully take him out of your possession in order to ride him to church. You inflict upon me no physical privation by refusing to let me have him, unless I can show that the benefit which I expect from having him is one which I have already been used to enjoy. As Physical Possession cannot confer a permanent title, so Beneficial Possession can only confer a permanent title to the extent of the benefit derived from it.

## II. Proprietary Rights

§ 86. The Right of Property, strictly so called, stands upon a wholly different foundation from the Right of Possession. It arises, not from the principle of personal freedom, but from the distinct and independent Axiom, that one human being has no right to deprive another of the Produce of his Labour. I believe it will be found that, of all the rules which I have stated as Axioms, this is the only one which has ever, as a general principle, been disputed by any one capable of understanding what a general principle is. It may even be doubted whether this exception is more than. an apparent one. Those theorists who have honestly opposed the principle of Exclusive Property have usually done so, not as denying its justice in ordinary cases, but as thinking that it may be with advantage superseded, in certain stages of Society, by a different and more artificial arrangement of rights. If the famous maxim, La Propriété c'est le Vol, was ever seriously asserted, it was probably by the consciously dishonest sycophants of some tyrannical Democracy.

§ 87. What then do we mean by the Produce of human labour? Literally speaking, there is no such tiling. No human being has the power of creating Matter. The utmost he can do is to effect new combinations of pre-existing elements. The object of human labour is therefore to do this in such a manner as to produce consequences favourable to human existence or enjoyment, and labour which succeeds in effecting this object is said to be Productive. By the Produce of human labour we therefore mean, if we have any intelligible meaning, the beneficial or pleasurable qualities which human labour confers upon the inanimate or irrational creation. And from this it follows that the Possessor of a thing, having by his own labour made it fitter for human use or enjoyment than it originally was, thenceforth acquires a right to its exclusive use or enjoyment.

§ 88. The Rights acquired by the possession and improvement of a portable or movable article may therefore be regarded as unlimited. The thing has become the exclusive property of the possessor, and he may do with it whatever he pleases without inflicting physical privation upon any one but himself. Not only he cannot be compelled to use it or to permit its use by any one else, but he cannot be prevented from destroying it. It is true that the English Law declares, and that most wisely and righteously, that the proprietor of a living animal shall not be permitted to inflict upon it any unnecessary suffering. But this exception is clearly founded, not upon any theory of a qualified interest retained by mankind in that which has become the property of an individual, but upon a far better and nobler principle. It arises from the recognition of a Moral Right in the creature itself; a Right which its irrational possessor may be unable to assert or to comprehend, but which any human being who witnesses its infraction is conscientiously justified in enforcing.

§ 89. The personal enjoyment of every Proprietor must inevitably terminate with his life; and therefore, as between himself and the rest of mankind, his decease will by physical necessity operate as a Dereliction or extinction of his title. Can this operation be qualified, as between the rest of mankind and any given individual, by the intention of the deceased? Suppose the case of a Proprietor who dies after solemnly declaring that his property shall belong after his decease to a certain person. This hypothesis brings us to the difficult question of Testamentary Authority; a question which the best Moralists have been content to solve upon principles of general expediency. The argument that industry is encouraged by the prospect of transmitting its produce, and that the power of Testation is therefore beneficial to a civilized community, is sufficient to justify the uniformity of modern Legislation upon the subject. But it is not sufficient to satisfy those who wish to account for their own instinctive conviction, that an honest man's right to dispose of his earnings is something more than a police regulation.

§ 90. We have already assumed that I have no right to deprive you of the produce of your labour. What then do we mean by Deprivation? Do we only mean such interference as will inflict upon you physical suffering or moral disappointment? If so, I may justify myself in reaping your wheat, or in shearing your sheep, by the plea that you have more than you can use and that you will never detect the loss. Surely Deprivation has a wider sense than this. The true meaning of the rule must be, that I have no right to prevent the produce of your labour from being used or enjoyed according to your ascertained intention. That intention being known, what difference can your death make? It may have put an end to your personal interest in the fulfilment of your directions, but so might a foreign voyage or a paralytic stroke. It will not enable me to deny the fact, that I am enjoying the benefit of labour which was intended for a purpose inconsistent with my enjoyment.

§ 91. It is indisputably true that this reasoning, if not wholly unknown to the primitive races of mankind, was wholly disregarded by them. At the commencement of History the subordinate members of a Family appear to have possessed no indefeasible legal rights, and it is therefore no wonder that they could dispose of none. Even the patriarchal despot himself may be considered to have occupied the situation of the chief magistrate of a State, or of the chief officer of a Corporation, rather than that of an individual Proprietor. In some cases, however, he was permitted to name, by a public and irrevocable act, his successor in authority. The Decemviral Code bestowed such an authority upon every Roman Paterfamilias without exception. Upon this Law the ingenuity of the later Roman Jurists constructed a system of Testamentary Donation, no less free and secret than that which is now practised in England. And from these facts we find ourselves required to infer that the reverence, now universally thought due to the last Will of a dying man, is an artificial habit and not a natural impulse.

§ 92. Surely such arguments may without disrespect be said to confute themselves. When we say that the Right of Testation is conferred by Natural Justice, we mean simply that the common reason of mankind connects the absolute power of disposition with the absolute right of alteration or destruction. If it can be shown that, in any age or nation, the title of a free and independent Proprietor has been considered to terminate of course with his life, this may possibly be evidence to the contrary. But what inference can be drawn from the practice of an age in which free and independent proprietorship was unknown? In order to find out what is natural to man, it is not enough to watch what men do under circumstances of unnatural restraint. It is not in the hold of a slaver that an artist can judge what are the natural attitudes of the human body; nor is it from the customs of men who had nothing which they could properly call their own, that a metaphysician can decide whether the validity of a Will is an opinion natural or unnatural to the human mind.

§ 93. Every Testamentary disposition must necessarily, so long as it continues such, be revocable at the pleasure of the Testator. Whether it can be made otherwise by communication and acceptance between the parties concerned, or in other words by ceasing to be an Individual act and becoming a Consensual transaction, will be hereafter considered. But in the meantime it is clear, not only that a Testator cannot reasonably be supposed to mean his Will as an irrevocable gift, but that he has, upon principles of Natural Justice, no moral power to make it so. The ancient Laws which only recognized Testation as valid when effected by a public and irrevocable act were wholly founded upon considerations of Civil policy. it concerned the commonwealth that the Chief of a Roman clan, or the Lord of a feudal castle, should not make a hasty or capricious disposition of his office. But that the man who forms an intention for the benefit of another becomes bound not to change his mind, has probably, as a doctrine of Right between individuals, never been seriously maintained.

§ 94. It is clear that this conclusion carries with it an important inference. Since every Testator has the power of revoking his Will by a distinct subsequent act, it seems to follow that every Testator has the power of providing that his Will shall revoke itself in case of the occurrence during his life of a distinct subsequent event. A declaration that the gift shall fail, or as it is commonly termed Lapse, if the Donee dies living the Testator will therefore be effectual; and so will a declaration that the gift shall be forfeited if the Donee does or fails to do a certain specified act during the Testator's life. And since every Testator has the power, not only of revoking his original Will but of substituting for it a new one, it further follows that an alternative gift to a third person, upon the occurrence of a specified event during the Testator's life, will be valid. If therefore I bequeath property to Brown, and in case of his decease or forfeiture during my life to Jones, it is clear that the gift to Jones ought to take effect if the contingency happens.

§ 95. The same principle is applicable to the description of the thing given. Whatever may be the natural interpretation of a simple Testamentary gift as regards the effect to be produced by the subsequent diminution or increase of its subject-matter during the Testator's life, it is clear that the Testator has authority to make it speak from whatever period he pleases. He may bestow all the property, or all the property of a particular description, which he shall possess at the time of his decease or at any previous time. Or he may bestow a specific article of property possessed by him at the date of the Will, with or without a proviso that, in case of its subsequent loss or destruction during his life, the Donee shall be entitled to receive compensation for its absence out of the residuary property disposable by the Will. The question, whether a given bequest speaks from the date of the Will or from the decease of the Testator, has been discussed with infinite subtlety by the Civilians, but they have always acknowledged that it must be decided by the actual or presumable intention of the Testator.

§ 96. Any property which is physically capable of beneficial use without consumption may be intelligibly bestowed upon two or more persons in Succession, the second Nominee succeeding either upon the decease or upon the forfeiture of the first. And in the case of articles which are easily identified and possess great durability, such as valuables and works of art, this is sometimes effectually done. But as regards most descriptions of movable property such a disposition would be of no practical value. Suppose, for instance, that a horse is bequeathed to Brown for life with Remainder to Jones. Jones is of course entitled, not only to claim the horse after Brown's decease, but to prevent Brown from killing or injuring the animal during his life. But, supposing that Jones lives in New England and that Brown chooses to take the horse on a journey to California, how is Jones to exercise his right of interference or to ascertain whether the property has been fairly treated or not? I shall therefore defer the examination of Successive Testamentary gifts until I have to speak of those descriptions of property which are indestructible and immovable, and to which the title of each Successor is therefore equally valuable.

§ 97. For the same reason, property which is physically incapable of being divided without losing its identity cannot be effectually given to more than one person at the same time. A watch or a gun, for instance, can only be enjoyed by means of actual possession, and the actual possession of such an article implies the opportunity of destroying or concealing it. But property which is in its nature distributable, as a flock of sheep or a tun of wine, may of course be bequeathed by its Proprietor, in any proportions he may think proper, to any number of persons. And in bestowing such a gift the Testator may effectually provide that, if any of the shares fail during his life by lapse or revocation, the entire property shall belong to the surviving or continuing Donees, or even that the share of a Donee who dies before the final division of the property shall survive to his co-Donees. For in this case the secondary disposition, being confined to the interval before possession is taken by the Donees, is alternative and not successive, and is therefore not liable to be disappointed by their interference.

§ 98. We now proceed to consider how far the Authority of Testation is affected by the fact of wrongful possession. It is clear that Jones can effectually bequeath his property to Robinson, although Jones is at the date of the Will wrongfully dispossessed by Brown. It is also clear that if the property taken from Jones is destroyed or injured by Brown, Jones can effectually bequeath to Robinson the compensation due from Brown to himself. For it would be unjust to allow one man to be deprived of the benefit of his labour by the wrongful act of another, and we have seen that a Proprietor whose power of Testation is taken away must be considered as in some degree deprived of the benefit of his labour. But if Brown, having dispossessed Jones, bequeaths the property to Robinson, the effect of the bequest will be to vest in Robinson whatever title Brown possessed. In other words, Robinson will become entitled, if Brown dies in possession of the property, to claim it against all the world except Jones; and therefore, if Smith takes possession upon Brown's decease, Robinson may justifiably dispossess him.

§ 99. The Roman Jurists investigate with metaphysical subtlety, indeed with more subtlety than common sense, the effect produced by the transformation or combination of substances upon the title of an antecedent proprietor. If we persist in regarding the Right of Property simply as the Right of exclusive Usage, the true principle will become sufficiently obvious. Whatever removes the possibility of the Usage in which the Right of Property consists must be considered to destroy the identity of the subject-matter and therefore to extinguish the exclusive right. The Proprietor will of course retain his claim for the value of the right which has been defeated. But the act of the wrongful possessor has irremediably deprived the proprietor of one thing, and there is neither sense nor justice in giving him another. Thus if Brown paints colours upon Jones's canvas, or writes letters upon Jones's paper, the picture or the manuscript belongs to Brown subject to Jones's claim for the value of the material. As canvas or paper the thing has lost its value, and as a picture or a manuscript Jones has no right to it.

§ 100. But when a wrongful though *bonâ-fide* possessor improves the property by his labour or blends it with materials of his own, so as to increase its value without destroying its identity, it seems clear that the rightful owner must elect whether he will take the whole, subject to the value of the wrong-doer's contribution, or yield the whole to the wrong-doer, subject to the value of his own. A further exception may perhaps be allowed when the subject-matter of the adverse claims is of such a nature that the wrongful possessor is able to replace it by an equal quantity of the same material. Thus if Brown carves a vase or a statue out of metal belonging to Jones, the metal has a fixed price to Jones while the work of art may be of inestimable value to Brown. In such cases the principle seems to apply which permits a full equivalent to be substituted for a specific act, where the former is an adequate satisfaction to the plaintiff and the latter would be an irreparable loss to the defendant.[17]

§ 101. It is clear that the title acquired by the Improvement of a movable article is both permanent and exclusive. Everything which is capable of physical possession is liable, not only to casual injury or destruction, but to inevitable consumption or deterioration by human use. Whoever uses an article which I have improved must thus necessarily consume some part of the useful qualities which I have conferred upon it, and thereby to a certain extent deprive me of the produce of my labour. The unintentional loss or abandonment of movable property is therefore insufficient to preclude the Proprietor from requiring restitution if he afterwards finds it in the possession of another person. But the Civilians rightly hold that, if, in such a case, the casual Occupant is found to have further improved the property by his own labour, the true Owner cannot re-

---

[17] See § 37.

claim it without making compensation for the additional value thereby conferred upon it. To deny this doctrine is to maintain that one man may, by his own carelessness or misfortune, become entitled to appropriate the work done by another.

§ 102. Whoever takes possession of a lost or abandoned article of property, with the knowledge that it belongs to somebody else and with the intention of making it his own commits of course the offence of Larceny. Nor is the character of the act altered substantially, whatever may be the case technically, where the finder, having taken possession without any dishonest intention, fraudulently retains it for his own benefit after receiving notice of the true owner's title. But whoever takes possession of lost or abandoned property, with the knowledge that it belongs to another, but with the *bonâ-fide* intention of restoring it to its owner may reasonably be held to acquire a right of Salvage; or in other words a right to retain the rescued property until he has received sufficient compensation from the owner for whatever trouble or suffering has been unavoidably sustained in the rescue; unless he had previously received notice from the owner that he did not desire the interference of any other person for the purpose.

§ 103. But a Proprietor's voluntary abandonment of Possession, accompanied by the intention of never resuming it, will of course operate as a Dereliction of his exclusive Title, and will restore the abandoned Property to its original condition as an unoccupied Thing. For it is evident that another man's occupation of what I never meant to use again cannot be said to inflict any privation upon me, whatever may have been my previous claim upon the thing occupied. It is even held by the Roman Civilians that accidental or compulsory Dispossession will amount to Dereliction, if consummated by the cessation in the loser's mind of all hope or anticipation of recovery. But this doctrine seems to confound Intention with Expectation. A man who has dropped his purse may never expect to see it again; but still, if I find and keep it, I am detaining something from him which he never meant to relinquish. It is safer, in such cases, to leave the extinction of the loser's Title to the sure operation of Time and Fact.

§ 104. The principles now laid down concerning the effect of Possession, or of the circumstances by which Possession may be accompanied, will carry us a great deal further. They will enable us to perceive how entirely fallacious is the theory of the Roman Jurists, which treats the fact of physical Possession, or the consciousness of physical power, as the foundation of all Property. Not only is Possession in itself utterly inadequate to confer an exclusive Right of Property, but an indisputable Right of Property may easily be acquired in many cases where no Possession has ever existed, or can by any possibility exist. There are many things in existence which are capable, without physical conflict or possession by any human being, not only of human use or enjoyment in their natural condition, but of improvement by human labour for the purpose of human use or enjoyment. Upon the principle of Enjoyment or Improvement, therefore, the appropriation of such things is easily explained, while upon that of Possession it cannot be explained at all.

§ 105. There can be no doubt, for instance, that a Right of Property is acquired by shooting or snaring a wild animal fit for human food. The death or capture of such an animal makes him fitter for human use than he was before, and therefore the person whose skill has effected the change has an exclusive right to its benefit. Not only is actual Possession unnecessary to complete the title thus acquired, but the power of actual Possession may continue doubtful without affecting it. The man who wounds a stag or wings a bird clearly acquires a Right of Property, which he may abandon by giving up the pursuit but which no one else has a right to defeat while he perseveres. The opinion of Gaius to the contrary is unworthy of a Roman Jurisconsult and astonishing to an English sportsman. It may even be plausibly contended that no man has a right to kill the deer which I am stalking until I have been allowed a fair trial whether I can secure him, because my discovery of the game is in itself an important step towards its conversion to human use.

§ 106. So there are many kinds of animal which may easily, without anything approaching to Possession, be so far domesticated as to be highly useful to mankind. Such an improvement is clearly sufficient to confer a Right of Property upon the improver. Suppose for example that I have, by my own trouble and risk, tamed a herd of wild cattle. Would it not be absurd to hold that the cows which I have milked and the calves which I have fed are mine but that the old bull, whom I dare not approach, may be shot by any one who pleases? Surety the answer is that the bull has been indirectly made serviceable by the domestication of his cows, and that I have therefore acquired a right to his services. Or suppose that I have hived a swarm of bees. Physical contact with them, if not impossible, would in all probability be highly unpleasant, but it surely does not follow that a stranger may destroy them to get their honey. In all such cases the test of title is not physical Power but physical Benefit.

## III. Occupatory Rights

§ 107. Many Jurists have thought it necessary to prove by elaborate argument that the irrational mundane creation is the absolute property of the human race, and, some of them have endeavoured to silence all doubt upon the subject by an appeal to Revelation. Blackstone in particular declares, with orthodox dogmatism, that the whole theory of Property rests upon a single text in the Book of Genesis, and that all attempts to establish it otherwise are airy metaphysical speculations. Those theologians who believe that revealed Religion was intended to enlighten us respecting another state of existence, not to supply the place of reason and experience in the present, will probably be of opinion that a settler in the primeval wilderness was morally justified in felling a tree or in killing a buck, although he had never heard of the Mosaic Scriptures. But, however this may be, it is clear that the question forms no part of Jurisprudence. That science only professes to define the Rights of human beings as between themselves. The Jurist finds mankind, as a fact, in the exclusive and undisputed enjoyment of so much of the Earth as they choose to claim. It is his business to settle the rules by which this prerogative is to be distributed, not to decide whether it has been usurped or ought to be abdicated.

§ 108. Experience shows that physical suffering is the inevitable consequence of physical Privation. If therefore one human being has no right to make any material object the means of inflicting suffering upon another,[18] it follows that no human being has a right to do any act which will make the surface of the Earth unfit, or less fit than it otherwise would be, for human occupation. It signifies nothing that there is no particular person upon whom present loss or pain is thereby inflicted. If Selkirk had wantonly burnt the forests or flooded the valleys of Juan-Fernandez, he would clearly have been guilty of a Nuisance against mankind in general. So the man who unnecessarily cuts down a fruit-tree or dams up a rivulet, or even who gathers unripe fruit or kills unseasonable game or fish, commits a Public Nuisance unless he has previously done something to acquire an exclusive Right of Property in the thing which he spoils. Whether the Earth belongs to the human race or not, it is obviously their appointed place of abode, and one man has no right to make it uninhabitable by another.

§ 109. Upon the same principle no human being has a right to do any act which tends to confine the natural freedom of mankind, or in other words to obstruct the facility of human locomotion over the surface of the Earth. A mis-

---

[18] See § 57.

anthropic settler in the wilderness, for instance, cannot justifiably disguise the fords or fell trees across the deer paths, and a mariner who discovers an uninhabited island may lawfully be prevented from making the anchorages or the landing-places inaccessible to future voyagers. Whoever commits such an act is therefore civilly responsible for whatever loss or damage it may eventually cause to any human being. And whoever commits a Public Nuisance with the general intention of injuring his fellow-creatures although without malice to any particular individual, is criminally responsible for the consequences. It is possible as we shall hereafter see, to acquire the right of excluding mankind from particular portions of the Earth; but no man has naturally such a right, and any man who attempts to exercise it without having earned it may lawfully be restrained from doing so.

§ 110. It will easily be apprehended that I should not have said so much upon so trifling a subject as that of Title by Physical Possession, if it had not acquired an artificial importance from the speculations of a very famous and ancient school of Jurisprudence. Taken upon its own merits, I should scarcely have thought it worth a single paragraph. No man can live for a day, without perpetually taking and relinquishing Physical Possession of innumerable worthless objects. A man of ordinary stature cannot walk a mile without taking Physical Possession of more than two thousand spots of ground. Such possession must of course be respected while it lasts. A man has a right to the soil which supports his foot, just as he has a right to the space which is filled by his body. Both rights are alike indispensable to the enjoyment of personal freedom. But I should have thought it superfluous to point out that a human being acquires new rights whenever he changes his attitude, if this simple and obvious inference had not been made the basis of a most disproportionate theory.

§ 111. The Roman Jurists deduced the whole institution of Property from the Title acquired by Physical Possession. They held that, if the fact of Physical Possession is accompanied by the Intention of permanent Occupancy, the thing possessed becomes the exclusive property of the Possessor; and the termination of his Physical Possession will not, unless accompanied by a corresponding change of intention, terminate his right. It is a doctrine as unfounded in principle as it has proved pernicious in practice. Not only would it be unjust to let one man's intention control another's freedom, but the intention supposed in the present case is wrongful in itself. The man who intends to withdraw a certain thing from the common stock without using it for his own benefit intends to commit a Public Nuisance; and an act done with that intention, so far from conferring upon him an exclusive right, would impose upon him an obligation to undo it. The Roman theory is founded upon an entire misapprehension, not only of what Intention can effect, but of what a human being can justifiably intend.

§ 112. If the intention of a Possessor cannot continue the effect of his Possession after it has terminated, still less can it amplify the effect of his Possession while it exists. The right of Physical Possession is nothing but the right of personal freedom. What does not interfere with the one is no infringement of the other. If I plant my foot upon a certain point of the Earth's surface, I acquire the right of standing there as long as I please. But I cannot, by casting round my eyes and saying All this is mine, acquire the right of preventing another man from standing opposite to me. The highest modern authorities are said to have laid down the rule, that consciousness of unlimited physical power is equivalent to Physical Possession. But an Australian farmer knows better. He knows that an unoccupied cattle-run is not to be appropriated by standing upon it and wishing for it. No such title, whatever may be the theory of metaphysicians, ever was or ever will be respected by the common sense of mankind.

§ 113. The great defect of the Roman principle is its entire inapplicability to Immovable Property. The surface of the Earth is obviously incapable of being occupied, in quantities sufficient for beneficial use, by physical contact. The Romans themselves do not seem to have admitted that any territory could be considered as wholly unoccupied. But the fact has irresistibly forced itself upon the attention of modern Publicists, and they have absurdly endeavoured to meet its consequences by an extension of the Roman doctrine of Occupancy. The result has been the well-known canon, that physical Power is equivalent to physical Possession. Its consequences have been found, not merely morally unjust, but intellectually ridiculous. How are the limits of physical Power to be determined? Can a mariner appropriate the whole Southern Ocean, or a chamois-hunter the whole summit of Mont-Blanc? Does the occupant of a field become proprietor of the subjacent strata of Earth, or of the superincumbent column of air? Above all, what is to prevent the first man who lands upon an unoccupied Continent from declaring himself exclusive proprietor of all its accessible territory?

§ 114. It is clear that every Beneficial Occupant acquires, not merely a right of undisturbed corporeal abode, but also a right of undisturbed Enjoyment, or what the Roman Law terms a Servitude. He acquires the right to say, not merely that nobody shall take away the thing possessed, but also that nobody shall interrupt the benefit which he is deriving from its Possession. Thus if I am riding upon a horse, no man has a right to mount behind me without my consent, because, even supposing him able to do so without personal annoyance to me, he thereby deprives me of part of the benefit which I am deriving from the powers of the animal. So if Diogenes sits down to bask in a sunny corner, he acquires both a right of Possession to the space which he occupies and a Servitude over the pavement around it. He is entitled, not only to stay in his corner as long as he pleases, but to prohibit Alexander from standing in his light.

§ 115. It is evident that the Appropriation of Territory

can only take place subject to whatever Servitudes or Rights of Usage may have been previously acquired therein by the enjoyment of any other person, since I have no right to improve the surface of the Earth for my own benefit so as to inflict privation upon another. The simplest form of Servitude is that which is termed a Right of Way, and which arises merely from the habit of personal presence upon the Territory in question. Thus although a savage, accustomed to traverse a forest or to sleep in a cave, cannot prevent a settler from occupying the soil, yet it is clear that the settler, having occupied the soil, cannot exclude the savage from his accustomed haunts. Distinct Rights of Way over the same territory may of course be acquired by any number of persons. But the Occupant is clearly entitled to limit them all to a single definite track, and to prohibit all departure from it unless it becomes impassable through negligence or accident, since by so doing he merely protects his own property from unnecessary damage without inflicting any physical privation or inconvenience upon the persons entitled to the Servitude.

§ 116. What the English Law terms Rights of Common, and the Roman Law Rights of Usufruct, consist in the prescriptive right of taking or consuming certain produce upon certain lands. Thus if I am accustomed to cut wood or turf, or to pasture my sheep or cattle, upon unoccupied land, I acquire a right of continuing to do so which will bind a subsequent Occupant. But, whatever my habit of Usage may be when the land subject to it is appropriated, such my right must thenceforward remain. If I afterwards attempt to extend it, I am depriving the proprietor of the benefit which he had reason to expect from his occupation of the soil. Thus I cannot justify myself in digging turf for sale by a Usage of digging turf for fuel, nor in felling timber to build a house by a Usage of cutting sticks to repair fences. It is clear, moreover, that an Occupant subject to a Right of Usufruct may set apart a portion of the property sufficient for the purpose, and may exclude the Usufructuary from the residue. It would be ridiculous to insist upon my keeping a farm of a thousand acres untilled in order to provide common of pasture for half a dozen cows.

§ 117. The Right of Sporting, which consists in the prescriptive right of capturing Game upon certain lands, is a Servitude of a very peculiar and sometimes oppressive nature. Its value is at the best very precarious, and its successful exercise is usually found inconsistent with the occupation and cultivation of the soil. The question in such cases may therefore be taken to be, whether the occupant is able to make sufficient compensation for the extinction of the Game. In some cases this is impossible. A riparian proprietor must not starve a fishing village by building a weir so as to exclude the salmon, nor must an immigrant farmer drive away an Indian tribe by clearing the woods which shelter the deer or by inclosing the prairies which pasture the bisons. But we cannot allow the feeding ground of a whole village to remain a morass because a few vagabonds have been used to shoot snipe there. They must be pensioned off with so many fowls or turkeys a year, and the soil must be drained at once.

§ 118. The Gothic Feudal Tenures, and the Roman Jus Emphyteuseos, were instances of the peculiar interest created by a qualified Transfer of immovable property. In the latter case the Transferor reserved to himself a certain portion of the produce, with a conditional right to compel restitution if the Transferee should mismanage the land. In the former the property was transferred by the Lord to his Vassal, subject to forfeiture in case the Vassal failed in the due performance of certain services to the Lord. But these forms of proprietorship, although I have been induced by their historical renown to point out the relation in which they stand to the general principles of Jurisprudence, are no longer of such practical importance as to make them worth examination. In England the creation of a Seignory in Fee, or in other words the reservation of feudal service upon an absolute Transfer of Real Estate, has long been forbidden by Statute, and the relation of Landlord and Tenant can now only be established by Lease.

§ 119. A Lease or Demise is simply a qualified Transfer, by which immovable property belonging to the Lessor or Landlord is temporarily vested in the Lessee or Tenant. Supposing the Tenant to die during the continuance of the Lease, it is clear that the Landlord, being out of possession and having parted with his immediate right of possession, has, until the Lease expires, no more claim to the unoccupied property than any other person, and that, even if he succeeds in reoccupying it, he may lawfully be ejected by the Tenant's testamentary Donee. And even if the Tenant is wrongfully dispossessed by a third person, the Landlord cannot justifiably eject the dispossessor until the expiration of the Lease, because, his own right of possession being suspended during that interval, the dispossession is not, as between him and the dispossessor, a wrongful act. The Tenant may of course surrender his Lease and give up possession of the property to his Landlord, and the Landlord may grant a renewal of the Lease, or even wholly release his Reversion, to the Tenant.

§ 120. It is usual, upon a Lease of immovable property, to reserve to the Landlord a certain proportion of the profits under the name of Rent. The effect of such a reservation is of course to confer upon the Landlord a qualified interest in the property during the continuance of the Lease. If therefore the Landlord dies before the expiration of the Lease, he may dispose by his Will of the Reversion and the Rent, and the Devisee will be entitled as Landlord to claim the Rent which becomes due after the Testator's decease. And if the Rent is not punctually paid by the Tenant, the Landlord will be justified in entering upon the property and in Distraining or seizing so much of the produce as may be sufficient to discharge the arrears. But it is also clear that a Tenant, by converting to his own use the produce of his tenement without accounting for the Rent due thereout, commits a wrongful act and becomes personally bound to make compensation to the Landlord. And the Landlord may, in addition to these remedies, stipulate that the Lease shall become void if the Tenant permits the Rent to run in arrear.

§ 121. Any part of the Landlord's proprietary rights may, upon the same principle, be effectually excepted out of the Lease. If the Tenant is willing to accept, and the Landlord is only willing to confer, a qualified title to the property, there can be no reason why their mutual intention should not be binding. Thus it is usual, in English Leases of agricultural land, to reserve to the Landlord the exclusive right of Sporting or killing Game upon the property. Cases have no doubt occurred in which this privilege has been so unscrupulously exercised as to inflict ruinous loss upon needy and unwary Tenants; and the consequence has been that certain Economists have raised a vehement clamour against something which they choose to call the Game Law, but which every reasonable being perceives to be the Law of Contract. Whether they seriously mean that no man is to be allowed to feed pheasants in his wood, or that no man who does so is to be allowed to lease an adjacent field without the wood, they have never explained and probably do not know. But is certain that such a conclusion would be neither more nor less rational than a proposal to forbid the manufacture of cotton because millowners sometimes oppress their workmen.

§ 122. We have seen that the wrongful possession of property may be ripened by Prescription into an indefeasible title.[19] This doctrine becomes particularly important in the case of immovable property, which might otherwise be identified and reclaimed at any distance of time. The consummation of title to such property does not consist in physical possession, far less in that symbolical quasi-possession which the Civilians term Occupancy, but in beneficial enjoyment. If therefore you permit me to enjoy

---

[19] See § 67.

certain territory in any manner which you have a right to prevent, during such a period of time as to raise the presumption that you have given up the intention of interfering with my enjoyment, you will confer upon me a title by Prescription to continue it. And thus the principle of Prescription may not only transfer the right of property, but may create or extinguish Servitudes or Easements as against the beneficial proprietor.

§ 123. But it is evidently necessary, for the purpose of establishing a title by Prescription, that the wrong-doer's Occupation should be distinctly adverse to the injured party's Right. If the one is not inconsistent with the other, there is no exclusion. It will not do to say that, although the defendant's Occupation was originally permitted by the plaintiff, the defendant made it adverse by wrongfully using it for his own benefit. Such reasoning may prove that the plaintiff has forfeited his right to make the defendant account for the arrears, but not that he has forfeited his right to turn the defendant out of possession. For that purpose it must be shown, not that the defendant has wrongfully used his occupation, but that his occupation originally was, or has since become, in itself a wrongful act; that is to say, that it was so intended by the one party and so understood by the other. It would be hard indeed if a proprietor who has neglected to discharge a fraudulent steward were to be held to have conferred upon him a prescriptive title to the estate.

§ 124. We have already seen that, where property belonging to one person is in the possession of another, a transfer by the rightful owner will confer upon the transferee the right of compelling restitution from the wrongful possessor. It is true that in this respect the Common Law ascribes, or did formerly ascribe, very peculiar consequences to the Disseisin, or exclusion by an adverse claimant entering with the intention of making good his claim, of a person entitled to immovable property. In such a case the title of the Disseisee was technically said to be converted into a Bare Right, which could not, until some act had been done to clothe it with the actual enjoyment of the property, be transferred by the person in whom it was vested. But this excessive rigour, though probably justified by the impolicy of permitting the feudal tyrants of former days to found pretexts for oppression upon the purchase of colourable titles, appears to a modern Jurist harsh and absurd.

§ 125. A Corporation, in its simplest form, is nothing but an association of individuals who have agreed to occupy property together for a certain purpose. The effect of such an agreement will be, that each individual will only acquire such a right of property in the common stock as the terms of the Association enable him to hold. In other words, his share in the Corporate Property will belong to him in his character as a member of the Corporation and not otherwise. Thus if he ceases to be a member of the Corporation, whether by decease or by retirement, his interest in the Corporate Property will at once determine, except of course where he is specially empowered by the terms of the association to appoint a successor in his room. And so when the terms of the association empower a certain proportion of the Corporate body to dispose of the Corporate property, the title of an individual member is liable to extinction without his co-operation or consent.

§ 126. Many familiar examples might be given of incorporated Associations. The most familiar and the most important of all is that of the great associations which are termed Political States. It is simply as an association of individuals for a certain definite purpose that England or France possesses a character, and therefore a capacity of occupying territory, distinct from that possessed by any number of Englishmen or Frenchmen as individuals. And there can be no doubt that half a dozen shipwrecked sailors would, by associating together for mutual protection against a tribe of cannibals, acquire a corporate character as distinct as that of the greatest Empire in the world. But I do not think it necessary to place the theory of National Rights and Obligations upon this foundation. I prefer to recognize as natural facts the States now actually existing upon the Earth, and to ascertain the effect of their existence upon the Rights and Obligations of mankind without any reference to the circumstances of their origin.

§ 127. A Corporation may of course be created, not merely by Association, but by Association combined with Delegation. A body of individuals, associating together and contributing property for a given purpose, may, if they think proper, commit the property and intrust the purpose to some one or more of their number exclusively of the rest. And the person or persons so appointed will by their acceptance of the appointment become a Corporation, and will hold the Corporate Property as such. A single person appointed to act in a Corporate capacity is termed a Corporation Sole, of which species of Corporation the King of a Realm or the Parson of a Parish are familiar instances. But all these different kinds of Corporation may coexist in the same Association and for the same purpose. A number of individuals may associate so as to form a Corporation Aggregate and may at the same time delegate certain special functions to a Corporation Sole, as in the case of Monks who combine to form a Monastery and to elect an Abbot. Or a body of associated individuals may appoint a Corporation. Aggregate and vest the supreme authority in a Corporation Sole, as in the case of a City whose inhabitants combine to elect a Town-Council presided over by a Mayor.

## IV. Dominatory Rights

§ 128. Let us now observe how readily the difficulties of Territorial Appropriation are solved by the simple maxim, that Property is the fruit of Labour. It becomes, easy, in the first place, to distinguish that which may be property from that which cannot. Those parts of the Earth which are capable of producing human food become of course the property of the first man who improves them by cultivation. Those which can only be used for rest or shelter can only be appropriated by being made more fit for that purpose. The navigator can only make use of so much of the sea as lies within the sweep of his cable, and the traveller of so much of the wilderness as is inclosed by the curtains of his tent. Therefore the navigator who lays down moorings upon a shoal becomes proprietor of the anchorage, and the hunter who builds a hut upon a mountain of the shelter, but of nothing more. And neither the High Seas nor the uninhabitable tracts of the Earth can become property at all, because they cannot be made fitter for human use than they naturally are.

§ 129. The same maxim will furnish us with a general principle for the solution of that most difficult question, What extent of soil is a single human being entitled to appropriate? That which he has actually improved is of course his own, but what precise amount of elbow-room is each successive immigrant bound to allow his predecessor? It is a question to be answered by the eventual facts of each case. Every man who fairly commences the improvement of unoccupied soil acquires by that act an exclusive Right to so much thereof as he shall ultimately succeed ill improving. If I interrupt the continuity of his labour by settling too near him, I render its consequences less beneficial to him than he had reason to expect when he commenced it, and do thereby in some measure deprive him of its benefit. The measure of appropriation is therefore the eventual power and perseverance of the occupant, and every settler is bound at his own peril to commence work out of the reach of all previous cultivators.

§ 130. Even the essential nature of a Right of Property in Immovable Things can be more accurately defined upon the principle of Improvement than upon that of Occupancy. The Occupant of land is entitled to the exclusive benefit of his own labour, and to nothing more. He therefore acquires no right whatever to restrain mankind in general from any interference with the occupied land which does not tend to deprive him of that benefit. The miner cannot prevent me from cultivating the surface over his head, nor the farmer from excavating it under his feet, unless he can show that by so doing I am impeding his operations. The English Courts have decided otherwise; though they admit that a landowner has no power to prevent a building from being erected so as to overhang his field, unless he can show that it interferes with his enjoyment. Under the Earth to Hell, above the Earth to Heaven, is the quaint language of some of the old feudal Grants; and it seems inconsistent to sever the proprietor's celestial from his infernal privileges.

§ 131. The first settler upon uninhabited territory must upon the same principle be held to acquire an unlimited right of using whatever lands he may occupy in whatever manner he pleases, provided he can show that its use is in some manner or other beneficial to himself. He must not make his acquisition of title the instrument of wantonly or maliciously destroying the utility of the neighbouring soil. He must not, without some motive of convenience, kindle fires upon his land so as to destroy the neighbouring woods, nor dam his watercourses so as to flood the neighbouring valleys. But he is not responsible for any injury which he may cause to the neighbourhood, while unoccupied, by the *bonâ-fide* use of his own property for his own intelligible purposes. He may obstruct a river by erecting waterworks, he may pollute the water or the air by working a manufactory, he may even make the whole vicinity a place of peril by setting up a powder-mill. Any undertaking which is lawful in itself may lawfully be commenced in any locality where, at the time of its commencement, it cannot be shown to injure or annoy any human being.

§ 132. So it is clear that an Occupant of land acquires no title to any movable article whose presence within the area of his property is not due to his own labour. If you lose or abandon movable property upon my land, I have no right to call it my own until I have found it and taken physical possession of it. The right which I acquire by building a house, or by ploughing a field, is an exclusive title to the benefit of the qualities which I thereby confer upon the soil, and has no connection with the title to a jewel picked up within the premises. The English Courts have taken this view of the question; but they do not seem to have perceived that the decision is inconsistent with the principle of Title by Occupancy, or that the right of an Occupant to minerals lying upon the surface of his land cannot reasonably be distinguished from his right to minerals concealed beneath it. The Roman Law divided the property found between the finder and the place-owner; an arrangement which Gibbon considers equitable, but which more practised Jurists will probably reject as an inconsistent compromise between two opposite principles.

§ 133. So the Occupant of land acquires no exclusive title to the Game, or wild animals fit for human food, which may happen at any given time to be found upon it. But the case is altered where, as sometimes happens, the proprietor has employed skill and labour to attract the presence of such animals. The landholder who constructs a decoy for wild fowl, or who provides food for pheasants, or even who protects the eggs of grouse or partridge which exist at his expense, is clearly entitled to the benefit of what be has done. That benefit consists in the right to say that you shall not deprive him of the chance of profit which may arise from his arrangements, or in other words that you shall not attempt to capture Game upon his land. To the free Game upon his land he has no more right than any other man; but whatever Game is actually captured there is more or less the produce of his labour, and of that produce no human being can justifiably deprive him.

§ 134. The question is one in which most Englishmen take a strong interest, and which no educated Englishman can impartially examine without becoming thoroughly ashamed of the nonsense which has been talked on both sides. But it has probably never been remarked, how much of this nonsense is due to a metaphysical theory of Property which was invented two thousand years ago. Either the absurd conclusion that all Game is Property, or the absurd conclusion that Poaching is consistent with Natural Justice, must clearly be deducible from the Roman doctrine of Title by Occupancy. If I have constructive Possession of the wood, I am of course proprietor by Occupancy of the animals in it. If I have not constructive Possession of the wood, how can I be said to have any interest in a bird of whose existence I am ignorant? By the plain rule, that I am entitled to the exclusive benefit of the qualities which I have conferred upon the wood and to nothing more, both absurdities are avoided.

§ 135. The principle of Appropriation by Improvement will at once enable us to detect the fallacy of the distinction which some Moralists have attempted to draw between the Right of Testation as applicable to Movable and to Immovable property. There is no reasonable foundation for the doctrine, that a man's clothes or his weapons are his own so long as they exist but that his field is only his own during his life. The Title acquired by the conversion of a stick and a stone into a hatchet, of a wild beast into a docile slave, of a swamp into an orchard or a garden, is precisely of the same nature. In each case the subject of the right is not the thing itself, but the beneficial quality which has been conferred upon the thing. In each case that quality, be it what it may, owes its existence to the labour of the occupant. In each case, therefore, he is entitled both to enjoy it during his life and to dispose of it after his decease.

§ 136. A person who becomes entitled to Immovable property by Devise or Testamentary gift stands of course in the place of the person from whom he received it, and is therefore entitled, as against the rest of mankind, to the same proprietary rights as his predecessor. Nor can a Devisor deprive his Devisee of any proprietary right which he might himself have exercised. There is no foundation whatever for the opinion, that the authority to impose such restraints is the logical consequence of the authority of Testation. No distinction can be more obvious than that which exists between the right of selection and the right of exclusion; between the power of saying who shall exercise a certain privilege and the power of saying that nobody shall do so. If I cultivate a garden I may leave it to whom I please, but I must leave it absolutely. I cannot prevent my Devisee from making it a wheat-field or a fish-pond. A dying man, in short, may dispose of his rights as he thinks proper, but he cannot take them with him.

§ 137. But, although an owner of Immovable property cannot deprive the human race of the full benefit of his acquisition, there is nothing to prevent him from providing that it shall devolve upon any number of existing persons in any order of Succession which he may think proper. Thus, if I leave my farm to Brown for life with Remainder to Jones, the disposition is clearly valid. If Robinson excludes Jones after Brown's decease, he is obviously defeating my Will as much as if he had excluded Brown himself. So my Will may apportion the benefits of ownership at my pleasure between Brown and Jones. It may empower Brown to deal with the property during his life according to his own uncontrolled discretion, or it may restrain him from making the slightest alteration without the consent of Jones. It may even empower Brown to dispose of the whole property after his own decease, in which case the Remainder to Jones will be a mere alternative in case Brown happens to die intestate. I may, in short, impose what restrictions I please upon either of my Devisees, so long as they are imposed for the benefit of the other. But I cannot prevent them from exercising together the entire right of property.

§ 138. The reversionary title thus bestowed upon Jones may be either Vested or Contingent. In the former case the property will belong absolutely to Jones subject to Brown's life interest, and will be disposable by his Will although he may die in the lifetime of Brown. But in the latter it will be void if he fails to survive Brown, and the property will therefore in that case remain unoccupied as if the Testator had died intestate. Or the will may contain an alternative Devise to Robinson in case Jones dies living Brown, and this alternative Devise may itself be either vested or liable to failure in the same manner as the Remainder to Jones. So the Devise to Jones may be made to depend upon the fulfilment of a Condition Subsequent, that is to say upon the performance or non-performance of some specified act by Brown during his own life. And in this case, as in the former, the conditional Devise may be either vested or contingent; and may, if contingent, be replaced by an alternative Devise to a third person.

§ 139. It is evident that a proprietor who has a qualified or partial title can confer upon his Transferee nothing more than that which he himself possesses. If. therefore immovable property becomes vested in Brown for life with remainder to Jones, a Lease by Brown to Robinson will only be effectual during Brown's life; unless it is confirmed either by the eventual recognition or by the original concurrence of Jones. But it is usual, in all settlements of valuable landed property, to bestow upon a tenant for life a Power of making Leases so as to bind the property in the hands of the remainder-man, the terms upon which alone they are to be valid being of course carefully specified so as to prevent the Lessor from obtaining any undue advantage at the expense of his successors. And a Lease duly made by a tenant for life in pursuance of such a Power will of course take effect precisely as if its execution had preceded that of the settlement.

§ 140. The Servitudes hitherto specified are merely Personal, that is to say they arise simply from the use or enjoyment of a particular Thing by a particular Person.[20] But, in all civilized countries, what the Civil Law terms Predial Servitudes, and the Common Law Easements, are of much greater importance. Such Rights arise from the

---

[20] See § 115.

principle, that every Occupant of territory acquires the right to its enjoyment without disturbance by the proceedings of any subsequent Occupant of territory in the same neighbourhood. Thus if I am the first to clear and cultivate a farm in an uninhabited district, all future settlers are henceforth bound so to use their own property as not to deprive mine of the natural advantages by which I found it attended. The miner must not cause the soil to subside, nor the manufacturer make the air unwholesome, nor the miller alter the flow of the watercourses. Whoever injures my property by such means is depriving me of the benefit of my labour.

§ 141. For the same reason, no subsequent Occupant in my neighbourhood can deprive me of the benefit of any artificial improvements upon my property which I had effected or commenced when he acquired his own. He must not build his walls so as to darken the windows of my house, nor cut his drains so as to spoil my well, nor irrigate his meadows so as to interfere with the working of my mill. Nor can he complain that his fields are flooded, or his air corrupted, or his drainage obstructed, by any improvements made or commenced upon my property before his occupation; provided of course that such alterations were of a kind which, as not being wantonly destructive to the common property of mankind, I had originally a right to effect; [21] because it is his own fault that he chose to settle upon lands which were already subject to such inconveniences. An artificial Easement binds a subsequent Occupant in the same manner as if it were a natural one.

§ 142. But it is clear that every Occupant of Immovable Property acquires the right, as against all prior Occupants in his neighbourhood, of retaining it in the condition in which he found it when he acquired his title. The Servitudes which he finds established, or in the course of being established, he must respect; but he is not obliged to allow

---

[21] See § 131.

the establishment of any more. Nor am I even bound to use my own property so as not to deprive a prior settler in my neighbourhood of the benefit of his improvements commenced after my occupation. His erection of a dwelling-house will not disable me from establishing a tanyard under his windows, or from building a wall before them. One neighbour cannot be permitted to impose, by his own voluntary act, a new and unexpected Servitude upon another. That can only be effected by some subsequent dealing between them, which may be construed to have imposed a Special Obligation upon the party whose volition it is sought to control.

§ 143. The right of a proprietor to prohibit such acts as interfere with his enjoyment can of course only be construed as extending to acts which cause, or tend to cause, physical inconvenience or material loss. The infliction of imaginary annoyance, or the loss of imaginary pleasure, is not to be regarded. A landowner cannot be prevented from spoiling his neighbour's prospect by building a wall or felling a wood, nor from invading his privacy by settling upon a hill which overlooks his garden. If such consequences can be allowed to interfere with the proprietary rights of others, it must be upon the ground of some clearly recognized and well understood Moral Usage. There would otherwise be no limit to the caprices of selfish sensibility. The poetical inhabitant of a Cumbrian villa has been heard to make public complaint of the railroads which enable our toilworn artisans to enjoy the scenery of the northern Lakes; and it is quite possible that, if such men had their will, the most beautiful scenery upon Earth might in many instances become the private pleasure-grounds of a few fastidious sentimentalists.

§ 144. The Common Law goes so far as to lay down the rule that a landholder, by using his own property in a particular manner without interruption from his neighbours, will in time acquire a Prescriptive Right not to be interrupted in his enjoyment, and may thenceforward prohibit his neighbours from using their property so as to interrupt it. Thus, if Jones builds a dwelling-house, it is held that Brown will in process of time become restrainable from building a wall so as to darken its windows; although he might have done so when first it was built. But it seems difficult to make out that this doctrine is founded upon any principle of Natural Justice. How can the fact, that Brown has not hitherto chosen to use his property for a certain purpose, raise the presumption that he has bound himself never to do so? Or what hardship will his act inflict upon Jones twenty years hence, which it would not have inflicted the day after the house was built? Continued submission to Wrong, the only foundation upon which a title by Prescription can be raised, is in such cases wholly absent.

§ 145. The same effect may be produced by a Contract, not to transfer immovable property, but to do, or to abstain from doing, some particular act relating to it. Thus if a landowner covenants with his neighbour to repair a certain wall, or not to fell certain trees, upon his property, a purchaser of the property with notice of the Covenant will be compellable to perform it, or restrainable from breaking it, in the same manner as the Covenantor himself. The only doubtful question is whether such a Covenant can be so concluded as to bind a purchaser *without* notice, in which case it is technically said to Kun with the Land. The English Courts hold that this may be done where the subject-matter of the Covenant is property actually in the possession of the Covenantor, though not where it is property to be afterwards acquired by him. But it may be doubted whether it ought to be allowed in the case of any *positive* Covenant. Such a Contract, whatever may be its terms, can surely be scarcely considered as conferring upon the Covenantee a right capable of being enforced without the further co-operation of the Covenantor.

§ 146. The Roman Jurists drew, and the English have adopted, a distinction between Corporeal and Incorporeal Rights of Property in things immovable. According to this theory, the proprietor of a field has a title whose subject-matter is so much soil, while the proprietor of a Right of Way over a field has a title whose subject-matter is nothing but an invisible privilege. Never perhaps did the blunder of one man inflict greater intellectual confusion upon another, than this metaphysical crotchet has done upon the English student. Its consequence is, that we find in all our text-books Easements or Servitudes classed as a kind of property distinct from Land; an arrangement which may be illustrated by supposing Vision or Articulation to be classed in a physiological treatise as a kind of animal distinct from Man. For the importation, or at least for the general reception, of this incredible absurdity we are indebted to the sketch of English Real Property Law contained in Blackstone's Commentaries; a performance which I do not hesitate to pronounce the worst and weakest specimen of Legal analysis with which I have the misfortune to be acquainted.

§ 147. A moment's reflection will convince us that the two forms of Title are in principle precisely similar. A landed proprietor is a person who has acquired a right to use, without interruption from any one else, certain territory in a certain manner. The owner of a Servitude is nothing more or less. The difference between them is only one of degree. The privilege of exclusively cultivating and reaping a field is much more valuable to its possessor, and much more burthensome to the rest of mankind, than that of walking across it at pleasure. But when we analyse the two conceptions, we find that the ideas which they contain are precisely the same. Each consists of a physical fact and a metaphysical truth. There is the material existence of a Thing and a Person, and there is the moral existence of an Opinion which connects them together. Both Rights are therefore Corporeal as regards the Thing to which they relate, and both are Incorporeal as regards the privilege which they confer. And the attempt to distinguish between them only shows that the Romans were no less contemptible as metaphysicians than admirable as practical Legislators.

# CHAPTER III
# STATUAL RIGHTS AND OBLIGATIONS

By the word Status we simply mean the circumstances or conditions under which a given human being is compelled to act or to exist. Every person must therefore possess a Status of his own, and what that Status is must be determined before the nature of his Rights and Obligations can be ascertained. The Roman Jurists understood this obvious truth, and their Institute therefore commences with the Law of Personal Status. But they did not understand the equally obvious logical principle, that the foundation ought never to be enlarged until the superstructure is complete; in other words, that the consequences of every distinct fact ought to be fully deduced before it is combined with another. They attempted to distinguish in the first place the different varieties of Status, and to explain in the second their respective Jural operations; and the result has been that famous division of all Law into Personal and Real, whose combined authority and absurdity has reduced the best modern Jurists to the despairing conclusion, that a logical system of Jurisprudence is a moral impossibility.

In the former part of the present Book I have examined the questions of Right which arise from such elements of Status as are common to all mankind. In the present Chapter I shall consider to what extent the principles thus ascertained ought to be modified in the case of those human beings in whose Status there is some special peculiarity. What then are the special peculiarities of Personal Status to which mankind are liable? Whatever they may be, it is obvious that they naturally divide themselves into two great classes. The distinction of Sex pervades the whole animal creation. The other peculiarities of Status by which a human being may be affected are all Casual; that is to say they consist, not in an alternative which cannot be escaped, but in a departure from the ordinary type of humanity which may or may not be perceptible.

What the normal or average faculties of a human being may be, is a question for the Physiologist. But, such as they are, it must of course be presumed, until the contrary is proved, that any given human being possesses and has exercised them. This presumption may, however, be repelled by evidence. It may be shown that a particular individual does not naturally possess the faculties of an ordinary human being. Or it may be shown that, admitting him to possess them, he has been deprived by circumstances of their free exercise in a particular transaction. In both cases the Status of the individual in question is or has been peculiar, but in the one the peculiarity is Circumstantial and in the other Personal.

We then proceed to consider the distinction of Sex. Every one knows that the whole human race is about equally divided into two classes, termed Men and Women. The physical and moral disparities which exist between them, and the peculiar intimacy and importance of the mutual obligations which they are consequently capable of contracting with each other, are alone sufficient to make a considerable difference in their relative moral duties, and thus to raise some of the nicest and most difficult questions in Jurisprudence. But this is not all. Experience proves that the birth of Children is the natural and usual consequence of Sexual Cohabitation; and the fact of Sex thus leads us to consider the Jural character of the Filial relation, as well as of the remoter degrees of Consanguinity which are its indirect consequences.

The present chapter will therefore consist of the following four Sections: I. Circumstantial Status. II. Personal Status. III. Sexual Status. IV. Filial Status.

## I. Circumstantial Status

§ 148. We have already seen that a human being can only alter his own natural Rights by his own Intentional Act. It now becomes necessary to inquire what we mean by

Intention. In a mere physical sense, every event may be considered as my act which is caused by, or which would not have taken place without, the exertion of my physical faculties. The fall of an avalanche may be intelligibly said to be the physical act of a traveller who sneezes while crossing a glacier. But an Intentional Act requires, not only the fact of physical, Causation, but the fact of Intention; that is to say, of Volition combined with Intelligence. The agent must do the physical act wilfully, and he must comprehend its necessary consequences, or he will not be responsible for it. If therefore it can be shown that a given act was done under circumstances which made the agent incapable of refusing to do it, or incapable of foreseeing its consequences when done, it follows that its effect upon his natural Rights will be more or less modified.

§ 149. That no man can possibly be held responsible for an act which he was physically unable to help doing, is a conclusion which does not require to be proved. But compulsion may be moral, as well as physical. A man may do an act, not because he wishes to do it for its own sake, but because he is anxious to avoid or to procure certain consequences with which he has been incidentally menaced or tempted by some other person. That no such evidence can be admitted to justify the commission of a Wrong, or even to mitigate the punishment of a crime, is perfectly clear. The man who wilfully injures another is equally inexcusable, whether he did so from selfishness or from malice. But an act which confers a benefit stands upon different grounds. In this case it may fairly be contended that, if the real motive of the benefaction was not the wish of the Benefactor to gratify the Beneficiary, the latter is conscientiously hound to make restitution and the former is conscientiously entitled to claim it.

§ 150. Thus it is evident that a gift or contract executed under Duress, that is to say from the wish to avoid the infliction of unjustifiable violence, is altogether a nullity. In such a case there is, in fact, no intention on the part of the agent to produce the ostensible effect of the act which he is doing. His only motive is alarm, and he goes through the form of a Jural transaction merely as a means of escape from danger. The highwayman, for instance, who by threats compels a passenger to deliver his purse acquires precisely the same title, and commits precisely the same offence, as if he were to wrest it from its owner by actual force. Even the purchaser or donee who takes advantage of the apprehensions entertained by a menaced proprietor to procure a free gift or an advantageous bargain may be compelled to make restitution. And since such a transfer is wholly void, it follows that the transferee is a mere intruder, and that a purchaser from him, whether with or without notice of the Duress, will acquire no title against the transferor.

§ 151. But the question, what combination of facts will amount to Duress, is one which has been discussed, both by the Roman and by the earner English authorities, in singularly confused and unsatisfactory language. They persist in attributing the nullity of an act done under Duress, not to the Circumstantial Disability of the agent, but to the crime or fraud of the adverse claimant; and they therefore draw endless distinctions between necessary and unnecessary alarm, and between alarm caused and alarm not caused by the fault of an interested party. The truth is, that Duress is a question of Status and not of Fraud. It depends simply upon the inquiry, whether the agent did the act because he meant it to have a certain effect or because he was too frightened to refuse. If the fact of intention did not exist, or if the agent's state of mind was such that it could not exist, the causes of its non-existence are wholly immaterial.

§ 152. A consent procured by Falsehood or Deception will, upon the same principle, be a nullity as between the parties, and an act done in pursuance of such a consent will be just as much a Wrong as if the consent had never been given. Not only will a transfer of property procured by the fraud of the transferee be no bar to his justifiable dispossession by the transferor, but the rule ought to be the same when the transfer takes place in consequence of a fraud committed by a third person, or even of the voluntary mistake or self-delusion of the transferor. For, in both cases the fact, whoever may be responsible for it, is that the transaction would not have taken place if the agent's state of mind had not been such as to disable him from making a free choice. But Fraud cannot, like Duress, be held to make the transferee a mere intruder. The intention to execute the transfer, however caused, has actually existed; and the consequence is that a purchaser for value ought not to be responsible for any fraud or mistake of which he had no notice.

§ 153. The English Courts of Equity hold that, when property already bound by a Real Obligation is placed by the obligor in the hands of a trustee for himself, the trustee receiving notice of the obligation becomes liable to the obligee and not to the obligor. Thus if Brown accepts a transfer from Jones in the name of Robinson, Robinson, supposing the transfer to prove fraudulent as between Jones and Brown, would be bound to hold the property as trustee for Jones; and if, after receiving notice of the fraud, he were to transfer it to Brown, he would become personally responsible to Jones in case of its loss. The decision has been questioned, but apparently not upon substantial grounds. It can make no real difference to Robinson whether he is trustee for Brown or for Jones, and the embarrassment of having to decide upon a disputed antecedent claim by Jones against Brown is not necessarily greater than that of having to decide upon a disputed subsequent assignment by Brown to Jones.[22]

§ 154. There is scarcely any subject upon which the speculations of Jurists have been so vague and unsatisfactory as upon the question, what amount of Fraud is sufficient to set aside a transfer of property. I cannot refrain from quoting two examples, the one from an eminent Ro-

---

[22] See §§ 102, 103.

man and the other from an eminent American authority, of the strange impotence of thought with which the subject has been discussed. Fraud, says the great Labeo, is any craft, deceit or artifice used for the purpose of circumventing, deceiving or misleading; a definition which simply substitutes five unintelligible words for one. Undue concealment, says Judge Story, is the non-disclosure of those facts and circumstances which one party is under some legal or equitable obligation to communicate to the other; a definition amounting to the satisfactory announcement, that undue concealment is concealment which is undue. Such passages go far to excuse the vulgar opinion, that the successful study of Law presupposes the extinction of common sense.

§ 155. The solution of the whole difficulty will be found in a simple distinction which has already been incidentally explained.[23] Natural Jurisprudence is founded upon moral Right, not upon moral Duty. It is by taking the defendant's conscience as the test of the complainant's claim to relief, that so many profound Jurists have failed to discover a satisfactory definition of Fraud. It is by taking the complainant's conscience as the measure of his own rights, that any man of sense may easily define it for himself. Now under what circumstances would an honourable donor think himself justified in reclaiming what he has intentionally given away? Surely when, and only when, he is conscious that he would never have parted with it if he had not been deceived. The measure of Fraud is therefore, not the degree of moral obliquity which can be detected in the adverse claimant, but the effect which the deception has produced upon the conduct of the deceived party. If he has done that which he would not otherwise have done, the counter-obligation is complete and the act is revocable.

§ 156. It is obvious that, if I do an act whose *physical* consequences I am prevented by circumstances from fore-

---

[23] Introd. II.

seeing, I shall not be responsible for them. The man who carries a light into a magazine cannot be held answerable for the explosion unless he knows that powder is kept there. So if a tradesman sends home one article by mistake for another, or if a bailee delivers up the bailed property in ignorance that something of his own is concealed within it, the recipient acquires no title whatever by the act. If the mistake is mutual, he is to be considered simply as a *bonâ-fide* but wrongful possessor. But if, after discovering the mistake, he retains the article with the intention of making it his own, he will be guilty, not perhaps of what the English Law defines as Larceny, but clearly of a punishable Fraud. And if he accepts the transfer with notice of the mistake and with the intention of profiting by it, he is, or ought to be, held guilty of actual Larceny.

§ 157. The case of a person who commits a wrongful act while prevented by circumstances from comprehending its *moral* consequences is in some degree different. Such a misapprehension cannot excuse the wrong-doer from making full compensation for the injury which he has done, but it may exempt him from punishment by showing that he did it without any wrongful intention. If, for instance, Don Quixote had really slain the inn-keeper whom he mistook for a Moorish enchanter, his honest delusion ought to have been a defence to a prosecution for murder, though not to an action for damages. Nor does it signify whether the mistake is one of fact or of opinion. Whatever may be the case where the parties are bound by Positive Law, it is clear that in a state of Nature every man is entitled to make up his own mind upon the validity of his own claims and to act accordingly, and that an error of judgment, though it may be a Wrong, cannot amount to a criminal offence.

§ 158. This brings us to consider the effect of a Doubtful or Disputed Wrong. Suppose that one person endeavours to exact compensation, or to inflict retaliation, for an act done by another which the agent believes to be justifiable. That whichever may be mistaken will be civilly responsible for whatever damage or loss he may in consequence of his mistake inflict upon the other party, cannot of course be doubted. But no Moralist has been able to resist the conclusion, that neither the disputants themselves, nor any other persons who may under the same belief assist either of them in the attempt, can be held punishable for any act of violence which may be found necessary to maintain their imaginary rights. And the inevitable consequence is that, however trifling may be the original cause of dispute, both parties are at liberty, without becoming criminally answerable to any human authority, to maintain the conflict until the extermination of their last partisan.

§ 159. The whole fabric of human Legislation may be considered as supported by the necessity of somehow or other evading this tremendous inference. Experience proves that there is no state of society in which the honest men find it difficult to put down the professed rogues. It is the disputes of professedly honest men which would speedily prove the destruction of any human community in which each claimant was permitted to decide his own cause. How terrible an evil such anarchy must be, may be conjectured from the tyrannical absurdity of the institutions which have, in semi-barbarous times, been eagerly adopted and zealously maintained as its alternative. And how intolerable a very slight degree of it has been found in civilized society, is proved by the ignominious state of political paralysis in which so many European states are habitually kept by their chronic dread of Revolution.

§ 160. The only principle upon which Private War can be effectually, or indeed justifiably, prohibited is that of Arbitration; and even Arbitration must derive its validity from the consent of the interested parties. Every human being is entitled to interfere on behalf of what he thinks justice, but no human being is entitled to treat resistance to his interference as an additional offence. But no contract can be more binding than the mutual consent of two disputants, that the question between them shall be referred to an impartial Arbitrator and that his decision shall be final. And it is clear that, supposing the decision to be honestly given to the best of the Arbitrator's judgment, the party to whom it is adverse cannot conscientiously resist it, although it proves to be mistaken. Municipal Law, in its simplest form, is in fact nothing but the establishment in a community of human beings of a permanent system of Arbitration; and the basis of all Law is therefore the express or implied consent of a certain number of persons to refer all their disputes to a certain Arbitrator.

§ 161. The next step is to suppose that a wrongful claim preferred by one party is admitted by the other. It is clear that in this case the rightful claimant may justifiably refuse to he bound by any act which he may do in confirmation of the wrongful claim, since he is disabled by his mistake from comprehending the consequences of such a confirmation. Nor ought it to make any difference whether the confirmation takes place in consequence of misinformation respecting the facts of the case, or of misapprehension as to their Jural effect. It is true that the Civil Law draws, and that the English Courts of Equity have adopted, a distinction between a mistake in Fact and a mistake in Law. But some of the most eminent continental Civilians have denied its soundness, and it may be doubted whether the denial is not justified by reason. The man who receives money which is not due is clearly bound in conscience to refund it, and the man who pays it does not seem bound in conscience not to reclaim it.

§ 162. From this it follows that upon principles of private Justice, whatever may be the case upon principles of public Policy,[24] no man can be held to have forfeited by Prescription a right which he did not know that he could enforce. It is impossible to maintain that I have any reason to rely upon the non-assertion of an adverse title as a sign that it will never be reasserted, unless there is proof that the

---

[24] See § 146.

person in whom it is vested is aware of its existence. The occupant who fraudulently suppresses his predecessor's will, or the thief who feloniously purloins his neighbour's movable property, cannot acquire any title by Prescription so long as the wrongful act continues undiscovered by the injured party. And even the testamentary heir of an adverse claimant cannot he excluded by lapse of time so long as he remains ignorant of his testator's rights, unless the bar was complete before his succession. No Jury can be asked to presume that which the circumstances of the case make morally impossible.

§ 163. But there is an obvious distinction between a Confirmation and a Compromise. The man who abandons a valuable claim which he thinks worthless is doing he knows not what, and may recall his mistake when he finds it out. But the man who for valuable consideration gives up his chance of being able to enforce a claim whose nature he fully understands cannot be permitted to rescind his bargain because it turns out that he would have been successful, any more than he can be compelled to refund its price because his opponent proves to have been in the right. In such a case each party has got what he contracted for. One has sold and the other has bought a chance, and both have avoided the expense and anxiety of litigation. The essence of a Compromise is the acceptance of a smaller certain, in lieu of a larger uncertain, benefit; and no such transaction could ever take place if the parties were not allowed to admit the element of uncertainty into their calculation.

§ 164. It is upon these principles that the English Courts of Equity act in maintaining or rescinding Compromises. They consider the object of the transaction to be the removal of a common doubt, arising from certain known facts. If it appears that the doubt was not common, or that the facts were not known, the transaction may justifiably be treated as invalid. Suppose, for instance, that Jones compromises a claim upon property in the possession of Brown. If Brown possessed, or had the means of possessing, any exclusive information respecting the facts of the case, or if Jones acted upon any misapprehension of fact not partaken by Brown, Jones is entitled to rescind the transaction. And if both parties acted upon a common mistake of fact, the transaction may be rescinded by either. So far as a Compromise is based upon assumption the assumption must be correct, and so far as it is based upon uncertainty the uncertainty must be equal.

## II. Personal Status

§ 165. We have now seen to what extent the responsibility of a human being may be qualified by evidence that he was prevented by circumstances from refusing to do, or from fully comprehending the consequences of doing, a particular act. It can of course make no difference whether this sort of disability was the effect of the circumstances under which the individual act was done, or of the habitual situation of the person who did it. A person who is incapable of controlling his own action, or of comprehending its consequences, is therefore to that extent irresponsible for them. And from this it follows, not only that there are many most important acts for which no human being is responsible, but also there are many human beings who are morally incapable of an intentional act of any importance, and who consequently cannot materially alter their own natural Rights.

§ 166. It is notorious that human beings are occasionally for a time reduced to a condition in which both Volition and Intelligence are utterly extinct, and it is possible that cases may occur in which they are permanently deprived of both. It is of course clear that the Rights of a person so afflicted, if Rights he can be said to retain, cannot possibly be affected by anything which he may do, except so far as his incapability of self-control may justify those around him in forcibly disabling him from violence. An epileptic patient, for instance, is clearly neither criminally nor civilly responsible for his acts during the spasms of his disease. And if there are, as there certainly were in times when the proper treatment of insanity was unknown, maniacs whose whole life is one continued epileptic paroxysm, the same principle must apply to them. Such victims of frenzy have ceased, not merely to be human beings, but to be sentient animals, and are as incapable of responsibility as so many inanimate machines.

§ 167. But Volition is not to be confounded with Motive. The man who loses the physical power of self-control becomes irresponsible, but the man who loses the moral power of self-control does so at his peril. That Moral Insanity may possibly exist, I shall not venture to deny. But that its existence can make the slightest difference in the responsibility of the moral Maniac to his fellow-creatures, I refuse to allow. My right of Retaliation arises from the facts that you have hurt me and that you meant to hurt me, not from the fact that you thought it was wrong to hurt me. If Brown kills Jones, he must justify his act or forfeit his life. That he was physically unable to avoid the act, or that he was intellectually unable to understand its physical nature, would be a good defence. That he was morally unable to comprehend its wickedness may possibly, in the sight of his Maker, be sufficient to excuse him from guilt; but it cannot possibly entitle him to complain because Jones's friends do to him what he did to Jones.

§ 168. The same distinction will apply to the doctrine of Physical Necessity, so dangerously exaggerated by the Casuists of a former age. That doctrine, if logically carried out, would lead to the most monstrous consequences. What do we mean when we say that a starving man has a Right to food? Do we mean that he is entitled to cut his way into a baker's shop? that if, in doing so, he slaughters half-a-dozen apprentices he is justified? and that if he loses his own life the baker is guilty of murder?. Either we mean this, or we mean nothing. A Right which a free man must not maintain sword in hand is no Right at all. Such a theory can only have arisen from that confusion between Casuistry and Jurisprudence which is so inveterate a habit among the Publicists of the school of Grotius. Humanity ought to be satisfied by the admission, that to relieve a starving fellow-creature, though not a Jural obligation, is an imperative Moral Duty; and that to punish him for taking necessary food, though not strictly speaking an Injustice, would be a heinous Sin.

§ 169. But, although no human being who is capable of physical Volition can exempt himself from general responsibility by pleading the moral weakness of his Will, yet he may justly do so as against a person who has taken undue advantage of that weakness. Thus if I accept an unequal bargain or compromise from a person whom I know to be offering it under the pressure of want or of debt, I am bound to show, not only that I abstained from all previous interference or persuasion, but that I previously ascertained his knowledge and comprehension of the sacrifice which he was making. And the same rule ought to apply to any transaction in which one of the parties becomes aware that the other is acting under the influence of any motive or habit which is likely to weaken his moral power of self-control. A fool cannot be prevented from dealing according to his folly, but whoever deals with him must first make sure that he understands its consequences.

§ 170. We will next suppose the case of a person whose Volition is unimpaired, but whose intellect is imperfect. This imperfection is in some cases so great as entirely to disable the person labouring under it from discerning the connection of Cause and Effect. In such a case the Maniac or Idiot is of course altogether irresponsible. Nothing that he can possibly do will affect any of his Natural Rights, whether by making him amenable to criminal punishment or to civil liability; except of course to the extent of the necessary right of self-defence acquired by his neighbours. But such entire intellectual obscuration is comparatively rare; and even where it does exist, the constraint which humanity renders necessary for the sufferer's own safety is usually such as to take away his opportunity of becoming either the victim of fraud or the agent of violence.

§ 171. How far then can a human being be held irresponsible for an act done by him, upon the ground that he was intellectually incapable of foreseeing its consequences? Of course so far, and so far only, as he would be held irresponsible upon the ground that he was casually prevented from foreseeing them. The man who breaks a Contract is only responsible for the loss thereby inflicted upon the Contractor so far as he had the means of foreseeing it,[25] and is therefore clearly irresponsible for so much of it as may arise from intermediate causes which he is incapable of comprehending. But the man who commits a Delict is liable for the loss which he inflicts, whether he could foresee it or not.[26] If, therefore, Brown beats Jones and thereby causes him to forfeit by his absence a conditional benefit. Brown is liable for the loss if he understood the nature and effect of a blow, although he may have been incapable of understanding the value of property or the meaning of a condition.

§ 172. Every human being is thus *primâ facie* responsible for his own wilful acts, so far as he is intellectually capable of comprehending their nature. It is not necessary that he should be intellectually capable of judging how far they are likely to be for his own advantage. If I go to market and sell a horse to a stranger for a high price, the purchaser cannot make me refund by proving himself to be incapable of understanding the value of a horse. If he knew what he was doing, I am not answerable for what he did. But incapability of judgment, or what the English Courts term Imbecility, is justly held to alter the Status of the Imbecile person as regards all those who are aware of its existence. If I privately offer a disadvantageous bargain to my

---

[25] See § 113.

[26] See § 7.

neighbour, knowing that he is incapable of detecting its inequality, he ought not to be bound by his acceptance; unless I can prove, either that I made him understand the nature of the transaction, or that he acted with the advice of some third person who was capable of doing so.

§ 173. Intellectual, like physical, disease may be either chronic and permanent or acute and intermittent. There are many persons who have been attacked by Lunacy and have completely recovered, and there are some who are liable to occasional paroxysms with intervals of apparently perfect sanity. There is of course no reason for holding that an attack of Lunacy inflicts any disability upon the patient except during its continuance. And if such a patient, after recovering his reason, confirms or recognizes a transaction concluded by him during his Lunacy, it is clear that he thereby takes upon himself the same liabilities as if he had been sane at its conclusion. But as periodical fits of the gout are an indication of latent bodily disease, so periodical fits of Lunacy can only arise from latent intellectual derangement; and it seems reasonable to attribute to a person so afflicted that degree of Imbecility which is required to set aside a disadvantageous transaction under questionable circumstances.

§ 174. There is one strange, yet not uncommon, form of intellectual disease which has, upon several occasions, excited very painful interest in English Courts of Justice. I mean that sort of derangement which is termed Monomania, and which seems to consist in a confusion between the memory and the imagination of the patient, whereby his mind is impressed with a *quasi*-recollection of facts which never took place. The rational principle in dealing with such cases appears to be, to examine how far the actual reality of the imagined events would have affected the responsibility of the patient. Thus it is clear that the homicide who kills an innocent passenger under the delusion that he is a lurking assassin must be acquitted. But if I shoot a Cabinet Minister under the delusion that I have been defrauded by the Government, or if I strangle my servant under the delusion that I am Emperor of China, I am guilty of murder; because neither Emperors nor victims of fraud are justified in killing their fellow-creatures. And in transactions unconnected with the patient's peculiar delusion we are assured that Monomania, so far from inferring Disability, does not even raise the presumption of Imbecility.

§ 175. It has been a frequent question among Jurists, how far the effect of intellectual derangement is altered when it is caused by the wilful folly of the patient; that is to say, by voluntary Intoxication. In the case of a Gift or a Contract, it is difficult to understand how there can be any doubt upon the subject. If a man is too drunk to know what he is doing, this amounts to manifest Disability, and his acts ought to be altogether void. If he is too drunk to have the use of his judgment, this amounts to Imbecility, and his acts ought to be voidable as against any person who takes advantage of his condition. But in the case of an Injury, whether by Delict or by Breach of Contract, the question of antecedent responsibility arises. Admitting the drunkard to have been entirely irresponsible when he did the act, which is seldom the case, it is still clear that he was not irresponsible when he did what caused the act. He therefore stands in the position of a man who wilfully turns loose a dangerous lunatic or a carnivorous animal. In other words he is civilly, and according to the degree of his negligence criminally, responsible for the consequences of his conduct.

§ 176. How far physical Infirmity can be held to raise the presumption of intellectual derangement, is of course a mere question of Fact. There are some bodily diseases, such as paralysis and violent fever, which necessarily infer temporary Imbecility if not absolute Disability; and in such cases the capacity of the patient to affect his natural Rights will be limited accordingly. There are also certain bodily afflictions or privations, such as blindness and deafness, which unavoidably produce a difficulty in exercising the judgment equivalent to the effect of a certain degree of intellectual Imbecility. But the effect of ordinary Disease, even when painful and incurable, in impeding the exercise of the intellect is very different in different persons. And the effect of Age, not only in producing intellectual weakness but even in producing that degree of physical Infirmity which is likely to be accompanied by intellectual weakness, is equally variable.

§ 177. But there is one particular form of physical deficiency which is so invariably accompanied by a certain degree of intellectual incapacity, that it is usually classed by Jurists as a Disability *sui generis.* I mean of course Infancy, that is to say physical Immaturity. Experience has established the facts, that bodily and mental Maturity are usually acquired together, and that the completion of the latter seldom precedes that of the former. The proportion between the two may not in every case be precisely the same, but there is always great convenience, and probably scarcely ever any material injustice, in taking the one as the measure of the other. The Common Law fixes the age of complete Maturity at twenty-one; the Civil Law, probably with better discretion, at twenty-five. But such arbitrary solutions, however recommended by expediency, are unknown to Natural Justice, which recognizes no test except the visible completion of physical growth.

§ 178. The degree of intellectual incapacity arising from Infancy is of course very different at different ages. But we are not without a test by which we may distinguish the period during which it amounts to absolute Disability, from the period during which it is gradually becoming qualified by the advance of intelligence. Nature has divided the period of growth into two nearly equal intervals by a great physical transformation, which is usually accompanied by a corresponding mental advance. Perhaps there would be little risk in holding that the age of Puberty may be considered as marking the commencement of Jural responsibility, and consequently that no act done by an Infant under that age ought to affect his natural Rights. His gifts and contracts ought to be wholly void, his release or neglect ought not to bar his claims upon others, and even his crimes ought only to be so far punishable as may be necessary for his own future reformation.

§ 179. Except in arbitrarily fixing the age of Puberty at a certain interval after birth, both the Civil and the Common Law generally ratify this doctrine. But they make one exception, and that a most odious and cruel one, with respect to criminal liability. They limit the period of absolute irresponsibility to seven years after birth; from which time until the age of Puberty, although they presume incapacity of criminal intention, they admit evidence to the contrary. And upon such evidence, as we are calmly informed by Blackstone, a child eight years old has been publicly put to death under the sentence of an English Court of Justice. But the days in which a crime so unspeakably horrible was likely to be permitted have long been over. Children under the age of Puberty are still tried and punished by the Magistrate, but it is well understood that in such cases the penalty is to be fixed with a view solely to the welfare of the culprit. And it may be doubted, to judge by the aversion which is sometimes expressed at the roughness of our prison discipline, whether even this test will not shortly be found too rigid for the endurance of modern philanthropy.

§ 180. The Common Law somewhat arbitrarily declares the complete criminal responsibility, and the almost complete civil irresponsibility, of an Infant between the ages of Puberty and Maturity; that is to say, between the ages of fourteen and twenty-one. The only exception which it admits consists in his capacity to make himself liable for the price of such articles as may be necessary for his maintenance during Infancy. Such a rule seems unnecessarily stringent. It is admitted that a certain degree of intellectual Imbecility is likely to accompany physical immaturity, but the presumption that it must necessarily amount to absolute Disability is surely inconsistent with fact. There can be no reason why a half-grown lad should not be allowed, with the assistance of competent advisers and upon the ordinary terms of the market, to effect a lease of land or an investment of money; and there can be no doubt that, by repudiating such a transaction when he came of age, he would be morally, if not legally, guilty of gross injustice.

## III. Sexual Status

§ 181. The question, how far the Rights and Obligations of a Woman ought to differ from those of a Man, is one which recently been agitated with vehement absurdity by the advocates of the one sex, and silenced with ungenerous ridicule by those of the other. There is no want of reality in the grievances denounced by the American platform; but it will be found that, as respects unmarried women at least, they arise from Social Usage rather than from Legal enactment. Nothing certainly can be more unjust than the prejudices which exclude Women from certain professions for which they are peculiarly fit, and nothing more paltry than the jealousy which has invented one vulgar nickname for female intellect and another for female courage. But Legislation has had as little to do with the one absurdity as with the other, and it may be hoped that English good sense is becoming ashamed of both. We shall in time become convinced, paradoxical as the opinion may now appear, that female independence is a benefit to society, and that the mothers of wise and brave men ought to be clever and spirited women.

§ 182. I am not aware that any civilized system of Jurisprudence has imposed any personal Disability upon unmarried Women. The doctrine of perpetual Female Tutelage, so tyrannically asserted by the Decemviral Code, was systematically evaded by the Imperial Jurisconsults; and long before the age of Justinian it had wholly ceased to exist. No such distinction between the sexes was ever recognised by the Common Law. An Englishwoman is responsible for Wrongs and punishable for Crimes, capable of acquiring and transmitting property, and personally bound by Contracts and Releases, precisely in the same manner as an Englishman. Nor do the Courts of Equity treat with suspicion her gratuitous or disadvantageous transactions, upon the ground of any inferiority of intellect or discretion presumable from the fact of her Sex. But Natural Justice, and to a considerable extent Positive Law, confers certain peculiar immunities upon Women; which may be generally described as privileges arising, either from the indulgence due to physical weakness, or from the respect due to moral purity.

§ 183. That the person of a Woman ought in all cases to be sacred from actual violence, the most chivalrous Moralist can scarcely maintain. Such violence may have become, by the wilful act of the sufferer herself, absolutely necessary for the safety of the person who inflicts it. The considerations which are commonly thought to justify the deprivation of life or of liberty are obviously applicable to both sexes alike. If the punishment of death is ever necessary, it is surely necessary in the case of such a criminal as Lady Macbeth. If the use of deadly weapons in self-defence is ever justifiable, it is surely justifiable against such an assailant as Brunechild or Clorinda. But it may perhaps be laid down, that no punishment whose efficiency consists in the physical pain endured by the criminal ought ever to be inflicted upon a female offender. This is a rule which the Common Law formerly disregarded, and which the police of some continental nations are still not ashamed to violate, but which I believe to be uniformly observed by the modern Legislation of Western Europe.

§ 184. A successful assault upon Female Chastity is considered, by all civilized Legislators, as a felony scarcely less atrocious than Murder; and even an unsuccessful attempt to effect such a purpose becomes, if actual violence is used, a most serious misdemeanour. And it may be added that any act or word by which the modesty of a woman is wilfully and maliciously insulted, is an outrage upon public decency which may fairly be thought to justify severe Retaliation. In all such cases the Common Law justly and generously refuses to take into consideration the moral character of the injured party, except so far as it may lead to the inference that the aggressor did not comprehend the true nature of the injury. No extremity of self-degradation can ever deprive a woman of the right to reassert, and to make others respect, the natural dignity of her Sexual Status.

§ 185. Before I proceed to investigate the Rights and Obligations which naturally arise from the voluntary intercourse of the Sexes, I think it necessary to repeat a remark which I have already made. I am at present discussing the consequences deducible from the principles of Natural Justice, combined with the facts natural or necessary to human existence. These consequences will not enable us to appreciate the peculiar sanctity which Christian Legislation in general, and English Legislation in particular, annexes to the Contract of Marriage. For that purpose it will be necessary to introduce the artificial element of Moral and Religious Belief, and this I propose to do in its proper order. But in the meantime I shall find myself compelled to admit, or to seem to admit, the validity of certain sexual connections which are justly held immoral and dishonourable by all Christian men. And I therefore wish to remind my readers that I do so, merely as being unable to perceive any ground upon which such a conclusion could be reasonably rejected by a Legislature recognizing no higher rule of Duty than Justice between man and man.

§ 186. The mere fact of Sexual Intercourse, taking place between a Man and a Woman by their mutual consent, cannot be thought to impose any obligation upon either party. But natural reason suggests, and the Civil Law allows, some difference between the situation of a casual paramour and that of a recognized Concubine. Cohabitation without Marriage is undoubtedly an immoral practice; but it would be absurd to deny that, as between the parties themselves, it imposes upon the Man the moral duty of making some provision for the Woman. That she has any moral right to insist upon such a provision cannot perhaps be maintained. But if he dies intestate pending the Cohabitation, she has surely a fair claim upon his property for such a maintenance during her future life as he was accustomed to allow her. Nor can it be disputed, except upon grounds of public policy or of religious scruple, that the fact of Cohabitation between a Man and a Woman is sufficient to form a valuable consideration for any provision which he may have expressly or impliedly agreed to make for her upon that condition.

§ 187. Cohabitation between a Man and a Woman, accompanied by a mutual Contract that it shall continue during their joint lives, is termed Marriage. It will scarcely be disputed that such a transaction is as clearly ratified by Natural Justice as by revealed Religion, or that, considered merely as a civil Contract, it is one of the most solemn and binding which a human being can undertake. There is probably no artificial obligation whose conscientious observance is so important to the happiness of the parties concerned, or whose breach by either of them is so incapable of effectual compensation. The duties imposed by Marriage are of course chiefly of such a nature that no human tribunal can compel their performance, or can even ascertain their non-performance. But there are some which are capable of being clearly defined, and upon whose fulfilment, however reluctant and ungracious, it might in many cases become absolutely necessary to insist.

§ 188. To what extent do the Rights and Obligations arising from Marriage depend upon the mutual intention of the Husband and Wife? Those antique systems of Positive Law under which Custom was everything and Contract nothing, returned a very brief answer to this important question. Marriage, in their view, was a solemnity and not a transaction; a solemnity which the parties might no doubt decline to perform, but whose natural effect when once performed nothing could alter. The Wife was the slave, or rather the property, of the Husband, and was as incapable of insisting upon the execution of a Contract made between them before she became so, as if she had actually been transformed into an inanimate chattel. To a Hebrew Priest, or to a Roman Decemvir, marrying a woman was an act as immutable in its character as killing a man; and a previous agreement between the parties, for the purpose of modifying the effect of what they were about to do, would have appeared as absurd in the one case as in the other.

§ 189. The liberality of Natural Justice arrives, although by a very different train of reasoning, at a somewhat similar conclusion. It considers Marriage as a Contract, indeed as the only Contract, by which two human beings are permitted to abandon for their mutual benefit their natural freedom, and to become to a certain extent each other's property. Strict equality of terms is the only condition upon which such a transaction can be held valid. To allow the contrary would be to let one human being become the slave of another. But the peculiar difficulty of Marriage is that, in order to secure virtual equality between the parties, we are compelled to insist upon apparent inequality. The physical, and in some respects the moral, difference between the sexes is naturally such, that a literal division of the matrimonial duties between Husband and Wife would inflict cruel hardship upon the one without conferring any corresponding benefit upon the other. Justice therefore requires us to apportion the burthen according to the respective faculties of its bearers.

§ 190. The essence of every Marriage, considered as a civil Contract, is the undertaking of the Husband to maintain the Wife. We know nothing of any form of human society in which this has not been the primary purpose of wedded life; and we have therefore a right to conclude that the disparity, or rather the dissimilarity, in which the practice originates is a natural and necessary one. This leads to the conclusion that a certain degree of obedience is due from the Wife to the Husband; not the obedience which a master requires from the slave who is his property, nor even the obedience which a preceptor requires from a pupil who is unable to take care of himself, but the obedience which the leader of an enterprise, or the manager of a partnership, is entitled to expect from a faithful and loyal companion. The breadwinner, as the proverb well expresses it, must be the master. In other words the husband, being bound to support the household, has a right to select at his discretion the place and manner of its support.

§ 191. From this it follows that a Husband may, notwithstanding his Marriage, bind himself by Contract with third persons in any manner which he thinks proper; because such a discretion is consistent with, and may be absolutely necessary for, the discharge of his obligation to maintain his Wife. But it also follows that a Wife cannot after her Marriage, except by the consent of her Husband, bind herself by any obligation whose fulfilment would be inconsistent with the due discharge of her duty to cohabit with and obey him. For if a married woman could, by entering the service of a person unaware of her Coverture, acquire the right to separate from her husband without his consent, Marriage would cease to exist as a Status. It further follows that a married woman cannot make herself responsible for necessaries supplied by a third person for her maintenance, since by so doing she would be undertaking the support of the household. But there is no reason why she should not be criminally punishable, in the same manner as if she were unmarried, for any crime which she may commit without her Husband's knowledge.

§ 192. Even where a married woman enters into a Contract with the consent of her husband, it seems difficult to maintain that she is personally bound, except so far as he may eventually authorize her to fulfil it. To that extent, if the Contract is such as would have bound her if she had been unmarried, she ought perhaps to be held liable. But her first duty must always be to her husband; and therefore, if he revokes his consent and requires her to break her engagement, she cannot be blamed for her obedience, although he will of course be responsible for his interference. But the doctrine of the Common Law, that a wife cannot be criminally punished for certain descriptions of Delict if committed by her husband's instigation, seems neither rational in itself nor consistent with itself. The fact of such instigation must in all cases be a palliation, and may in some be a complete excuse; but it is too much to lay down the rule that a female thief throws off all future responsibility by marrying a male thief.

§ 193. We now perceive the true meaning of a doctrine which has been very vehemently, but very thoughtlessly, condemned. I mean the rule of the Common Law which declares that every husband becomes personally liable, during the joint lives of himself and his wife, for the fulfilment of her prenuptial obligations. That rule is nothing but the logical consequence of the principle, that Marriage is a Status and not merely a Contract. Every woman who marries devotes herself to the domestic service of her husband. Therefore every man who marries a woman withdraws her from the necessity of fulfilling her previous obligations, and by doing so clearly becomes bound in justice, during the interval of her exemption but no longer, to fulfil them himself in her room. How far a husband, having married without notice of his wife's obligations, is entitled to insist upon her personal assistance in fulfilling them, is a different question; but its practical importance is not such as to make it worth discussion.

§ 194. As the Marriage of a female obligee disables her from fulfilling her obligation, so the Marriage of a female obligor disables her from enforcing her right, except with the consent of her Husband. The duties of Cohabitation and Obedience can scarcely be reconciled with the necessity of compelling performance or of exacting compensation from third persons. It is therefore reasonable to presume that every Wife has, by the act of Marriage, authorized her

Husband to require, in her name and for her benefit, the fulfilment of whatever obligations may have been due to her while unmarried. And it may even be contended that, as a consequence of this implied authority, the Wife's obligee will be discharged by a compromise concluded between himself and the Husband, provided he had no previous notice of the Wife's dissent. But it is clear that the Husband's gratuitous release of the Wife's obligation will not preclude her from enforcing it if she survives him; because authority to enforce a right does not imply authority to throw it away. Nor, since the Wife has no means of compelling the Husband to enforce her obligations, ought any lapse of time pending her Coverture to be considered as a prescriptive bar to her claim after his decease.

§ 195. It is evident that the nature and purpose of a Marriage do not impose any restraint upon the parties as regards the property of the wife. The husband is necessarily bound to maintain the Wife, but the Wife is not necessarily bound to confer any benefit upon the Husband except her personal assistance and obedience. With that duty the management or enjoyment of her property has no connection. She is therefore at liberty to stipulate for his entire exclusion, and for her own absolute and independent ownership. She may reserve the income to her separate use during their joint lives, and may provide that the principal, in case of her decease during Coverture, shall devolve or be disposable by her will as if she had never been married. The effect of such a stipulation is simply to place the Husband in the same situation as if the Wife had possessed no property at all; and if Natural Justice does not forbid me to marry a poor Wife, there is no reason why it should forbid me to renounce the benefit of marrying a rich one.

§ 196. To what extent can a married woman, while reserving to herself the beneficial rights, retain or decline to retain the obligations of an independent proprietor? The English Courts of Equity allow a latitude in such cases which seems scarcely consistent with principle. They assist a Wife to make herself by her Marriage-Contract the inalienable owner of her separate estate, and by virtue of this stipulation to receive the income for her own benefit in defiance of her most solemn and equitable engagements. This extraordinary severance of enjoyment from responsibility is justified by the singular argument, that the separate ownership of a married woman is the Creature of Equity, and therefore exempt, as we are probably meant to infer, from the rules of common sense and common justice. But upon the other hand the same Courts hold that, in default of a proviso against alienation, a married woman is absolute mistress of her separate property, and is therefore capable, not only of binding it by Contract as if she were unmarried, but of surrendering it altogether by a gratuitous and irrevocable gift to her Husband.

§ 197. There is surely no necessity for either of these extremes. A married woman ought in justice to be considered as the absolute proprietor of her separate estate as against all mankind except her Husband. Not only ought her separate income to be necessarily subject to her debts, but there seems no reason why, after her Husband's decease, her person and the residue of her property should not be liable. There are probably few debtors who usually require or deserve less indulgence than a married woman who outruns her income. But the power to exercise her right of ownership is one question, and the power to surrender it is another. It is most dangerous to hold that a Wife, by reserving to herself a separate interest in her property, enables herself to make an irrevocable transfer or disposition of that interest for her Husband's benefit. A testamentary gift or a transaction upon strictly equal terms is the utmost which ought to be permitted between them, and that only through the intervention of some independent adviser.

§ 198. On the other hand, the nature of a Marriage-Contract does not necessarily preclude the Wife from thereby making a donation of her property to the Husband. Although she cannot personally undertake to assist in maintaining herself, he is clearly at liberty to stipulate that she shall allow him an equivalent for undertaking to maintain her. She may therefore bestow upon him, if she thinks proper to do so, the enjoyment of her property during their joint lives and the reversionary title to it in cape he survives her. And no arrangement which she may make for the purpose of withdrawing any part of it from the effect of such a donation can, unless sanctioned by or known to the Husband before the Marriage, be permitted to exclude his marital claim. But a Wife cannot, without some further consideration than the mere fact of Marriage, bestow upon her intended Husband the power to dispose of her property so as to bind her if she survives him; because your obligation to maintain me while you live is no sort of equivalent for a gift which leaves me destitute after you are dead.

§ 199. So long as the Husband continues to maintain his Wife according to the terms of the Marriage-Contract, the Wife does not necessarily acquire any interest in the Husband's property. His Contract is to maintain her, not out of any particular fund, but merely as he maintains himself. Nor does the operation of this Contract necessarily continue beyond their joint lives. There is no reason, apart from express or tacit stipulation, why a Widow should be held entitled to maintenance out of her deceased Husband's property, any more than a Widower out of his deceased Wife's. The mutual duties of Cohabitation and Support are at an end, and if anything more can be claimed it must depend upon the intention of the parties. And even if a Husband makes a postmortuary settlement upon his Wife, or bestows upon her a separate allowance during Coverture, the provision must be considered as a mere voluntary gift and therefore as revocable at the pleasure of the donor.

§ 200. But a Prenuptial provision by a Husband for his Wife is always, if known to and accepted by her before the Marriage, considered as a transaction for value; although there may be no equivalent for it except the Marriage itself. The Husband may secure to the Wife the enjoyment, after his decease, of the whole or any part of his property by way of Jointure during her life or Widowhood. He may even, if he thinks proper to do so, settle upon her the absolute reversion in case she survives him. He may also bind himself to allow her what English Conveyancers term Pin-money, that is to say an allowance or annuity during their joint lives for the discharge of her exclusively personal expenses. But this he can only do to the extent of his own present or future income subject to the necessary expenses of his household; for a Wife must not, under pretence of stipulating for Pin-money, divest her Husband of the ownership of his property and make herself the manager of his estate and the ruler of his family.

§ 201. The inability of a Wife to bestow an irrevocable Postnuptial gift upon her Husband necessarily implies her inability to make a disadvantageous bargain with him. But there can be no reason why a Husband and Wife should not be permitted to exchange property for their mutual accommodation, provided. that the terms of the arrangement are strictly equitable. If therefore a Wife chooses to give up her fortune to her Husband in consideration of a Jointure of equal value, the transaction ought to be held as binding as any other purchase. An intended Husband and Wife may of course make mutual settlements of their property, but in this case the intended Marriage itself necessarily forms part of the consideration. It is therefore for the parties themselves to determine whether this circumstance will justify any and what inequality in the provisions exchanged, and likewise whether the failure of the provision made by the one party is to authorize a corresponding diminution in that made by the other.

§ 202. Can property be so bestowed upon a married woman by the gift of a third person, as to exempt it from the claim of her Husband under the Marriage-Contract? The English Courts of Equity hold that it may; but this is because they consider the Legal claims of the Husband as inequitable, and are therefore anxious to evade them. But if we are satisfied that the true construction of the Marriage-Contract has been ascertained by the Law, we shall find it very difficult to hold that such an evasion ought to be allowed. The Wife has bestowed upon her Husband a certain interest in her property; and we are now asked to permit her enjoyment in defiance of her own Contract, because a third person has forbidden her to fulfil it. It is true that, when property is bestowed upon an unmarried woman with a declaration that it shall be exempt from the marital claim of any Husband whom she may hereafter marry, a Husband marrying her with notice of the exclusion and without having procured its rescission will be bound; but this is merely because the circumstances of such a Marriage amount to a tacit consent by the Husband that the exclusion shall be valid.

§ 203. We have now gone through the principal consequences which arise from the simple fact of Marriage. It remains to consider how far these consequences can be altered by the eventual Breach of the Marriage-Contract. The essence of that Contract is, as we have seen, the undertaking of the Husband to maintain the Wife. If he fails to do so, she clearly becomes his creditor. She acquires a claim upon his whole property for compensation, and this claim she may enforce by taking any part of it in execution. In such a case, the provision allotted to the Wife is termed by the English Civilians her Alimony. If the Marriage-Contract has conferred upon the Husband any interest in the Wife's property, that interest ought clearly to be subject to her right of maintenance. Neither the Husband nor his creditors, nor even a purchaser from him with notice of the Wife's title, ought to be permitted, so long as her claims are unsatisfied, to retain anything which belongs to her. And finally a Husband who wilfully neglects to maintain his Wife, and who has no property with which she can maintain herself, must be considered as guilty of a criminal offence.

§ 204. The obligation of a Husband to maintain his

Wife cannot of course be considered as unconditional. By such an undertaking two conditions are tacitly implied. The first is Conjugal Cohabitation. No man can bind himself to maintain a woman as his Wife who does not live with him as such. And therefore a married woman who disobediently and causelessly leaves her Husband's house, after communicating to him her intention never to return, forfeits her right of maintenance and cannot recover it unless he consents to receive her again. The consequence will of course be the same if, after leaving her home by her Husband's permission, she deliberately refuses to return at his request. And from this it follows that a married woman will forfeit her conjugal rights by her absence from home, in disobedience to her Husband's express commands, for such a length of time as may be sufficient to raise the presumption that she has formed, and means him to understand that she has formed, the deliberate intention never to return.

§ 205. But circumstances may easily occur under which the Wife will be justified by the Husband's misconduct in refusing to cohabit with him, and in this case she may of course do so without forfeiting her right of maintenance. Cruelty or Adultery is the cause usually alleged for such a separation. It is clear that a woman is not bound to cohabit with a man who inflicts upon her any personal ill-treatment. Nor, whatever may have been the absurd maxims of a semi-barbarous age, is it possible to conceive a case in which ill-treatment, such as would not be justifiable if inflicted by one independent human being upon another, could be justifiably inflicted by a Husband upon his Wife. It is equally clear that a woman, is not bound to cohabit with a man who has been guilty of infidelity to her person. But the Canonists rightly hold that a Wife who, having suffered from her Husband's Cruelty or being aware of his Adultery, deliberately does anything which shows an intention not to withdraw from Cohabitation with him, must be considered as having condoned his offence; in other words that she has waived her right to separate from him, and cannot afterwards assert it without forfeiting her claim for maintenance.

§ 206. The second condition of marital maintenance is Conjugal Fidelity. As a woman is not bound to cohabit with a man who is the husband of other women, so a man is not bound to maintain a woman who is the wife of other men. How far the misconduct of an Adulteress, or of her paramour, ought to he considered as a criminal offence against her Husband, or as a palliation of violence committed by him, is a question scarcely to be discussed without introducing those elements of social and moral prejudice which in modern society make so unreasonable, but still so practically important, a distinction between Marital and Conjugal Infidelity. The Marriage-Contract, it is clear, is in both cases broken. But the injured Husband may elect either to repudiate his Wife and give up her property, or to maintain his marital rights and allow her a sufficient maintenance; because it is unreasonable that the unfaithful Wife should be permitted to acquire, by her own misconduct, the right of exercising any control or of gaining any advantage over her Husband.

§ 207. But the effect produced by the Adultery of a married woman may be in a great measure removed by the previous misconduct of her Husband. Her offence, however disgraceful in itself, ceases to be a crime against him if he has facilitated its commission by intentional connivance or by wilful negligence, or even if he has provoked it by his own infidelity or by such cruelty as would have justified her in refusing to cohabit with him. In these cases he must repudiate her, if he elects to do so, upon such terms as she would have been entitled to claim if she had chosen to separate from him upon justifiable grounds. In other words, he must permit her, at her own choice, either to retain her full right of maintenance or to claim restitution of all her property. The principles thus laid down will perhaps explain the true meaning of a scandalous proceeding said to have been formerly practised in some parts of England; the public sale of a Wife by her Husband. All parties to such an abominable transaction would of course be punishable for a gross breach of public decency; but there can be no doubt that its effect, while unrevoked, would be to deprive the Husband of all right to complain of the Wife's subsequent misconduct.

§ 208. If Marriage is to be regarded as a Status and not merely as a Contract, a Remarriage by a man or woman already married to a living person is clearly a mere nullity. Whatever may be thought of Polygamy in a moral point of view, it is evidently, unless justified by express stipulation or by recognized Usage, a breach of Natural Justice. How, in the absence of such special means of explanation, can a declaration that I will cohabit with you for life be understood to mean only that I will permit you to be one of several persons with whom I intend to cohabit? Or how can you, by agreeing to cohabit with me, be held bound to cohabit with any stranger whom I may choose to admit into the partnership? Nor, supposing the Remarriage of a person already married to be void, can there be any doubt that, if effected without notice of the previous Marriage, it becomes punishable as a criminal fraud on the part of the Bigamist.

§ 209. Supposing the actual Wife of a Bigamist to die before his second or void Marriage is repudiated by the other party, there seems to be no reason why the second Marriage should not, if the deceived person elects to confirm it be considered as valid. The Bigamist is undoubtedly bound in conscience to fulfil his contract if he can do so without prejudice to the rights of his first Wife; and the second Wife, not having been a party to the fraud committed upon the first, may justifiably insist upon his doing so. The Casuists of former times are said to have ruled that a man married to one woman is not morally bound to fulfil a promise of Marriage made in case of her decease to another. Such a decision can only have proceeded, either from a most extravagant conception of the sanctity of Marriage, or from a most deficient sense of common truth and justice. The promise is one which the promissor has a perfect right to make and the promissee to accept; and, so far from being morally void, it would clearly, if supported by a sufficient Consideration, become a Contract for whose breach full compensation ought to be legally recoverable.

§ 210. But will the Repudiation of a Husband or a Wife, upon justifiable grounds, enable either or both of the divorced parties to contract a valid Remarriage with another person? The English Statute Law has decided that it will; and, so far as justice between individuals extends, the decision is clearly right. There can be no doubt that the man who marries a divorced Wife acquires and creates the rights and obligations. of a Husband, or that the woman who marries a divorced Husband acquires and creates those of a Wife; and that whether the second took place with notice of the first Marriage or not. One divorced Spouse retains, no rights which can impede, or which can be infringed by, the consummation of another Marriage by the other. The true objection to such Remarriages, and it is an objection which, whether rational or irrational, is likely to be found a very serious one, is of a nature which cannot be explained until we come to the subject of Conventional Jurisprudence.

§ 211. The Papal Canonists most absurdly attributed, and perhaps still attribute, the effect of an actual Marriage to a Precontract, or mutual Promise of Marriage unaccompanied by actual consummation or Cohabitation. They held that a man might be justified in repudiating the companion of his life and the mother of his children, upon proof that by marrying him she broke a previous engagement. By the English Law this odious crotchet has long been utterly rejected. As between the parties to the Precontract, its breach may no doubt be injurious or even criminal. But there can be no equitable comparison between the rival claims of the Promissee and of the Promissor's innocent Wife or Husband. It would be quite as reasonable to annul a Marriage upon the ground of a previous contract for Service or Partnership, as upon that of a previous Promise of Marriage.

§ 212. A Husband and Wife may of course, if they think proper to do so, cease by mutual consent to cohabit; and in this case the Wife, having been guilty of no disobedience to her Husband, will retain her right of maintenance. She may consequently, by contract with her Husband, commute this right for a fixed allowance during the separation; and such a contract will of course bind the husband's property in the same manner, and to the same extent, as it would if concluded upon any other valuable consideration. But it may be doubted whether a Husband can effectually bind himself to maintain his Wife while separated from him otherwise than by his own permission. And if this be so, a separation between Husband and Wife is only valid so long as both parties continue to desire its validity; and the Wife, by refusing to return to her Husband at his request, would forfeit her separate maintenance.

§ 213. But Marriage, considered as a civil contract, cannot possibly be held otherwise than dissoluble by mutual consent. Such a dissolution is termed a Divorce, and, if freely and deliberately concluded and consummated by mutual separation, is undoubtedly valid as between the parties themselves. There is no principle of Natural Justice upon which it can be maintained that either the Husband or the Wife acquires any inalienable claim by their Marriage. I need not say that such a claim is conferred upon both parties, subject to certain necessary exceptions, by the Law of every Christian country; but it is upon grounds of public policy or of religious belief that such Laws are to be justified. Nor can I at present explain why a fraudulent offence is committed by a divorced Husband or Wife, who marries again without giving notice of the previous Marriage, or even why in such a case the second Marriage is not to be held binding upon the other party. The injury done by such a deception is one which Natural Justice can only recognize through the medium of Moral Usage.

## IV. Filial Status

§ 214. The simple fact, that one human being is the Son or Daughter of two others can scarcely, upon grounds of Natural Justice, be held to create any obligation between them. A full-grown Child, possessing the ordinary faculties of a man or woman, has no claim upon its Parents for maintenance or protection; nor, in the absence of any express or tacit stipulation between the Parents themselves, has it any title by survivorship to their property. Those systems of Law which have disabled Parents from disinheriting their Children appear to have done so from reasons of public policy alone. Neither the Entails and Majorats of the Feudal Law, nor the distributive Successions of ancient London and modern France, were founded on any idea of private equity. In England the Testamentary power has, ever since its first existence, been capable of exercise without any restriction for the benefit of the Testator's Children. The rights acquired by the existence of a Child are therefore confined to his chance of succession as Heir to his Parent in case of intestacy.

§ 215. The different modes of analysis adopted by the theoretical and the historical Jurist are nowhere more directly opposed than upon the subject of Inheritance *ab intestato.* The theorist commences with the principle that whoever acquires property acquires the right to dispose of it as he pleases, and thus arrives at the inference that property of which no disposition is made ought to devolve according to the probable intention of the owner. The antiquary ascertains the fact that no man could in primitive times acquire property except for the benefit of the Family to which he be- longed, and thus perceives at once how inevitable it was that the common stock should remain unaltered by the decease of the individual partner. Both are so far perfectly right, but either may easily become wrong. We must not reason upon principle until we deny facts, nor upon facts until we forget principle. What Law ought to be, and what Law has been, are distinct co-ordinate questions which must never be confounded with each other.

§ 216. I believe that no human community is known to have recognized the institution of exclusive Property, without also recognizing the principle that the Child is the natural Heir of the Parent. This fact entitles us to assume, not indeed that the Parent's property ought necessarily to devolve upon the Child, but certainly that a Parent who dies without expressing a different intention may fairly be presumed to have meant it so to devolve. And from this it follows, not only that the property of a Parent who dies intestate must devolve upon his Children, but that an unmarried Testator, making his Will without express reference to the possibility of his marriage, must be presumed to have only intended the disposition to take effect in case of his continuing single. The principle of Ascending or Collateral Succession stands upon a much less obvious foundation. But still the general prejudices of mankind may be considered to authorize the position, that any Kinsman, however remote, of an unmarried Intestate ought, if recognized by him as such to be considered as his Heir in preference to a casual occupant of his property.

§ 217. The principle of Lineal and Collateral Inheritance is therefore, assuming it to be well founded, one of general Probability and not of Natural Justice. The various rules by which the rights of the different classes of Heirs may be determined as between themselves, stand upon still narrower ground. They depend, or ought to depend, upon the various methods of testamentary disposition which may be found to prevail in different human societies. Whether those methods are in themselves equitable or expedient, is nothing to the purpose. The question is, not what the deceased proprietor ought to have done with his property, but what he would probably have wished to do with it. To prescribe a certain course of devolution, approved by the Legislature and unalterable by the proprietor, may be inconvenient, but is consistent and intelligible. But it would be absurd to permit free Testation, and at the same time to regulate Successions *ab intestato,* without regard to the ordinary usage of Testators.

§ 218. This brings us to one of the most abstruse and difficult questions in Jurisprudence. To what extent does Natural Justice admit the validity of an indefinite Entail?. It is obvious that the relation between Parent and Child enables a Testator intelligibly to point out, as the objects of his bounty, classes of persons not in existence at the date of the Will. This can manifestly be done in a form which, if allowed to stand good, might render the property inalienable for many centuries. An estate may for instance be bestowed upon a certain person and his male lineal Descendants successively for their respective lives, with the proviso that the elder of two or more Co-heirs shall be exclusively entitled. Such dispositions are termed Entails, and were, in almost every European nation now existing, formerly held valid by the Feudal Law. Public policy and commercial convenience have now restrained them to very narrow limits. It remains to inquire whether justice and reason ought not originally to have done the same.

§ 219. A proprietor ought to have the power of Testation because, by losing the anticipation that his property will devolve at his decease according to his wish, he loses, to a certain extent, the benefit of his labour in acquiring it.[27] But do we mean by this, that every proprietor has a right to feel sure that his capricious injunctions concerning his property will be respected until the end of Time? Our meaning, if rational, is surely more confined. We mean that a man may be said to enjoy the fruits of his labour, not only when he consumes it himself, but also when he bestows it upon those whom he knows and loves. We therefore conclude that a man is deprived of the fruits of his labour, if he is not permitted to expect during his life that those whom he knows and loves will enjoy it after his decease. Further

---

[27] See g 42.

than this there is no necessity to go. The enjoyment of a proprietor means his enjoyment in his own person, or in the person of some one actually known to him. He may give away hie property as he pleases, but it must be to a fellow-creature and not to an abstract idea.

§ 220. Now let us see how this principle applies to the question of indefinite Entail. If I leave my property to Brown, I am clearly conferring a benefit upon a human being in whose welfare I may be supposed to take a personal interest. If I leave it to Brown for life, with remainder to his Children or Issue living at the date of my will or born during my life, the case is still the same. But suppose that Brown is childless at the date of my will, and continues so until after my decease. Even in this case I am bestowing a distinct personal benefit upon Brown, by providing after his decease for Children or Issue for whom he might otherwise have thought himself morally bound to provide during his life. But the same rule no longer applies, when I undertake to make an independent provision for a generation of Brown's Descendants who may not come into existence until after his decease. I am now endeavouring to bestow a benefit upon a class of objects for whom I cannot pretend to feel any sympathy, and such a disposition is not a gift but a Law. We thus arrive at the conclusion that Natural Justice confirms the well-known dogma of the English Courts, that property cannot he entailed upon the unborn Issue of a person not in existence at the Testator's decease.

§ 221. The peculiar form of ownership known to English Conveyancers as an Estate-Tail is an exception, though as it at present exists by no means an important exception, to this general rule. It is usual, in what are termed Strict Settlements of landed property, to limit the estate to the Father for life, with remainder to his unborn Sons successively in Tail-Male. The consequence is that, if nothing is done to alter its devolution, it will descend to the eldest Son and his male lineage, and upon their failure to the second and other Sons in the same manner. During the Father's life, the next in succession under the entail cannot dispose of the property so as to bind the other Sons or even his own Descendants. But after the Father's decease, or with his consent and assistance during his life, the next in succession may by a formal Resettlement put an end to the Entail and become absolute owner. The effect of an English Estate-Tail may, in short, be summed up by saying that a Tenant in Tail in Remainder is practically a Tenant for life, and that a Tenant in Tail in Possession is practically an absolute owner without the power of Testation.

§ 222. The validity or invalidity of an Entail of course carries with it the validity or invalidity of any ulterior disposition which the donor may attempt. If I may bestow an independent interest in my property upon a certain generation of Brown's unborn Descendants, it is clear that I may, in the event of their non-existence, bestow the property upon Jones. But if the gift to Brown's Descendants is invalid because too remote, the gift over to Jones is necessarily, unless otherwise confined within proper limits, invalid likewise. Thus if I devise property to Brown for life, with remainder to his Issue born during his life and in default of such Issue to Jones, this is a mere substitution of Jones for Brown's Issue as successor to Brown at his decease, and is therefore valid. But if I devise property to Brown, and upon failure of his Issue at any future time to Jones, this might clearly entitle Jones's great-grandson to claim an independent interest in the property upon the extinction of Brown's lineage a century after his decease. In this case therefore the devise over to Jones is invalid, and Brown succeeds me as absolute owner.

§ 223. A Postnuptial Settlement by a Parent upon his or her Children actually in existence will of course, if unsupported by any special consideration, be merely gratuitous. And a Postnuptial Settlement by a husband or wife upon the future Children of the marriage would be not only gratuitous, but revocable at pleasure by the Settlor until the birth of some Child capable of claiming under it. But if a husband and wife were to join by mutual consent in making a settlement upon their Children of property belonging to both of them, the reciprocal agreement ought to be considered as constituting a valuable consideration on both sides; and the disposition ought not, even before the birth of a Child capable of claiming under it, to be revocable except by mutual consent. And a Postnuptial Settlement by the husband upon the Children, executed in consideration of a benefit conferred upon him by the wife out of her own property, is clearly a purchase by the wife from the husband for the benefit of her Children, and will bind both parties accordingly.

§ 224. A Premiptial settlement upon the Settlor's Children by a particular marriage ought to considered, if the marriage actually takes place upon the faith of its validity, not merely as an irrevocable gift but as a transaction for value received. Either party is entitled to stipulate that the other shall make a postmortuary provision for their Issue, and the consummation of the marriage is a sufficient consideration for the acceptance of the stipulation. Nor can such a settlement be defeated by the joint act of the husband and wife after marriage; because the wife, being then under the potential control of her husband, can no more consent to disinherit her Children for his benefit than to impoverish herself. But during the interval between the execution of the settlement and the consummation of the marriage, there is no reason why a revocation, executed by both parties upon due deliberation and without any suspicion of undue influence, should not effectually defeat the claim of the Children under the settlement.

§ 225. It is sometimes provided by a Prenuptial settlement that the wife's property, in default of Issue of the marriage, shall devolve upon some third person named by her. The fair construction of such a provision is obvious. It is an expedient to supply the absence, or to avoid the coercion, of her testamentary authority. As between herself and her husband it is therefore a transaction for value, but as between herself and her Nominee it is a voluntary gift. During her coverture she can neither defeat, nor enable her husband to defeat, her gratuitous disposition, any more than she can relinquish her own reversionary claim to her property. But if she should become a widow, it is clear that a purchaser from her would acquire a title preferable to that of the Donee under the settlement. And it may even be doubted whether, since the donation was merely intended to provide for the event of her decease living her husband, it ought not to be held revocable at her pleasure when that event becomes impossible.

§ 226. That a Father is morally entitled to exercise for his own benefit any control over his Children, is an opinion which was probably never seriously maintained by any human being. To what an atrocious length the old Roman Law carried the Paternal authority is well known. But it is by no means necessary to suppose that the power of the republican Paterfamilias to sell or to murder his adult Son was derived from any idea, however perverted, of natural equity. It is far more likely that the Patria Potestas was a relic of those pre-historic times in which Families, or tribes professing to consider themselves as Families, lived a vagrant pastoral life in perpetual fear of violence from one another. It is easy to understand that a prerogative, which soon became intolerable when exercised by the chief of a peaceful civic household, may have been indispensably necessary to the captain of a clan of wandering savages.

§ 227. The existence of the Filial relation has hitherto been considered as an isolated fact. But of course it may, and indeed for a certain time after its commencement must be complicated by the personal disability of the Child to provide for itself. In this case it is clear that the Child is morally entitled to require from its Parents such maintenance and personal care as may be necessary to keep it in life and health during the interval of its disability. To prove this it is not necessary to refer to those natural instincts which are common to the whole animal creation. It is sufficient to lay down the general principle that, if I wilfully place a fellow-creature in such a position that he requires my assistance to keep him from perishing, I become bound to give it. As between the Parents themselves, it seems reasonable that the Father should be held responsible for the Child's maintenance and the Mother for her personal aid and protection. But as between the Child and the Parents, each is no doubt com-pellable to do, to the utmost of his or her power, whatever may be found necessary for its support.

§ 228. What authority a Parent is morally justified in exercising, or morally bound to exercise, over his Children for their own benefit, is a question which, as I have already pointed out,[28] does not properly belong to the science of Jurisprudence. But the obligation of a Parent to maintain his immature Children must necessarily be held to confer upon him a reciprocal right of control over them, which he may exercise, not for their benefit, but for his own. If I am bound to do something for you, it follows that you are bound not to prevent me from doing it. Every Parent who maintains his Children Is therefore to a certain extent morally entitled to make them obey him. He may insist, not only that they shall refrain from doing anything which interferes with his profit or comfort, but that they shall assist, so far as they are able, in providing for themselves. Further than this his beneficial authority can scarcely be thought to extend. A Child ought not to be a burthen to his Parents if he can avoid it, but a Parent has no right to derive absolute profit from the labour of his Children.

§ 229. A Child whose Parents die before he is capable of maintaining himself may reasonably be held entitled to maintenance out of their property so long as his disability shall continue. But, except for this purpose, he will of course be unable during his immaturity to dispose, so as to bind himself or his Heirs, of anything which he may have

---

[28] Introd. II.

inherited; and it is evident that the fact of this inability affords a sufficient ground for permitting the further protraction of an Entail upon either Parent. Suppose, for instance, that lands are devised to Brown for life, with remainder, not to his Children absolutely, but to such of his Children as shall attain maturity, and in default of such issue to Jones. It is clear that in this case the gift to Jones is valid. The qualification of maturity merely annexes to the provision for the Children a condition which would have been impliedly annexed by the fact of their immaturity, and the gift to Jones has no effect except to substitute him for the Heir of the surviving Child.

§ 230. The English Law rightly attributes to a living but unborn child the full Status of an existing human being. Wilfully to extinguish the life of such a child is therefore a criminal offence, and that although the extinction takes place with the consent or by the volition of the Mother herself. A Child *in utero* may upon the same principle be the object of a gift or disposition as a person in existence; and a devise to Brown's unborn Child for life, with remainder to his or her Children, will therefore be valid. We are thus enabled to perceive the true grounds upon which the famous English Rule of Perpetuity, apparently so arbitrary, is founded. According to that rule, no disposition of property is valid which can possibly render it inalienable for a period exceeding twenty-one years and nine months after the expiration of some specified life or lives in being at its commencement. This simply means that property may be bestowed upon the unborn Children of any living person, and that the vesting of the gift may be postponed until the periods of gestation and immaturity are complete.

# BOOK II
# CIVIL JURISPRUDENCE

We now proceed to inquire, in what manner the natural Rights and Obligations of mankind are affected by their division into independent States. A State is an Association of human beings for the purpose of mutual defence against Wrong. It is evident that, according to this definition there is more than one subdivision of the present Work which might be made to embrace the subject of Civil Jurisprudence. If the Political association is distinct and express, it becomes a Contract. If it is tacit and indefinite, it becomes a Usage. In either case the parties creating or adopting it would clearly constitute a Corporation, and would alter their natural Status accordingly. Nor can it be doubted that, if a really independent State were to be formed by such means at the present day, it would in process of time be recognized and treated as such by all those which already exist.

But there is no practical value in such speculations as these. The formation of an independent State by the voluntary act of a number of private individuals is a phenomenon which may possibly have taken place, but which History certainly does not record. The earliest traditions of antiquity represent the human race as already divided into Tribes; that is to say into fraternities connected, or professing to be connected, by descent from a common ancestor, but kept together in point of fact by some common purpose or necessity. Every Political community with whose origin we are acquainted appears to have been directly or indirectly founded by some primitive Tribe. Those which at present exist are the result, not merely of long and incessant change, but of many violent conquests and many unjust compromises. But we know nothing of any phase of human society in which they, or that from which they are derived and which they therefore represent, did not exist.

I shall therefore, as I have already said, consider the subject of Civil Jurisprudence as arising, not from the possibility of certain Contracts or Usages, but from the actual existence of a certain class of definite Facts. I do not think it worth while to inquire how far the Rights of mankind would be affected by the transformation into an independent State of a hunting-party in the wilderness or of a boat's crew upon a desert island. Such a transaction would no doubt possess a certain Jural significance of its own. But, in the absence of its recognition by the rest of mankind, the physical weakness of the contracting parties would make one very important difference in its effect. That fact would naturally lead to the conclusion, that the formation of the community was a colourable and not a *bonâ-fide* act; and would therefore justify its treatment, in the event of its, attempt to exercise the authority of an independent State, as a gang of pirates and not as a political association.

The natural order of thought upon the subject of Civil Jurisprudence is as follows. We begin by inquiring what are the Jural relations which exist between one independent State and another. We then proceed to consider what effect the separate existence of each State ought to produce upon the mutual Rights of the Citizens who compose it. Finally, we introduce the additional element of Territorial Sovereignty. Every Political association, or at least every Political association now existing among civilized men, has a twofold purpose. It is the acceptance of a personal obligation as between the parties concerned, and it is the occupation of a National territory as against mankind in general. The subject will therefore be completed by the questions, what peculiar effects the National Occupation of territory ought to produce where it exists, and in what peculiar cases it ought to be considered as existing. And the present Book will thus contain the following four Chapters: I. International Rights and Obligations. II. Municipal Rights and Obligations. III. Territorial Rights and Obligations. IV. Extra-Territorial Rights and Obligations.

It will of course be convenient; whenever it becomes necessary to suppose the co-existence of two or more independent States, to distinguish them from each other by specific names. It is obvious that the symbols selected for this purpose ought to be familiar to every English reader as names of political communities, but that they ought not to be associated with the actual or historical existence of any political community in particular. For these reasons, and not from that childish anxiety to make a jest of serious subjects which all rational beings now regard with such richly-earned dread and aversion, I shall take leave to designate the members of our imaginary political world by the famous titles of Lilliput, Blefuscu and Brobdignag.

## CHAPTER I
## INTERNATIONAL RIGHTS AND OBLIGATIONS

It is obvious that the mere formation or existence of an independent State can only affect the natural Rights of its Citizens as between themselves. It must, before it can be thought to affect their Status as regards the rest of mankind, be followed by some Corporate or National action on the part of the State, capable of imposing a Foreign or International obligation upon its Citizens. The manner in which such action must take place in order to be effectual for this purpose will of course in some measure depend upon. the internal constitution of the State in question. But its external operation must necessarily consist, either in the commission of an International Wrong or Delict for which the Delinquent State is responsible, or in the communication of an International Consent which the Consentient State is bound to fulfil.

What will amount to an International Delict has already been sufficiently discussed, since it is evident that any act which would amount to an Individual Delict, if committed by one private person against another, will amount to an International Delict if committed by the authority of one independent State against any Citizen of another. But the peculiarity of International Delicts consists in the singularly dangerous and destructive character and consequences of the Remedy which, in the present condition of mankind, they must unfortunately be admitted to justify. That remedy is only to be found in the acts of International violence known by the name of Reprisals, and its usual though not invariable consequence is the condition of mutual retaliation and resistance which is properly termed War.

The subject of International Consent naturally commences by the inquiry, how far the rules which apply to a Consensual transaction between individuals are applicable to a similar transaction, between independent States. But when this question is answered another remains. There are certain Consensual transactions which cannot possibly take place between individuals, but which may take place between independent States. A Consensual Obligation can only be said to exist when the parties to it are ascertained or ascertainable. A Contract between an individual and the whole human race is therefore impossible, because the human race is an indefinite body of human beings. But a Contract between all the independent States in the world is possible, because the independent States of the world are a known and recognized body of Corporations. The Consensual act which is termed Legislation, and which can only take place between individuals after they have been separated from the rest of mankind by the formation of an independent State, may therefore take place between independent States which have no antecedent connection with each other; and with this form of International Consent the subject will conclude.

The present Chapter will therefore consist of the four following Sections: I. International Reprisals. II. International War. III. International Consent. IV. International Legislation.

## I. International Reprisals

§ 231. The Status of Hostility has already been incidentally mentioned as one whose justifiable existence between two individuals living in a state of Nature may easily he conceived.[29] But the consequences of such Hostile action as this would be of little practical importance to the rest of mankind. Not only would Intervention and Arbitration be easily accessible, but the contest, if suffered to proceed, would probably be decided by a single battle, dangerous to no one except the combatants themselves. But the case becomes very different when one powerful and resolute Nation conscientiously affirms, and another conscientiously denies, the existence of an intolerable International Wrong. Such Hostilities sometimes outlast an entire generation, and their prosecution perpetually raises questions of Right which more or less affect the interests of the whole human race. The solution of such questions according to the principles of Natural Justice is therefore one of the most interesting and beneficial tasks which can be undertaken by an enlightened Publicist.

§ 232. It is easy to assert, and impossible to disprove, that this theoretical idea of mutually justifiable Hostility is never realized in practice, and that, in every International contest which ever took place, one at least of the Belligerents has been guilty, not merely of unconscientious and inhuman rashness or obstinacy, but of distinct Injustice. Every reasonable Moralist will admit that this is probably the case in all Wars, but few reasonable Historians will undertake to pronounce that it has unquestionably been the case in every particular War. It is easy to imagine a War in which both parties would be morally justifiable, and it is possible to point out some Wars in which neither party can be proved to have been morally culpable. But the truth is, that such casuistical speculations are of no practical value. However

---

[29] See §158.

unscrupulous the conduct of Sovereigns and Statesmen may sometimes be, it is scarcely possible to convict an entire community of conscious and intentional Wrong. And indeed, when we consider the ease with which public opinion can in most communities be misled, it becomes probable that very few cases occur in which such a conviction would be just.

§ 233. The only legitimate object of International Hostility is Satisfaction for International Wrong. Hostilities undertaken for any other purpose are not merely an immoral and inhuman act, but a manifest offence against International Justice. The purpose of inflicting a certain amount of suffering upon the Delinquent State, as a punishment or retaliation for the injury sustained by the Complainant, is an obvious breach of natural Equity; since it cannot possibly be fulfilled without more or less making one human being criminally responsible for the offence of another. Even the purpose of inflicting such an amount of suffering as may be sufficient to extort from the Delinquent some concession which depends upon his own will, though less obviously immoral, is equally unreasonable and therefore equally unjustifiable. It enables him, by the mere exercise of passive obstinacy, to protract War until it becomes a struggle for extermination; in which each party, without being conscious of its own final object, blindly and desperately strives to inflict the greatest possible amount of misery upon its antagonist.

§ 234. It is scarcely necessary to point out that the infliction of a Wrong by one independent State upon another is not sufficient to justify any Citizen of the Injured in exacting, by his own private authority, Reprisals from the Delinquent State. Every human being is of course entitled to stand up for what he thinks right; but in doing so he must be prepared to show, either that he is himself wronged, or that he is acting by the authority of some one who is so.[30] Pri-

---

[30] See § 11.

vate revenge is not to be permitted because its object happens to have injured a third party. Now it is obvious that a Wrong may easily be committed against the State to which I belong, without inflicting any personal injury upon me. And therefore if I take upon myself, without the authority of the State, to inflict Reprisals for such a Wrong, I am gratuitously usurping the rights of the injured party; and by so doing am committing, whatever may be the merits of the dispute, an act of unjustifiable violence.

§ 235. What then are the peculiar Rights incident to Hostilities undertaken by the authority of an injured State for the purpose of procuring Satisfaction? The first object of the Complainant is to prevent if possible the infliction, or to compel if necessary the discontinuance, of the Wrong which constitutes the Casus Belli. His next attempt will be to exercise Reprisals; or in other words to exact full compensation, not only for the injury which he has directly sustained from the Delinquent, but for the expense which he has been compelled to incur in resisting it. For this purpose he may lawfully seize upon and confiscate all property belonging to any Citizen of the Delinquent State upon which he can lay hands, and will for that purpose be justified in employing whatever violence may be found necessary. This doctrine has been denounced as an injustice by many well-meaning philanthropists. They point out, with perfect truth, the cruel hardship of ruining an innocent merchant because his Government has done wrong. But it is strange that they have never perceived that the true injustice in such cases is inflicted, not by the Captor, but by the State to which the spoliated proprietor belongs.

§ 236. The attempt to capture private property by way of Reprisal will necessarily expose the Captor to the risk of Resistance or of Recapture by the spoliated proprietor. The seizure of my property by the authority of a State to which I do not belong and which has no exclusive jurisdiction over the locality in which I am, for the satisfaction of a claim whose justice is not recognized by the State to which I belong, is amply sufficient to justify me, or any person acting on my behalf, in using whatever violence may be necessary to recover possession. Nor, if I make the attempt, can the Captor justifiably inflict any violence upon me, beyond what may be necessary for the retention of his capture. But the Captor may lawfully, until he has secured his Prize, place me under such restraint as may be necessary to prevent me from effecting or procuring a Recapture; and if, to escape such restraint, I undertake to waive my right of Recapture, I shall of course commit a criminal offence by afterwards using violence for the purpose of enforcing it.

§ 237. The right of seizing private property by way of Reprisal leads to a very obvious conclusion; to a conclusion, indeed, so obvious that I have thought it superfluous to point it out in discussing the subject of Natural Jurisprudence. It is surely clear that, if I have acquired a claim upon your property, you cannot defeat it by placing your property in the hands of a third person. And therefore the State of Lilliput, having issued Reprisals against that of Blefuscu, has undoubtedly a good *primâ-facie* right to seize property belonging to a Lilliputian Citizen, although found in the custody of a Brobdignagian carrier or agent. As a general principle of Justice, indeed, this has never been denied. The celebrated dogma, Free bottoms free goods, rests upon an entirely different foundation. That foundation is, as we shall hereafter see, a legal fiction annexed to the doctrine of Territorial Jurisdiction; and a fiction so arbitrary in its character that it was probably invented as a mere pretext for the exemption of a numerous and powerful class of mankind from the calamities of War.

§ 238. The right of capturing hostile property in the hands of a Neutral carrier necessarily implies a further right, or rather remedy, which is termed by Publicists the Right of Visitation. It is held that any Person or Ship, duly commissioned by the Complainant to make Reprisals upon the property of the Delinquent, is entitled to arrest and search for that purpose all Persons or Ships who may be encountered upon the High Seas or within any other extra-National territory. A Neutral trader, being thus seized and carried into a foreign port for adjudication, becomes of course entitled to full compensation from the Captor for the expense and delay caused by his detention. But this will not justify him in making resistance by force of arms. If, having notice of the issue of Reprisals and being aware of the character and intention of his Captor, he uses violence to prevent himself from being captured, he is considered to commit an act of hostility, and to have made himself, though otherwise fully entitled to the character of a Neutral, liable to confiscation as an enemy.

§ 239. It may be conceded that, in the case of a Neutral ship which really has on board property belonging to the Delinquent, this practice is perfectly just. Such a ship, if she fights to resist Visitation, fights to protect the property of the Delinquent from seizure by the Complainant, and thereby becomes an active partisan of the former. But the case of a Neutral ship which has nothing liable to seizure on board is surely very different. Upon what principle can a foreign State be held capable of acquiring, by its own independent act, the right of punishing the owner of such a ship for not choosing to obey commands founded upon a groundless suspicion? or why is not one party, as much as the other, entitled to stand upon his own rights and to act at his own peril? The Cruiser, if he forcibly captures the Neutral under the *bonâ-fide* belief that there are Hostile goods on board, is guilty of no offence although he proves to be wrong. Why then is the Neutral, if he forcibly resists capture upon the plea that there are no Hostile goods on board, to be held, except upon the possible ground of useless and vindictive bloodshed, guilty of an offence although he proves to be right?

§ 240. It is scarcely necessary, or rather it is astonishing that it should ever have been necessary, to point out that the Complainant will not be justified in confiscating any property of which he may take possession by way of Reprisal, except so far as it is *bonâ fide* the beneficial property of the Delinquent. If he captures a Hostile ship, he is bound to make restitution of all Neutral property which may be found on board, subject of course to whatever claim the owner would under the circumstances have retained. And even if he captures Hostile property on board a Neutral ship, he can only retain it upon payment of whatever may be due from the proprietor to the shipowner. The contrary opinion has been supported by the argument, that it is the interest of the Captor to display his naval superiority by proving the inability of his enemy to protect the property in his custody. And this is undoubtedly true. It is also his interest, at least his immediate and apparent interest, to seize and confiscate Neutral property which does *not* happen to he in Hostile custody. But a civilized Publicist would just as soon think of recommending the one expedient as the other.

§ 241. Instances have occurred, and may possibly occur again, in which one State has been permitted by another to exact full Satisfaction by way of Reprisals. A timid and imbecile Government has been known to remain a passive spectator, while foreigners were inflicting upon its subjects the penalty of an aggression which it was itself afraid to retract and unable to maintain. In such a case the duty of the Complainant is clear. He is bound to consider himself as a creditor taking in execution the property of his debtor. He must keep an accurate account, on the one hand of his demand for damages and expenses, and on the other of all property captured by him from the Delinquent. And when the latter account exceeds the former, he must discontinue all further Reprisals and refund the surplus. It then becomes the duty of the Delinquent State, though perhaps a duty which few Delinquent States would under such circumstances be likely to fulfil, to distribute the refunded surplus among its spoliated citizens in proportion to their losses, and to make good the deficiency by general contribution.

§ 242. The issue of Reprisals by the Complainant will of course justify the issue of Counter-Reprisals by the Delinquent. And it is possible to conceive that this sort of predatory Hostility might in some cases be protracted for an indefinite time without any actual collision between the two States. It is possible to imagine two barbarous aristocracies carrying on a hereditary feud by robbing each other's defenceless vassals, without choosing to take the risk and trouble of protecting their own. Such conduct would, as between the predatory chieftain and the spoliated peasant, be as atrocious a breach of faith as could possibly occur. But, as between the one horde of banditti and the other, it would not be an offence against International Justice. It does not lie in the mouth of the aggressor to complain that his enemy, instead of deciding the quarrel sword in hand, lies in wait to inflict retaliation without facing danger. The selfish cowardice of the weak may be a crime against his own dependents, but it would be hard to term it an offence against the rights of the strong.

§ 243. Neither the issue of Reprisals by the Complainant, nor that of Counter-Reprisals by the Delinquent, necessarily infers the existence of what is properly termed War. The spoliation of the defenceless may be a miserable necessity, or it may be a disgraceful crime, but it can scarcely be a dangerous or difficult enterprise. A contest of mere piracy and devastation, however ruinous to the parties concerned, is not likely to endanger the peace of the world. It is only when two powerful communities are resolutely bent, the one upon effecting and the other upon preventing some important national undertaking, that they acquire the peculiar privileges of Belligerents; because it is only in such a case that the rest of mankind become bound in justice, either openly to take part with one of the combatants or scrupulously to maintain the most rigid impartiality between the two. War therefore, properly so called, can only be considered to have commenced when an armed force, acting under the authority of one hostile State, is forcibly resisted, in an attempt to inflict Reprisals or Counter-Reprisals, by an armed force acting under the authority of the other.

## II. International War

§ 244. All civilized Publicists have long ago abandoned the detestable opinion, that War puts an end to all Jural relations between the parties concerned; and that there is no form of annoyance or destruction so wantonly atrocious that, if one Belligerent is allowed by his conscience to employ it, the other has a right to complain of its employment. War is now universally regarded as nothing more than a temporary suspension, as between the Belligerents, of such of their ordinary Rights and Obligations as are inconsistent with the necessity of deciding by force of arms a certain definite controversy. The task of circumscribing the limits of this great evil by precise rules is one in which, for the last two or three centuries, good men and great Publicists have been incessantly engaged. Their labours have not yet been fully successful, for the ferocious habits of the middle ages have left melancholy traces upon the modern usages of War. But the steady and uniform improvement which they have effected presents an encouraging contrast to the failure of the indolent dreamers who believe, or affect to believe, that the evil passions of two exasperated Nations are to be checked by sentimental phrases or by conventional formalities.

§ 245. We will now suppose that War has actually commenced, and that the armed forces of two independent States are, with a definite object in view, physically opposed to each other. It is evident that a State which is, or which *bonâ fide* believes itself to be, unjustly attacked or resisted, may lawfully deprive its opponent of whatever instruments he is using, or intends to use, for the purpose of such attack or resistance. Each Belligerent is therefore at liberty to confiscate all property, whatever may be its nature or locality, of which the enemy is preparing to make use in maintaining the War. Thus naval stores intended to fit out a fleet, or provisions intended to victual an army, may be captured or destroyed for the mere purpose of preventing their hostile employment. And, since it must be presumed that the enemy intends to employ in the War whatever warlike resources he may possess, all property which is exclusively serviceable for military purposes is necessarily liable to be treated as Prize of War.

§ 246. But the civilized Belligerent will reject with abhorrence the barbarous doctrine, that the enemy may lawfully be deprived of all resources which *can possibly* be made available for the maintenance of the War. He will scrupulously refrain, not only from all wanton mischief, but from all acts of destruction which are not obviously required to prevent danger to himself. He will hold it utterly disgraceful to lay waste an agricultural district or to bombard an unfortified town, and still more so to perpetrate any of those diabolical acts of devastation by which a particular locality may sometimes be made permanently unfit for human habitation. It is by the intention of making it the instrument of an unjust resistance, not by the mere possibility of doing so, that a thing becomes Prize of War. And History has recorded that, whenever the principle of vindictive destruction has been substituted for that of necessary security, it has been by Belligerents who, whether despotic kings or democratic mobs have shamefully failed in the firmness required to meet a brave enemy in the field.

§ 247. These principles are very generally admitted by modern Publicists, but to their admission there is one singular and apparently indefensible exception. It is still the universal practice of Belligerent cruisers to destroy merchant-ships which they have captured from the enemy, and which they find it inconvenient to carry into port. This practice can only be defended by arguments which, if logically carried out, would justify the most pitiless atrocities ever committed by a cannibal war-party. That Commerce feeds Resistance, and that by the destruction of Commerce Resistance may possibly be starved, is unquestionably true. But the same may as truly be said of Population. Are we therefore justified in the massacre of all children who may possibly become soldiers, and of all women who may possibly become the mothers of soldiers? Or if the rejection of such horrible wickedness is to be considered as a concession to Humanity and not as a compliance with Natural Justice, what possible reason can be found for destroying Commerce and sparing Agriculture?

§ 248. The same distinction will enable us to determine the question, how far one Belligerent is entitled to exclude the rest of the world from communication with the other. Such a prohibition will be justifiable so far as, and no further than, the communication may be *directly* serviceable in the maintenance of the War. The monstrous doctrine that all Commerce with a Belligerent is an indirect assistance to him and therefore a breach of Neutrality towards his antagonist, if it was ever seriously maintained, has long been abandoned. But the case becomes altogether different when a Neutral trader is intercepted by one Belligerent in the act of conveying military supplies to the other. The Neutral is in this case guilty, not necessarily of a directly hostile act, but certainly of an act which the adverse Belligerent has a right to prevent. He is transferring property to a Belligerent which would in that Belligerent's own possession be lawful prize of War,[31] and this he can only do subject to the right of the other Belligerent to intercept the transfer. If the stores are of such a nature as to be useful for the purpose of War and for no other, they are liable to confiscation. If they are of such a nature as to be useful for the purpose of War and for other purposes likewise, the Intercipient is entitled to purchase them upon fair terms for his own use.

§ 249. From this it is clear that the theoretical Jurist need not trouble himself with any minute examination of the various commodities which are, or which are not. Contraband of War. The question, whether a given article is Contraband or not, will depend wholly upon two plain facts; the Opinion of the Intercipient and the Intention of

---

[31] See § 245.

the Neutral. It is true that the opinion can only be formed, and that the intention must usually be inferred, from the physical character of the article; but it must be remembered that this character is altogether dependent upon the existing state of military science. It is possible that, a century hence, gunpowder may be thought good for nothing but for fireworks, and that cotton or tallow may be the most dangerous contraband substances known. There is therefore no conceivable commodity which is necessarily Contraband or necessarily otherwise. The first question in every such case is, Does the Intercipient consider it as Contraband? If so, he is entitled to pre-emption. The second is, Did the Neutral intend it as Contraband? If so, he is liable to confiscation.

§ 250. The same principle evidently forbids a Neutral traveller or trader to make himself the medium of any communication between a Belligerent State and any person acting on its behalf, which is intended to be directly serviceable in carrying on the War. By doing so he becomes liable, not merely to confiscation as a dealer in Contraband; but to capture and detention as an active enemy. But he cannot be justifiably prevented from carrying despatches or messengers from a Belligerent to his own or any other Neutral State, even though the object of the communication may be to solicit the interference of the Neutral in the War. For not only does the existence of War confer upon the one Belligerent no right whatever to prohibit the pacific intercourse of the other, whatever may be its purpose, with the rest of the world, but the attempt to do so might well be interpreted as arising from the consciousness of an unjust cause.

§ 251. To what extent will the express commands of one independent State justify its Citizens in committing acts of wilful hostility against those of another? So far only as the State which gave the order was itself justified in doing so. A mode of warfare which exposes the State by which it is authorized to be treated as an universal enemy, exposes the commander by whom it is executed to be treated as a pirate. No human authority can exempt from punishment the man who inflicts wanton and useless suffering upon his fellow-creatures. The slaughter of non-combatants, or even the malicious destruction of property, are acts for which a General is as strictly answerable as a private malefactor. And supposing, if we may suppose an extremity of infamy which till lately would have appeared impossible, that a Soldier were to violate a woman by the express permission of his officer, there can be no doubt that both Soldier and officer, if made prisoners by the enemy, might most justly be executed as common felons.

§ 252. But no limit can be fixed to the amount of violence which Soldiers, acting by the authority of adverse Belligerent States, are at liberty to employ against each other. In such a collision it is the duty of the assailant to effect his object, and that of the assailed to prevent it, by every means in his power. For this purpose each party is justified in endeavouring to compel, by any mode of destruction or annoyance which he can find, the retreat or surrender of the other. Whatever will extinguish life, whatever will render life intolerable, may be lawfully used for this purpose. Nor is there any reasonable ground for the horror which philanthropists sometimes affect when they are informed that new and terrible expedients of attack have been invented by military commanders. Whether a fleet is destroyed by bombardment or by fire-ships, whether the garrison of a mountain fortress is blown up by gunpowder or suffocated by charcoal, is altogether immaterial. The end is sanctioned by the sincere belief of the combatant that it is just, and the means are sanctioned by his sincere belief that they are necessary.

§ 253. Still it must never be forgotten that the Soldier who carries on military operations, like the State which directs them, can only justify himself by showing that they were intended to obtain some definite and possible result. The combatant who fights for the mere purpose of vindictively inflicting loss or suffering upon his enemy is justly held to have broken the Laws of War. Thus the Guerilla who prowls round a hostile camp to shoot stragglers or sentries is treated by all civilized Belligerents as a mere assassin. Even the Commander who persists in defending a stronghold which he has no prospect of finally preserving cannot complain if he is refused quarter when it is captured, unless he can prove that the delay caused by his resistance was likely to be of real importance to his party. And there can be no doubt that the practice, too common among French cruisers during the Imperial War, of firing a broadside before surrendering to an irresistible force, might in many cases have been justly punished as an act of wanton murder.

§254. For the same reason, a Belligerent Commander is never justified in attacking his enemy without giving him the option of surrendering. And for this purpose every assailant is bound fairly to disclose his means of offence, if he has reason to believe that by so doing he can induce his enemy to surrender. A fortress which is surprised, or a detachment which is surrounded, ought to be shown their danger and offered quarter before fire is opened. Nor, when a battle is actually commenced, ought either party to inflict any violence upon the other which is not absolutely necessary for the purpose of winning it. No honourable enemy who offers to surrender as a prisoner of war must receive any injury. No honourable enemy who is clearly disabled as a combatant must receive any further injury. Victory, not slaughter, is the object of War, and slaughter is only justifiable so far as it is necessary to Victory.

§ 255. Such non-combatants as happen to be unavoidably present during a hostile engagement must of course accept the risk of their situation. The enemy cannot reasonably be expected to relinquish his attack, or to surrender without resistance, in order to preserve them from danger. But a military commander who compels non-combatants to take refuge in a fortress which he is about to besiege, or who refuses to allow a free passage through his lines to non-combatants who find themselves within a fortress which he has already besieged, in the hope that their presence may exhaust the provisions or shake the resolution of the garrison, acts just as atrociously as if he ordered them to be executed by his Provost-martial. The first of these hateful stratagems was unsuccessfully attempted, amid universal abhorrence, by a French general in Ireland. The second was successfully practised, without exciting any perceptible indignation, by an Austrian general and an English admiral in Italy. But in the estimation of common sense the conduct of each was equally wicked, and that of neither is distinguishable from deliberate murder.

§ 256. But the peculiar rights acquired by a Belligerent State are, as we have seen, merely the privileges which Natural Justice concedes to a community of human beings exposed to imminent peril by the necessity of fofcibly maintaining a *bonâ-fide* claim. And from this it is clear that there are two conditions in whose absence the existence of War ought not to be recognized, that is to say the actual Prosecution and the obvious Necessity of military operations. Two States which are not attacking each other cannot claim Belligerent Rights because they profess to be at War, for in this case the perils of War are not incurred at all Nor can two States claim Belligerent Rights because they are fighting for the mere pleasure of mutual destruction, for in this case the perils of War are only incurred by the wilful folly of the parties. It cannot be expected that mankind will endure the restraints of Neutrality, because two angry combatants are too weak to make War and too proud to make Peace.

§ 257. A Belligerent, having by force of arms exacted full Satisfaction from his opponent, becomes bound in justice, not only to desist from all military operations except such as may be necessary for his own defence, but to signify his readiness to discontinue the War. And a victorious Belligerent who neglects to give notice that he is satisfied ought not to consider himself entitled to claim compensation for any further attack which may be made upon him by the enemy, since it is highly probable that no such attack would have been made if the enemy had been aware that he had himself nothing more to fear. But the mere fact that the claims of a Belligerent are satisfied will not disable him from retaining possession of any fortresses or other military advantages which he may have captured during the War, provided they are necessary or useful for his own defence; because it is of course impossible to foresee whether the enemy will not renew hostilities for the purpose of, in the opinion of the successful party, wrongfully recovering that of which he has been rightfully deprived.

## III. International Consent

§ 258. No human obligation is more sacred, because none is more important to the welfare of mankind, than the observance of International Good Faith. There can be no doubt that one independent State may bind itself to another for any purpose which would be valid between two individuals, or that any undertaking, whether express or implied, which would bind an individual will bind an independent State. One State may therefore contract by Treaty with another to do or not to do a specified act. One State may become the Debtor of another for a fixed value. And one State may release to another a doubtful or disputed claim; from which it follows that a lapse of time, sufficient to raise the presumption that the intention of enforcing an International claim has been abandoned, will be sufficient to extinguish it by Prescription. In every such case the Consensual Obligation assumed by the Contracting State will be as binding as a Natural Right, and its breach will justify any measures by way of Reprisal or War which would have been justified by a corresponding offence against International Justice.

§ 259. Can one State justifiably refuse to be bound by a Treaty with another, upon the plea that it was concluded under circumstances of Duress or intimidation? [32] The negative opinion is usually maintained, and the case has been compared, with more ingenuity than accuracy, to that of a compromise for the avoidance of private litigation. But there exists, or there must be supposed to exist, an obvious connection between the legality of a private claim and the event of a lawsuit to establish it. No such connection is perceptible between the justice of a national cause and the event of a War to maintain it. The Litigant who compromises his claim must therefore be taken to do so because he doubts its legality. But a State may find itself compelled to make a concession which it believes to be gratuitous, because it finds itself physically unable to sustain a War. There is therefore nothing unreasonable in maintaining, that a State will not be bound by a Treaty, if concluded as the only means of avoiding a War which could not be undertaken with reasonable hope of success. Nor perhaps would such a doctrine be so dangerous to the peace of the world as is generally supposed. There would be many advantages in a general understanding, that no strong State can, with any confidence of ultimate benefit, drive a hard bargain with a weak one.

§ 260. But of course it does not follow from this, that a State will be justified in reasserting, whenever it has the opportunity, a claim which it has released because the prospect of enforcing it appeared hopeless. For in such a case the Relessor acts by his own free choice. He is not threatened by any pressing danger if he refuses to accept terms. He is at perfect liberty either to make what he can by abandoning his claim, or to take his chance of being able to enforce it. If he chooses the former alternative he is clearly bound. The choice is mere matter of calculation, and the calculator cannot step over his word because he finds himself mistaken. The utmost which can be conceded in such a case is, that *mere* lapse of time ought not to extinguish by

---

[32] See § 150.

Prescription an International claim which cannot be effectually maintained by force of arms. But if it can be shown that the claimant has, during the interval, knowingly obtained any benefit by his apparent acquiescence, this will be sufficient to extinguish his right.

§ 261. There can be no doubt that the commencement of a War must suspend all pre-existing Treaties between the Belligerent States. Contractual cannot be considered as more sacred than Natural Obligations, and it would be absurd to maintain that I am bound to give you with one hand what I am entitled to take away from you with the other. It may even be doubted whether a Treaty concluded for the express purpose of mitigating any future War between the parties could, if found to confer an unfair advantage upon one Belligerent, be held binding upon the other. For if the ordinary usages of War were really equitable, it would surely be thought an unreasonable stipulation that one State may for the future injure another without entitling the injured party to claim their full benefit. But this reasoning does not apply to a Convention made in contemplation of a particular War between the parties, because there is no difference between an act done as a preparation for a given event and an act done after its actual occurrence.

§ 262. A Treaty between two Belligerent States for any purpose unconnected with the War would be so obviously inconsistent with their relative situation, that it could only be considered either, as an absolute nullity or as an implied abandonment of the War. But no Treaties ought to be held more sacred than those which are intended to terminate or to mitigate the evils of an International conflict. Two Belligerents may therefore put an end to the War at their own discretion by concluding a Treaty of Peace upon any terms which they are mutually willing to adopt. They may agree upon a temporary interruption of the War by a Truce or Armistice for a fixed interval of time. They may, pending the prosecution of the War, mutually abandon any particular Belligerent Rights which they may consider, under the circumstances of the case, likely to cause useless suffering to both parties. Or they may compromise, by a Surrender or Capitulation, any special advantage which one party seems likely to gain by force of arms over the other.

§ 263. A Treaty of Peace, in its simplest possible form, consists in a Proposal, made by one Belligerent and accepted by the other, to discontinue the War. Such a Treaty is evidently a Consent by each party, whether because he is content with what he has got or because he despairs of getting anything more, to abandon all chance of procuring further Satisfaction from the other. Each party has therefore become bound in justice to refrain from the subsequent enforcement of any claim founded upon the facts which constituted the Casus Belli. Each party is also bound to refrain from the subsequent reassertion of his title to anything which has been captured from him during the War. And it is even held that, since the rights of every Citizen must be bound by the Contracts of the State to which he belongs, a proprietor recapturing his captured property will be liable to make restitution if it appears that Peace was concluded during the interval between the capture and the recapture.

§ 264. The conclusion of a Treaty of Peace will of course, as between the Belligerent States, make all subsequent hostilities wrongful from that moment. Each State is therefore bound to make compensation for all damage afterwards inflicted and restitution of all property afterwards captured, and likewise to inflict due criminal punishment upon the assailant or captor if he can be shown to have acted with notice of the Peace. But, as between each Belligerent and the servants of the other, subsequent hostilities without notice of the Peace must be considered as justifiable; because the commands of the employer cannot make the agent liable for disobedience until he has actually received them. In cases where War has been carried on in remote parts of the Earth, it is usual to fix a certain interval of time within which all captures are to be held valid; but it has been justly and honourably decided that such a stipulation must be construed as only applicable to captures made without notice of the Peace.

§ 265. The question, how far the restoration of Peace will revive such pre-existing Treaties between the parties as have been suspended by the War, is one which has been much disputed but which seems capable of a very obvious solution. A simple offer and acceptance of Peace is, as we have seen, an acknowledgment by each Belligerent that he is satisfied with what he has got by the War. In other words, it is a transaction by which each party consents to leave in the hands of the other whatever actual profits the War has placed there. It is easy to see that by such an agreement those pre-existing Contractual Rights are revived, and those alone, which continue clothed, at the time of the Peace, with actual enjoyment. Suppose, for instance, that the Lilliputian State has bound itself by Treaty to pay a fixed tribute to the Blefuscudian State, or to allow certain privileges to Blefuscudian citizens resident at Lilliput. It is clear that such an obligation will be finally extinguished by a War between the parties, unless its renewal is expressly stipulated by the Treaty of Peace. If Peace does not entitle you to reclaim what I have taken from you, much less can it bind me to make compensation for what you have failed to exact from me.

§ 266. The existence of a War between two independent States cannot of course invalidate the conclusion of a Treaty between either of the Belligerents and a Neutral. But such a Treaty will no doubt, if it should be found to interfere with the Belligerent Rights of the hostile State, constitute a Casus Belli between that State and the Neutral. If therefore a Belligerent knows, or has reason to believe, that a secret treaty or understanding exists between his antagonist and any Neutral State, by which the Neutral is bound to interfere directly or indirectly in the War, he is clearly entitled to take precautions for his own security against the Neutral as against a declared enemy. It was upon such information that the English Government seized the Danish fleet in 1807. That information is now known to have been correct; and we are therefore acknowledged, except by our most implacable foreign enemies and by those cosmopolitan philanthropists whom we always find more implacable than any foreign enemy, to have met that perilous emergency like wise and brave men. But had we been mistaken we should not have deserved the reproaches which were heaped upon us, because the indisputable facts of the case were sufficient to justify the belief upon which we acted.

§ 267. But of course it does not follow from this, that the Intervention of one independent State in a War between two others is necessarily, or even presumably, a breach of International Justice. The adverse Belligerent, thinking himself right and his opponent wrong, is entitled to treat the Intervenient State as an enemy; but the Intervenient State has clearly a right to be of the contrary opinion. A nation, like an individual, is justified in interfering whenever wrong is being done, provided the prevention of the wrong is the true and sole motive of the interference. A declaration of War in aid of a weak State against a strong one, or an armed mediation by a strong State between two weak ones, is therefore justifiable or unjustifiable according to the honest or selfish purpose of the Ally or Mediator. It must therefore, in ordinary cases, be taken as justifiable. The Intervention of Sardinia in the Crimea was applauded by all who thought Russia in the wrong; and even the Intervention of France in Italy, precipitate and suspicious as it was, could only be conscientiously opposed by those who thought Austria in the right.

§ 268. It is manifest, whatever may have been the subtle absurdities of medieval diplomacy upon the subject, that a Treaty made between two States in contemplation of War with a third cannot be distinguished from a Treaty made after the commencement of such a War. Not only can no conceivable Treaty entitle a Neutral to depart from strict Neutrality without incurring the responsibilities of a Belligerent, but the existence of a Treaty which purports to do so will be in itself a clear Casus Belli as between the adverse Belligerent and the Neutral. Nor is this all. Such a Treaty, if made in contemplation of a particular War, may be considered as merely a legitimate Alliance; but, if made in contemplation of *any* future War, it will be a manifest breach of International Justice. An Offensive or Defensive, or even a general Defensive, League between two independent States is nothing less than a mutual undertaking that they will stand by each other, right or wrong, in every controversy against the rest of mankind. Such an undertaking amounts to a declaration that the contracting parties no longer intend to be bound by the ordinary rules of Justice; and there can be no doubt that a declared enemy of the human race may lawfully be disarmed by any State, or by any combination of States, which has the physical power to do so.

§ 269. One independent State may, upon the same principle, bind itself by any Contract with a private Citizen of another which would be valid if concluded between two individuals. And in such a case the State to which the Contractee belongs will be justified in compelling the fulfilment of the Contract, or in issuing Reprisals for his benefit if it is broken. But it does not follow that the Contractee has any moral right to insist upon such an interposition. His situation is altogether different from that of a Citizen belonging to one State, whose natural Rights have been infringed by the act of another. The man who traverses the High Seas, or even the man who resides within the territory of a foreign State, may be doing so under the pressure of necessity. But the man who makes a bargain with a foreign Government is voluntarily placing confidence in its good faith, and cannot complain if he is allowed to suffer for his mistake. The English traveller in Spain is entitled to the protection of England against the oppression of Spanish Corregidors and Alguazils. But the English erectors of Spain have been not unjustifiably left to take the consequences of that peculiar course of dealing which is styled by Spanish Publicists the well-known loyalty of their nation.

§ 270. The existence of a War need not prevent one of the Belligerents from binding himself by special Contract to a private Citizen of the other. Thus captured property is often redeemed by the Proprietor under a Contract of Ransom with the Captor, and foreigners are sometimes permitted to travel or reside under a Safe-conduct within the territory of a State which is at War with their own. But there can be no doubt that the commencement of a War suspends all pre-existing Contracts between either of the Belligerents and any citizen of the other. It would be ridiculous to hold that circumstances, which justify me in seizing your property wherever I can find it, do not justify me in retaining it when it is actually in my hands. An exception, it is true, is universally allowed by modern International Usage in favour of debts due upon loan from one Belligerent to the Citizens of the other. But this exception is clearly due, not to any immutable principle of Natural Justice, but to the, obvious impolicy of a mode of Reprisal which would depreciate the national Securities by making them unsaleable abroad.

§ 271. Every person who is authorized to use his own discretion in carrying on military operations on behalf of an independent State for a certain purpose, is necessarily authorized to bind that State by any Treaty or Convention which he may conclude for the same purpose. The General who is instructed to drive the enemy out of a certain province may allow it to be evacuated upon any terms which he thinks proper to offer. The officer who is detached to capture a fort may bind his commander by accepting terms of capitulation. Even the soldier who charges the enemy by the order and under the eye of his superior is at liberty to offer quarter and to make prisoners. From the same principle it follows that every unsuccessful commander has authority to make terms with the enemy or even to surrender at discretion; and that, if he does so without treachery or collusion, his employers will be bound to observe the Contract, however disadvantageous it may be, so far as it relates to any forces of which he was empowered to dispose for hostile purposes.

§ 272. This brings us to consider the Status of a Prisoner of War. Such a Prisoner is simply a hostile combatant who has consented to desist from further hostility upon condition that he shall suffer no further personal violence. There is no other understanding on either side. The Captor is justified in keeping the Prisoner in custody, and the Prisoner in escaping from the Captor's custody and resuming hostilities. But while the custody continues both are bound. If the Captor inflicts unnecessary suffering upon his Prisoner, or if the Prisoner uses violence in attempting to escape from his Captor, an offence is committed against International Justice. And so long as the Prisoner is detained against his will, the Captor is clearly bound to allow him the necessaries of life without requiring from him any labour in return. But a Prisoner who is discharged from custody upon his promise to remain within the Captor's territory, or who is set at liberty upon his promise not to recommence hostilities, may of course be justifiably treated as a criminal if he is again taken in arms during the War.

§ 273. A Prisoner of War cannot be justifiably detained in custody, except by express stipulation between the parties, after the conclusion of Peace. In one memorable instance such a stipulation was made and accepted. The elected Sovereign of a great Empire had become a Prisoner of War, and it was found that his selfish ambition and his wonderful genius had become as formidable to his subjects as to his enemies. It was most righteously decided that, if both nations expressly agreed to exclude this man from the benefit of the Peace, he would have no right to insist upon his liberation by virtue of its conclusion. He was banished to a remote island, where, if the sincere intention of his Captors was faithfully fulfilled, he passed the rest of his life in courteous and liberal captivity. By that just and resolute act an example has been set to the world, which the world may yet find occasion to remember, of the manner in which the incorrigible scourges of humanity ought to be treated. It is a precedent of which, whatever courtiers may pretend to think, England has never repented and will never repent.

§ 274. A wilful breach of the Laws of War by one Belligerent may fairly be considered to discharge the other from whatever Conventions may have previously existed between them. If for instance the Lilliputian General puts to death a Blefuscudian Prisoner, the Blefuscudian General may, if he thinks it necessary and if his conscience will permit him, retaliate by putting to death any Lilliputian Prisoner captured before the act of the enemy was known. And it may even be doubted whether a prisoner who surrenders upon the express condition that he shall not be liable to such retaliation can claim as a Right to be exempted from it, since a contract not to punish a future Wrong is clearly invalid. But of course no right of Retaliation actually in existence can justify the breach of a subsequent obligation voluntarily assumed. Thus it was wrong in William III. to detain M. de Boufflers contrary to the capitulation of Namur, upon the plea that Louis XIV. had previously detained a Dutch garrison contrary to that of Dixmude. Faith once pledged may be released by subsequent treachery on the part of the Promissee, but cannot be justifiably broken upon the pretext of misconduct already known to the Promissor.

§ 275. The principles which are applicable to Treaties between a Belligerent and a Neutral State, are likewise applicable to Contracts between a Belligerent State and a, Neutral individual. Suppose, for instance, that Lilliput and Blefuscu are at War. It is clear that a Brobdignagian Citizen does not cease to be a Neutral by contracting to drain a fen or to build a cathedral for the Blefuscudian Government. But a Brobdignagian trader who undertakes to carry troops or despatches or to procure intelligence for the Blefuscudian Government must, pending the undertaking, be considered as a Blefuscudian Citizen; and will therefore be liable to have his ship and cargo seized and confiscated, if not to be detained as a Prisoner of War. So a Brobdignagian officer who enters the military service of the Blefuscudian State may lawfully be treated by the Lilliputian State, not of course as a pirate or an assassin, but as a public enemy. And a Brobdignagian Citizen who, while bound by an undertaking to assist the Blefuscudian State in the War, holds intercourse with the Lilliputian forces in the character of a Neutral, clearly exposes himself to criminal punishment as a Spy.

## IV. International Legislation

§ 276. The questions of International Justice noticed in the present Chapter have naturally been the subject of frequent and eager discussion among the independent communities into which mankind are now divided. Upon some of them there have been differences of opinion which are not yet reconciled, but upon the greater number the practice of all civilized States has now become uniform. It has therefore been found possible to draw up a considerable body of rules which, whatever may be their theoretical defects, no doubt practically represent the results of universal International Usage. And these rules the most powerful States now existing have taken various public opportunities of declaring their intention to maintain, if necessary, by armed Intervention. A declaration so made and so sanctioned certainly comes within my definition of a Legislative act; and the rules thus ascertained and adopted may therefore, as distinguished from those of abstract International Justice, be in my opinion accurately designated as Positive International Law.

§ 277. The late Mr. Austin, with his usual precision of thought but also with what I cannot help thinking his usual superfluous nicety of definition, has disputed the strict propriety of this phrase. He will not allow that the rules deduced from International Usage can properly be termed Positive Law, because they are not prescribed by a political Superior to a political Inferior. He does not even admit them into that class of Positive Moral Rules which he considers as Laws properly so called, because he denies that they are prescribed by any determinate rational being or body of rational beings. He maintains that their observance is enforced, not by the expectation of compulsion or of punishment from any ascertainable person, but merely by the fear of some indefinite evil which may possibly be the consequence of the general illwill likely to be excited by their transgression. He therefore classes them among those Positive Moral Rules which are only prescribed by general opinion, and pronounces that, like the Laws of Honour or of Fashion, they can only be designated as such by an analogical extension of the term.

§ 278. I venture to think that Mr. Austin's definition of Positive Law is one of those laborious refinements which might, if they were less admirably ingenious in themselves, be almost said to incumber the writings of that accomplished Jurist; and which seem to proceed from an unnecessary anxiety to make the scientific coincide with the popular meaning of the terms which he uses. It is unquestionably true that, according to my definition, the Irish peasant who defies the chivalry of Donnybrook to tread upon his coat-tail is prescribing a Law, and that the despot who compels half Asia to worship his statue is doing no more. It is also true that in common conversation it would be perfectly natural to speak of the Assyrian, and exceedingly absurd to speak of the Irishman, as a Legislator. But it does not follow, because an expression would be popularly unintelligible, that it must be scientifically incorrect. It would be equally absurd to say, without explanation, that Captain Munro was torn to pieces by a Cat, or that Mungo Park was near being devoured by a Lizard. But we are not therefore bound to insist upon defining Cats so as to exclude Tigers, or Lizards so as to exclude Crocodiles.

§ 279. The distinction between those Positive Moral Rules which are Laws properly so called and those which are only prescribed by public opinion, is in my opinion due to an inaccurate, or rather perhaps to an over-accurate, appreciation of existing facts. I do not even admit that the Laws of Honour or of Fashion are, strictly speaking, Laws improperly so called. For, although the entire class by whose opinion those Laws are enforced is no doubt an indefinite body, yet each individual who is expected to observe them is primarily responsible for their breach to his own acquaintance; or in other words to a certain number of known persons, who have expressly or tacitly declared that they will in that event inflict a certain penalty upon him. But, be this as it may, Mr. Austin's definition of Positive Moral Rules which are Laws properly so called will certainly not exclude International Law. For that Law is sanctioned by the express declaration of all the civilized States in the world that they intend to maintain it by force; and the civilized States of the world are an ascertained number of corporate bodies, each consisting of an ascertainable number of individual Citizens. That the execution of this intention has often been prevented by selfish policy is too true, but it is surely impossible to hold that the definition of Law must depend upon the efficiency of the Police.

§ 280. The only division of Law which I can admit to be of the slightest importance as regards our present subject of inquiry, is the distinction between Law de Facto and Law de Jure. Law de Facto has already been defined as any rule prescribed, with the intention of compelling its observance, by one human being to another.[33] But Law de Jure only exists when the person who prescribes the rule does so by virtue of an authority previously recognized by the person to whom it is prescribed. And it is only when this authority is irrevocable and unlimited, that the Legislator is said to possess Sovereign Authority over the persons for

[33] Introd. III.

whom he legislates. There is, as we have already seen, only one relation whose existence can be allowed by Natural Justice to bestow upon one human being such authority as this over another. This relation is that which exists between an independent State and the individuals by whom it is constituted. And therefore the word Law, in its highest and at the same time its most familiar sense, is confined to Law prescribed by an independent State to its own Citizens.

§ 281. From this it is clear that the rules deducible from International Usage, though in the strictest sense Laws, are not Laws de Jure. For not only have two independent States no more natural authority than two individuals to make Laws for a third, but it cannot be reasonably held that one independent State, by occupying territory contiguous to that of two or more others, has entered into any implied undertaking to respect their International Usages. The authority of Positive International Law, considered as distinct from abstract International Justice, is thus derived, not from the previous subjection of the Law-receiver to the Lawgiver, but from the subsequent acquiescence of the Law-receiver in the Law itself. And therefore an independent State may justifiably refuse to comply with a rule of International Law which it considers unjust and in which it has not acquiesced. The action of the parties who prescribe International Law is unquestionably Legislative, but the obligation of the parties who are bound by it is merely Consensual.

§ 282. The practical consequences of this distinction will be found very important. There is a great difference between the reasonable interpretation of a Law which derives its authority from the previous Sovereignty of the Lawgiver, and that of a Law which derives its authority from the subsequent assent of the Law-receiver. A Legislator de Jure is at liberty either to enact special rules or to enunciate general propositions. If he chooses to declare that every black man is to be considered as an irrational animal, or that every foreign ship is to be considered as a wandering fragment of foreign territory, all who recognize his supremacy will be bound by his decision. But a rule which is deduced from practical usage cannot be otherwise than special. Acts cannot establish principles. The man who takes advantage of a particular practice is bound to submit to it in his turn, but he is not bound to accept its logical consequences. He is perfectly free to say: I stand upon my natural rights so far as I have not actually abandoned them. My acquiescence in a given Usage only proves that I did not think proper to resist it, and you have no right to argue that, by consenting to admit one bad custom, I have bound myself to admit another.

§ 283. It is curious to observe how dexterously this transparent fallacy was employed, in the negociations which preceded the Treaty of Washington in 1842, by the able Jurist and most dishonourable man who effected that memorable fraud on behalf of the United-States. It will be found that the American Minister invariably commences his arguments upon Maritime International Jurisdiction, by assuming the general principle that every Ship carries about within her the exclusive jurisdiction of the State to which she belongs. From that assumption he deduces, with undeniable point and force of reasoning, the conclusions, that English deserters are secure on board American merchantmen on the High Seas, and that Negro slaves must continue in bondage on board American merchantmen in English harbours. The answer to this plausible sophistry, although it did not occur to the respectable nobleman in whose hands the interests of England were then unfortunately placed, is of course perfectly obvious. We deny, it might have been fairly said, that Natural Justice has conferred any peculiar privileges upon the hold of a floating vessel; and we therefore deny that any such privilege ought to be recognized, except in the special cases in which it has been practically established by International Consent.

§ 284. But, although an independent State cannot be blamed for asserting its natural rights in defiance of a rule of International Law in which it has not acquiesced, its Contractual rights stand upon a different footing. A State, like an individual, is bound, in making or accepting a Proposal, to take into consideration the meaning which it knows that the other party is attaching to the transaction, and to exclude that meaning if it is not intended to take effect.[34] All International Contracts must therefore, in the absence of any express stipulation to the contrary, be interpreted according to International Usage. It is, for instance, universally understood that money lent to one State by a private Citizen of another is not to be confiscated by the Debtor in case of a War between the two. I have already given my opinion that this rule is rather one of policy than of justice.[35] But, be this as it may, it is clear that any State which repudiates it after raising money upon the faith of its existence will be guilty of an infamous fraud. And such is the opinion of all mankind, buccaneers and French Anglomaniacs excepted, upon the stoppage by Prussia in 1752 of the interest due to English subjects upon the Silesian Loan.

§ 285. The distinction between Law de Jure and Conventional Law leads moreover to the conclusion, not only that an independent State cannot be blamed for not acquiescing in a rule of International Law which it thinks unjust, but that an independent State may lawfully revoke its acquiescence in such a rule. This of course can only be done under circumstances which exclude all suspicion of fraud or surprise. No human being can be allowed, first to accept the benefit of a conventional rule, and then to find out that his conscience will not allow him to let others do the same. The mere renunciation, however public or deliberate, of an unjust or immoral International practice is not sufficient. That may merely mean that the renouncing party has got all the good out of it which he expects, and therefore thinks it need no longer be permitted. Renunciation for the future

---

[34] See § 53.
[35] See § 270.

must be accompanied by reparation for the past. Whatever special advantages the renouncing State may have acquired by acquiescing in the renounced Usage must be restored, or reasonable compensation made for their retention. The position of that State will then become the same as if its acquiescence had never taken place.

§ 286. We will select as an example the African Slave Trade. Great pains were taken by many distinguished foreign Publicists to show that International Usage did not authorize England to punish that atrocious practice as piracy. And in this they were undoubtedly correct. The only wonder is, that they should have thought any such authority necessary. Natural Justice entitles me to interfere when I see one man handcuff another and stow him under hatches, nor can any Usage in which I have not acquiesced deprive me of this right. But was not England, in the present case, deprived of her own rights by her own act? For a long time this was unquestionably so. That one State, after stocking her own colonies with slave labour, should prohibit another from doing the same, was of course not to be borne. But our position became very different when we had emancipated, at the public expense, every Slave in the possession of an English colonist. It then became our right, there are moralists who would say that it then became our duty, to declare that we had washed our hands of Slavery, and that we would thenceforward acknowledge no difference between a Spaniard caught kidnapping Guinea Negroes and an Algerine caught kidnapping Neapolitan fishermen.

§ 287. It still remains to inquire, by what acts an independent State can be said to have acquiesced in a given rule of International Law. The question is one which might well have been thought too easy to require an answer, and the necessity of its discussion is due entirely to the exceptional quality of the nonsense which philanthropists have recently talked about the Laws of War. The principle for which they now contend, or rather the principle which underlies the assumptions which they now habitually make, is that the non-assertion, for whatever reason, of a contested claim amounts to an admission of its injustice. They invariably take for granted that a Belligerent, having abstained from a particular mode of hostility in one case, is guilty of wilful oppression if he attempts it in another. It never seems to strike them that the oppression, may possibly be all the other way, and that the inconsistent Belligerent may stand in the position, not of a man who claims more than his just rights from the weak, but of a man who dares not vindicate his just rights against the strong.

§ 288. The true principle of Acquiescence is perfectly obvious. No man can be allowed to resist a rule, however absurd or unjust, so long as he enforces it against others. If therefore a Belligerent insists upon confiscating Neutral ships for trading with his antagonist, he is bound in justice not, when he himself becomes a Neutral, to resist the confiscation of his own shipping upon the same ground. But it by no means follows that, if the Neutral does not resist the confiscation of his shipping by one Belligerent, he is bound in justice to permit it by the other. The man who maintains wrong must submit to wrong, but the man who submits to a first Wrong need not therefore submit to a second. The only reasonable inference from his submission is, that he intends to waive his claim to redress for the individual Wrong which he has actually suffered. But this inference does not apply to a succession of Wrongs. There is no presumption or probability whatever that a State which endures an insult from Brobdignag intends to endure one from Lilliput.

§ 289. There can scarcely be a more striking instance of this fallacy than the recent discussions upon Belligerent Rights of Capture. It is well known that Belligerents by land find it necessary for their own safety to use great caution in issuing Reprisals or levying Contributions within such hostile districts as they may occupy, while Belligerents by sea perceive no danger, and therefore feel no scruple, in seizing hostile ships wherever they can be found. And upon these facts it is argued, first that the Laws of War prohibit the capture of private property upon land, and secondly that they ought upon the same principle to prohibit it at sea. It is scarcely worth while to remark the practical absurdity of a rule which would make it literally impossible to extort Satisfaction from a State having no public revenue, and which might therefore leave a nation of pirates at perfect liberty to rob and murder mankind with impunity. The silliness of the conclusion, remarkable as it is, vanishes when compared with that of the reasoning. It may be doubted whether any conceivable intellectual contortion would be too grotesque for Moralists who seriously maintain that a dog which dares not seize a hedgehog must not seize a rabbit.

§ 290. The existence of a recognized Code of International Law has encouraged some sanguine philanthropists to hope that, by the further establishment of a Code of International Procedure, the decision of a controversy between two independent States will shortly become as simple a matter as that of a private lawsuit. The realization of this noble project, though not impossible, is probably far more remote than its advocates believe; because what is required to realize it is, not the Consent, but the moral improvement of mankind. It is only when the intervention of every civilized State in support of International Law can be confidently relied upon, that any conceivable system of International Arbitration will possess the slightest practical authority. We are still very far from such a state of things, but it may be hoped that we are tending towards it. Its attainment is not one of those Utopian visions which ignore the selfishness of human nature. It only requires the world to become resolute, rational and provident in its selfishness; and of such a change, miraculous as it now seems, the philosopher need not despair.

§ 291. These things may or may not be probable. But one thing is certain. Constituted as the civilized world now is, there are no accessible means of International Arbitration to which any independent State is morally bound to submit. The effect of such a submission would simply be this, that if I lose the award I am bound in conscience to give up my claim, and that if I win it I am no better off than before. The private Litigant gets his *quid pro quo.* He knows that if he fails he will lose what he thinks he ought to get or to keep but he also knows that if he succeeds he is sure of getting or keeping it without any further trouble. He therefore gladly accepts the chance of an unfavourable judgment, because by doing so he escapes the chance of an unsuccessful fight. But, in the present state of international morality, a litigant Government would obtain no such equivalent. It could not possibly rely, in case of a favourable award, upon such a general Crusade to enforce it as would make all resistance by its adversary hopeless. How then can it be expected to allow the extinction of its rights by the authority of a tribunal which has no power to establish them?

§ 292. It is possible to go much further than this. It is possible to maintain, not only that there are at present no means of International Arbitration which an independent State is morally bound to accept, but that there are none which an independent State would be morally justified in accepting. For there is another advantage upon which every Litigant is bound in conscience to insist, and which no private Litigant ever fails to obtain. Every private Litigant, in surrendering his judgment, throws off his responsibility. The same irresistible authority which secures him from disappointment if he wins, delivers him from casuistical scruples if he loses. The ejected landlord cannot trouble his conscience about his tenantry, nor the bankrupt merchant about his family. He has lost his property, and there is an end of the matter. But surely his feelings would be very different if the question were, whether he ought to give up his property, against his own opinion, in obedience to that of a person who has no power to make him do so. And such might be the situation of an independent State, if required to cede a province in compliance with an International

Award.

§ 293. I shall hereafter mention the peculiar Status of the English Government in India, as one which could not at present be conscientiously resigned. How differently it is regarded by our continental neighbours we all know. Now, upon the principle of International Arbitration, it would long ago have been necessary to submit the entire question of our Indian Empire to a jury of foreign Publicists; and such a reference was in fact, during the Mutiny of 1857, actually recommended by one or two of the very feeblest of our pacific sentimentalists. Upon the absurdity of expecting such a tribunal to be otherwise than consciously and intentionally partial, it is needless to dwell. But, putting this out of the question, imagine the necessity of deserting seventeen thousand myriads of human beings, whom we have wronged and who look to us for redress, unless we can convince a knot of envious bigots that their prejudices against perfidious Albion are unfounded. There is something shocking in the profound ignorance of right and wrong which is implied by the opinion, that one human being can get rid of his natural responsibility by voluntarily obeying another no wiser than himself.

## CHAPTER II
## MUNICIPAL RIGHTS AND OBLIGATIONS

I have already pointed out that by the term Independent State I mean, not generally any community of human beings associating for the purpose of mutual protection from Wrong, but individually some one of those existing communities which are actually recognized by mankind under that title. Now there is one phenomenon which all these communities, however widely their habits and institutions differ, will be found in some shape or other to present. They are all composed of persons living together upon the mutual understanding that each of them shall observe certain rules established, whether by custom or by enactment, for the convenience of the rest. Every person who belongs to such a community, or who behaves so as to make the members of such a community believe that he intends to belong to it, is therefore bound by its rules whatever they may be. In other words, every Citizen of a State has, tacitly if not expressly, made himself party to a Contract upon certain terms with his fellow-Citizens.

I trust that this conclusion will not be attributed to any intention of reviving the forgotten controversy upon the *Original* Social Contract. In no point of view is that theory worthy of a moment's attention from any man of sense. By what means the first artificial societies of human beings were formed, would no doubt, if there were the slightest chance of answering it, be a most curious and interesting question. They may have been created by mere accident and consolidated by mere habit. They may have been solemnly inaugurated, with the mystic oaths and bloody rites of some forgotten idolatry, by congresses of patriarchal chieftains upon the plains of Upper Asia. They may have been nothing but the natural development of the practice of Adoption; the clan imperceptibly becoming a community, and the bond of consanguinity being preserved in fiction long after it had ceased to exist in fact. But it is a question whose solution would not exercise the slightest influence upon the Status of any existing human being. No conceivable transaction, at a meeting of Caucasian flockmasters fifty centuries ago, can possibly be thought to affect the duty of a modern Englishman to his Queen and country.

The Social Obligation of which I speak is one of a very different kind. It is founded simply upon the undeniable fact of mutual confidence and the undeniable duty of mutual good faith. The obligation of a citizen to pay his taxes, the obligation of a clansman to stand by his comrade, does not arise from a covenant under hand and seal. It arises from his knowledge that he has been hitherto permitted to live in his town or in his tribe, upon the understanding that he will, whenever it may become necessary, perform the duty of a ratepayer or of a warrior. Whatever may have been the visible circumstances under which Political Societies first came into existence, their essence is, and always must have been, the mutual reliance of the individuals who compose them. In the fact of that mutual reliance consists the true Social Contract; a Contract not solemnized once for all in the twilight of fabulous antiquity, but implied by the daily life of every Citizen of every State in the world. Those who have taught themselves to believe that parchments and formulas are the substance of human transactions may think such an obligation vague and shadowy enough. But to those who know that the force of a Contract depends upon the mutual faith and the mutual benefit, its sanctity will appear such as could receive little addition from any conceivable quantity of manuscript or solemnity of imprecation.

It is evident that an Association for mutual defence against Wrong must, like every other human association, be intended to effect two consequences; first the immediate purpose for which it exists, and secondly the continuance of its own existence. In other words, the two great ends of Social Life are Private Justice and Public Policy. What Private Justice is we have already examined. We are now to inquire, first how far its general rules ought to be modified by the peculiar relation existing between Citizens of the same State, and secondly in what cases and to what extent its sacrifice to Public Policy may justifiably be imposed by the State upon the Citizen. And the subject will be concluded by considering in what portion of the Citizens, whether upon general principles or by virtue of special Institutions, the Authority of the State must in case of Civil Dissension be held to reside.

The best modern authorities upon Jurisprudence have however pronounced, to my utter perplexity, that the distinction between Private and Public Law is altogether unintelligible, and that the terms themselves ought to be banished from the science. The reason given for this exclusion is the arbitrary uncertainty of thought with which the division has been worked out by the Civilians, and the consequent impossibility of attaching to it any determinate meaning. That consequence I am prepared to deny. I think that the term Public Law admits of a perfectly clear and very useful definition. It may be taken to signify that branch of Civil Legislation which determines the relative Rights and Obligations of the State and the Citizen. Not only does this definition appear to me perfectly natural and obvious in itself, but it leads, as we shall soon see, to certain very important practical consequences. No distinction can be more simple than that which exists between a man's duty to his neighbour and his duty to his country, and no rule more rational than that which makes the interpretation of a Law depend upon the Legislator's motive for enacting it.

It has been remarked, and with perfect truth, that every department of every conceivable Civil Code must necessarily contain a mixture of Private and Public Law. But surely it does not follow that Private and Public Law are undistinguishable. We do not infer, because every portion of the sea is a mixture of salt and water, that salt and water are not distinct substances. The true analysis of such a science as that of Jurisprudence is to be performed, not by dissecting its surface into arbitrary compartments, but by resolving its materials into their component elements. Those elements are the Facts of each case, and the intention of a Legislator in prescribing a given rule is a plain question of Fact. If he did so because he thought it fair between man and man, it is Private Law. If he did so because he thought it necessary for the good of the State, it is Public Law. But if he did so from both motives combined, it is clearly Public and not Private Law; because the question is, not whether the Public or the Private element in a given Law predominates, but whether the Public element enters into its composition or not.

That it may be impossible to decide with confidence what was the original motive of a given rule of Law, I am perfectly ready to admit. But this uncertainty arises from the nature of human evidence. Tell me what the facts are, such is the utmost which Juridical Science can undertake, and I will tell you what the Law ought to be. Tell me the intention of a given Statute, and I will tell you whether it is Private or Public Law. It may be that you are unable to do so. The circumstances which led to an enactment may, like those of any other transaction, be undecipherable and undiscoverable. In all such cases of doubt, the rational course is to substitute general calculation for particular conjecture, by adopting some arbitrary test upon which Presumption may be raised. But this is the business of the practical Legislator. Given the facts, the principle is clear. It then becomes easy to divide all Civil Law into two distinct categories; rules wholly founded upon the intention of Private Justice, and rules wholly or partially founded upon the intention of Public Policy.

I therefore persist in dividing the present Chapter into the following four Sections: — 1. Municipal Arbitration. II. Municipal Allegiance. III. Municipal Authority. IV. Municipal Government.

## I. Municipal Arbitration

§ 294. The whole necessary difference between the relation of fellow-creatures and that of fellow-Citizens may be stated in a single sentence. As against my fellow creatures I am morally justified in enforcing what I think my rights by force, but as against my fellow-Citizens I am bound to submit them to the Arbitration of the State. We do not know, nor can we conceive, that any National community ever existed in which this was not required. Every Citizen is therefore bound, whatever may be his real or supposed claims upon his neighbours, to abstain from enforcing those claims except through the authority of the

Law. He will of course be justified in defending his person and property by force against Wrong. But if the Wrong is once successfully consummated, he must not exact Satisfaction, far less inflict Retaliation, upon his own private responsibility; and the attempt to do so, however clear the question may be in his favour, will be in itself a criminal offence.

§ 295. The first and simplest function of every State is therefore the administration of Private Justice among its Citizens. The discharge of this function is associated, in the mind of an English reader, with all the complicated machinery of modern Litigation and Legislation. But this association is altogether artificial. There have been, and there probably still are, small and rude communities among whom private questions of Right were decided by the votes of the assembled Citizens; each man forming his own opinion according to his own instinctive ideas of natural equity. Nor are we even now so far removed from this primitive method of Arbitration as is usually supposed. Whatever may have been the fictions of antiquity concerning the inexhaustible traditions of the Common Law, it is certain that a large portion, and in the opinion of every competent judge by far the more valuable and durable portion, of English Jurisprudence was constructed by the unfettered reason of the English Magistracy.

§ 296. A Judicial Decree, in its simplest and most primitive form, is nothing but a declaration by the State that it intends to compel a certain person to do or not to do a certain act, because it is of opinion that he is already so bound by Natural Justice. Its primary effect is therefore to determine what the mutual rights and obligations of the parties must henceforth be taken to be. Whatever the real merits of the case may originally have been, the losing party is now to be considered as in the wrong. If, having notice of the Decree against him, he disobeys it, he becomes bound to make full compensation for whatever loss or damage he may thereby inflict upon his opponent. And if he forcibly resists its execution, he justifies his opponent in using whatever violence may be necessary, and becomes criminally answerable for whatever injury his own resistance may cause. In such a case it is no excuse that the loser knows himself to be in the right, or even that the winner knows himself to be in the wrong. The authority of the State has extinguished the right of the one, and has removed the responsibility of the other.

§ 297. A Judicial Decree being merely the authoritative recognition of a pre-existing obligation between the parties, it is clear that the nature and consequences of the obligation so established must afterwards continue what they previously were. The right to execute a positive Decree may therefore be extinguished by Release or by Prescription, that is to say by such a lapse of time as will raise the presumption of an intended Release, in the same manner as the claim upon which the Decree was founded might have been. But since the Decree has recognized the existence of the obligation at a certain date, it is equally clear that no Release or Prescription which took place previous to the Decree can be pleaded as a bar to its execution. For the Decree, while it stands unreversed, must obviously be taken as establishing, not only the original validity of the claim upon which it is founded, but the invalidity of all subsequent objections thereto.

§ 298. Such would be the simple consequences of a Judicial Decree procured without previous Litigation. And there may no doubt be communities in which this is actually possible. We can imagine the elders of an Indian village settling the disputes of their neighbours over the council fire, with as little trouble or delay as the head of a family finds necessary in ruling his own household. But in a civilized nation, however small and simple, disputed questions of Right will inevitably become so numerous that some interval of time must necessarily pass between the first application and the final Decree. During this interval of time the successful suitor must be taken as having been kept out of his rights by the fault or the mistake of his adversary, and the Court is therefore bound injustice to place him as nearly as possible in the same situation as if this had not happened. In other words, the Decree ought to provide that the loser shall make compensation to the winner, not only for the delay caused by the pendency of the Suit, but also for whatever trouble and loss of time he, or any one acting by his authority, may have incurred in stating and proving his case to the satisfaction of the Court. From this plain principle arises the whole question, so important to modern suitors and lawyers, of Litigatory Costs.

§ 299. The prosecution of a Suit may moreover easily require, without prejudice or reference to its ultimate event, various provisional or Interlocutory exercises of authority by the Court. It may be reasonable to require from the Defendant sufficient security, whether by making a deposit of property or by procuring a responsible surety, that he will abide and comply with the Decree. It is always necessary, in cases where the facts are in dispute, to compel the attendance of such Witnesses as either of the parties may think proper to summon, and to punish their refusal to give evidence or their wilful falsehood. And it is the invariable duty of the Court to prevent, or in aggravated cases to punish, any act of either party which tends to make impracticable the execution of a final Decree against him. By which party the Costs of procuring and executing an Interlocutory Decree must ultimately be borne, will depend upon the reason of the application for it. If its necessity arose from the original nature of the Litigation, they ought to be Costs in the Cause; that is to say, they must be paid by whichever party is finally unsuccessful. But if it arose from the negligence or the obstinacy of the adverse party, he ought to pay them before he is allowed to proceed with his Suit.

§ 300. Of course the pendency of a Suit will no more prevent the claim upon which it is founded from being satisfied or compromised by a private transaction between the parties, than the pendency of War will invalidate a Treaty of Peace between the Belligerents. But the question, whether a claim can become obsolete by Prescription pending a Suit to enforce it, is sometimes a very difficult one. As a general rule, it is clear that a Defendant against whom a Suit is pending must be supposed to know perfectly well that the Plaintiff intends to insist upon his rights. But there is sometimes great danger that, by protracting the steps of a Suit, a merely colourable claim may be kept alive until the evidence necessary to repel it is out of reach. If therefore the forms of the Court are such as to permit such dilatory proceedings on the part of the Plaintiff, it will be just to compute every interval of unnecessary delay as so much added towards the lapse of time sufficient to extinguish his claim. But there can be no doubt that, under a rational system of procedure, the Defendant ought always to have the power of insisting that the Suit shall, in the absence of any special reason for standing still, either go on or leave off at once.

§ 301. A Judicial Decree may of course be reversed or modified by the authority of the State which pronounced it. But even if reversed it must still be considered as having worked, during the interval of its existence, a certain alteration in the rights of the parties. The Appellee did undoubtedly obtain, from a Court of adequate Jurisdiction, a solemn declaration that he was in the right and the Appellant in the wrong. He cannot be blamed for maintaining the advantage given him by this declaration, until he is deprived of it in due course of Law. The Decree of Reversal ought therefore to exempt him from making compensation for the consequences of the reversed Decree, and likewise from bearing the Costs incurred by the Appellant in the prosecution of the Appeal. In the case of a negative Decree, or of a positive Decree which has been carried into execution, the loser's right of Appeal may of course be extinguished by his Release, and is therefore liable to become so by Prescription.

§ 302. We have hitherto, for the sake of simplifying the

question, supposed the case of a purely Personal Decree, that is to say of a Decree commanding or forbidding a purely personal act. But the cases in which such Decrees are actually made are of course very rare and very peculiar. Except in family disputes about the custody of minors or lunatics, and in some few proceedings relating to conjugal rights, there is scarcely any conceivable Judicial Sentence which would not directly or indirectly affect the property of the parties concerned. Even in cases of purely personal Injury, the payment of pecuniary damages must almost always form a part of the reparation awarded to the plaintiff, and in fact the tendency of modern Litigation has been to treat every kind of private wrong as capable of being paid for in money. The most important consequence of an ordinary Judicial decision is therefore its operation upon the proprietary rights of the defendant. And we will now proceed, avoiding as much as possible all technical language, to ascertain the principles which determine what that operation ought to be.

§ 303. The simplest possible form of a Real Decree consists in the judicial recognition or rejection of an adverse claim preferred by one person to property in the possession of another. The only alteration which such a proceeding can make in the rights of the parties concerned relates to the apportionment of the Costs. When the successful title is subdivided into successive or concurrent interests, and the unsuccessful party is unable to pay the Costs of its establishment, it becomes a question whether the expence which has been incurred for the common benefit ought not to be borne by the common fund. There seems to be no reason why a Co-proprietor should not be permitted to make his partners in estate contribute to discharge the Costs incurred by him in defending the common title, or why the representatives of a deceased tenant for life should not, under the same circumstances, claim a lien upon the inheritance. When the interest of the successful Litigant is derivative and subordinate, his right to entire exoneration from the expence of defending it against a paramount claim is of course indisputable. It is acknowledged that a Creditor may add to his debt the costs incurred in defending the title of his Debtor, and that a Tenant may call upon his Landlord to protect him against an adverse claim to the inheritance.

§ 304. A Decree commanding the execution of a Real Obligation is of course in substance, whatever it may be in form, a Decree establishing a Real Title; and its consequences will therefore be equally simple. But, according to the procedure of the English Courts of Equity, one very important alteration in the rights of the parties is effected by such a proceeding. They hold that every Purchaser of immovable property is bound by a previous Decree establishing a Real Obligation against the Vendor, and that every Purchaser of immovable property pending a Suit to enforce a Real Obligation against the Vendor will be bound by the Decree. The practical effect of a Suit to enforce a Real Obligation is therefore to convert it, if eventually established, into a Proprietary Title[36]. But it is evident that the Justice of this rule is entirely a question of Remedial Practice. It depends altogether upon the consideration whether the arrangements of the Court are in point of fact such as to give every Purchaser an opportunity of discovering, with sufficient ease and certainty, the existence of a Decree or the pendency of a Suit concerning the property for which he has contracted.

§ 305. It frequently happens that a Decree for the execution of a Trust is rendered necessary, not by the Trustee's refusal to perform it, but by his uncertainty whether the Plaintiff is really the person for whose benefit it ought to be performed. In such cases, if the claimant is successful, his Costs must clearly be paid, not by the Trustee personally, but out of the Trust property; because the Suit is a part of the expences necessary for the due execution of the Trust. So under a Decree for the Distribution of a Trust-fund

---

[36] See § 76.

among two or more persons, the Costs of all the successful claimants must first be paid out of the entire fund, after which the surplus must be divided among them. For the expence of ascertaining all the persons entitled is a necessary preliminary to the execution of any part of the Trust, and it is therefore probable that the creator of the Trust intended it to be borne equally by all. But when Brown is entitled to a fixed value and Jones to the residue, Jones cannot claim his costs until Brown's claim, costs and all, is fully satisfied; because, if the fund is not more than sufficient for that purpose, it is evident that Jones has acted wrongly in applying to the Court at all.

§ 306. The effect of an erroneous Payment or Distribution in pursuance of a Decree for the execution of a Trust is clearly to discharge the party paying and to render liable the party paid. If Brown, in compliance with a Decree, pays money to Jones which he ought to have paid to Robinson, Robinson may make Jones refund but has lost his claim upon Brown. For the beneficial claimant makes his claim at his own peril and must give up what he gets by it if it proves to be a mistake, but the Trustee has acted under compulsion and ought therefore to be exempt from responsibility. The rule is of course the same when the Decree is only partially erroneous, as where a deceased person's property is divided between Brown and Jones as his Coheirs and it afterwards proves that he died indebted to Robinson. But in this case Robinson ought only to be permitted to recover one half of his claim from Brown and Jones respectively, and should either of them prove insolvent the loss must fall upon Robinson; because it was through Robinson's own mistake that he was not paid before the Distribution took place. Nor can the accidental circumstance, that one of the shares is still unpaid when Robinson prefers his claim, make any difference in this respect.

§ 307. The same principles are applicable in the case of a purchaser under an erroneous Decree for the Sale of Trust property. He stands in the position of a purchaser by private contract without notice.[37] If therefore the Proprietary Title of the Vendor was invalid, the Court which pronounced the Decree cannot restrain the true owner from ejecting the Purchaser. But, unless the Purchaser has been privy to some fraud or collusion used in procuring the Decree, he cannot be affected by any Real Obligation which bound the property in the hands of the Vendor. To all such claimants he is at liberty to say: I paid my purchase money under the direction of a Court of Justice. In doing so I was bound to suppose that your claim, if valid, would not be neglected. If it has chanced otherwise, apply for redress against those who have received what ought to have been yours. But do not expect me to pay my purchase money twice over, because, by the mistake of those who were entitled to command my obedience, I have paid it erroneously.

§ 308. It remains to consider the effect which ought to be produced by a wrongful Decree considered as a Judicial Precedent. We will suppose that the decision is acknowledged to have been erroneous in principle, but that circumstances have made it irreversible in fact. In such a case what ought the State to do? Not certainly to persevere in doing injustice because injustice has once been done. The first step to be taken is a public announcement that the erroneous Precedent will not be followed and must not be relied upon. But this announcement will not necessarily apply to transactions which have taken place in the meantime. If it can be shown that the parties to such a transaction were aware of the erroneous Decree, it is clear that they must be considered to have mutually acted upon the faith of its validity and consequently to have made it binding as between themselves. And even where a Suit upon a previous transaction has been commenced or resisted in reliance upon the erroneous Precedent, the party who has done so may fairly be exempted from payment of his oppo-

---

[37] See § 76.

nent's Costa.

§ 309. The earliest and rudest form of Judicial Arbitration was probably an appeal to the instinctive equity of an entire community. Its latest and most perfect form may possibly be an appeal to the instinctive equity of a select body of Jurists, trained by long practice in solving questions of Right and enlightened by the study of former precedents and opinions. But between these two extreme phases of rude and refined simplicity there is a great gulf fixed; a gulf so great that History cannot be said to record the commencement of its passage, and that Philosophy cannot venture to foretel its completion. The primitive system of Arbitration has never been found to continue. Either its caprice and uncertainty become intolerable and there is a general cry for the enactment of Statute Law, or its accumulated precedents harden into National Usage and become recognized as Customary Law. In both cases we have reached the point at which the State, in determining the Rights and Obligations of its citizens among themselves, begins to substitute Private Legislation for Natural Justice.

§ 310. What Private Law ought to be, is one of the principal questions discussed throughout the present Work. But what it is, must be considered entirely as a matter of fact. The Natural Justice of the case is now immaterial We have only to inquire what the Legislator actually meant, or rather what, judging from the language which he has used, the Citizen may reasonably suppose him to mean. That interpretation the State is bound in justice to declare and to enforce. Absurd and inequitable as in itself it may be, it forms nevertheless the basis upon which men have been making their Wills and their Contracts, and their confidence in its validity cannot without gross injustice be deceived. It is of course true that the authority which makes Law can unmake it, and that it ought to do so if the Law proves unjust or inconvenient. But the repeal of a Jural Law, however bad in itself, ought not to be retrospective; and, when it is found necessary, the justifiable expectations of those persons who have made their arrangements upon the faith of its enactment will always be carefully protected from disappointment by every civilized Legislature.

§ 311. No man, says the Roman maxim, can excuse himself by pleading ignorance of the Law; and upon this ground both the English Courts and the best foreign Civilians have maintained the rule, that money paid under a mistake in Law cannot be recovered. A more unsatisfactory distinction could scarcely have been invented. That a man who has parted with an advantage because he thinks himself bound in justice to do so cannot be permitted to change his mind, may with some plausibility be contended. He has decided against himself, and has acted upon the decision. But ignorance of Positive Law is really nothing but ignorance of Fact. What difference can it make whether I pay a debt because I do not know that it has been paid already, or because I do not know that a Statute has been enacted by which it is extinguished? In both cases the question arises because I do not happen to have heard of something which took place ill my absence. And why am I necessarily bound to know more of what is done by the Legislature than of my own private affairs?

§ 312. But upon the entire subject of Private Legislation I must repeat the opinion which I have already expressed,[38] that no single problem of pure Jurisprudence ever has been, or ever will be, satisfactorily solved by the enactment of verbal rules. That such enactments may, in rude and simple Societies, be useful as temporary expedients, I do not deny. Among people who cannot comprehend abstract principles, verbal regulations are better than none at all. But the inevitable consequence of all Dogmatic Legislation is the substitution of disputes about Words for disputes about Ideas. Instead of endeavouring to convey to each other our conceptions of justice and common sense, we begin to wrangle about the due interpretation of the

---

[38] Introd. XVIII.

formula which the Legislature has used. Where the Law is an arbitrary rule adopted for the sake of convenience, there is no disadvantage in this. But where it is an attempt to define a Jural principle, the mischief becomes serious. We are now imposing upon human language a task to which it is altogether unequal. The end of the attempt will infallibly be, either that we shall cramp Reason in obedience to Dogma, or that we shall stretch Dogma in obedience to Reason. In the former case our whole system of Law will become a public nuisance, in the latter our verbal Statutes will become a troublesome delusion.

§ 313. Precedent is the only true exponent of Principle. Practical difficulties require practical solutions. Tell us the facts of the case and the facts of the judgment, what passed between the parties and what the Court did in consequence, and you lay down a rule which may be wrong but which can scarcely be misconstrued. Add the reasoning upon which the decision was founded, and the Precedent is complete. But in doing this be it carefully remembered that the words of the magistrate are explanations and not Laws, and that the only purpose for which they are preserved is that of indicating the conception of principle upon which he acted. A system of Law thus constructed might no doubt be a bad one, but if so it would be deliberately and unavoidably bad. Its faults would proceed from the moral or intellectual perversity of its architects, not from their inability to explain their real meaning. It would therefore be an accurate representation of their opinions, whether right or wrong, upon the subject of Jurisprudence. In other words it would, considered simply as a Legislative expression, approach very nearly to perfection.

§ 314. The Dogmatic and Judicial principles of Legislation have been respectively adopted by two of the imperial races of mankind; the one hitherto the acknowledged pattern of civilized Jurisprudence, and the other probably destined to become so hereafter. The Roman Law consists wholly of verbal enactments and definitions, and the practical cases which it contains have been justly described as problems solved by authority for the purpose of throwing light upon its antecedent rules. On the other hand, that part of the English Law which is founded upon the principles of pure Jurisprudence consists almost wholly of recorded Precedents. The pathless wilderness of the Statute-Book contains comparatively few enactments which were intended to limit or curtail the discretion of the Courts in deciding questions of Right between man and man, and it will be found that these few were only admitted because they were imperatively required to correct the pedantic perversity of our ancient Magistracy. Roman Jurisprudence, in short, teaches by Precept, and English Jurisprudence by Example.

§ 315. I do not hesitate to declare my own opinion, that, precious and almost perfect as the substance of the Roman Law undoubtedly is, its principle of construction is radically false, and its entire result a brilliant and beautiful failure. The system is admirable in detail, but its whole composition is tainted by the vice of Pedantry. From the time of the Proculians and Sabinians whose controversies perplexed the Augustan Prætor down to that of the modern disputants about Real or Personal Statutes and Effectual or Ineffectual Blockades, we trace the inveterate tendency of the Civilian mind to turn away from facts and fasten upon sounds. That the same tendency has been shown by the teachers of the Common Law, and even that it anciently led them into depths of barbarous stupidity which the comparatively enlightened Roman would have despised, cannot of course be denied. But the difference between the two systems is this, that the one tends to intensify and the other to eliminate this great intellectual fault. The man who is guided by Enactment may be a great Jurist and the man who is guided by Precedent a pedantic fool, but neither can act as such beyond a certain point.

§ 316. It is true that there are able Jurists who altogether deny the practical value of this distinction. They tell us that neither Roman nor English Jurisprudence has any existence except as a body of Written Law; and that the true difference between them consists in the fact, that the Legislation of the Codes is concise and perspicuous and that of the Reports diffuse and obscure. But it is strange that any philosophical mind should be satisfied with so merely verbal a resemblance. That both English and Roman Jurisprudence can only be extracted from written books, is not only a truism but a self-evident necessity. But the true question is, upon what principle the extraction is to be effected. Now the Roman Codes are Imperative and the English Reports are Narrative. The former impose commands and the latter record facts. The Roman Lawyer had to find out what Gaius or Ulpian said. The English Lawyer has to examine what Mansfield or Eldon did. Here lies the; practical difference between Precept and Example.

§ 317. It is perfectly natural that those Jurists who believe, or who endeavour to believe, that all the questions of Right which have arisen from human affairs can really be crowded into the narrow receptacle provided for them by the Roman Institute, should watch with alarm what they affect to term the frightful accumulation of English Case-Law. Precedents are naturally frightful to those who cannot arrange them, just as roast beef is frightful to those who cannot digest it. But this is not the language which we usually hear from practical men. We do not find pilots complaining of the frightful accumulation of charts and buoys, or chemists of the frightful accumulation of experiments. Or if such language has ever been used in connection with such subjects, it has been by theorists anxiously clinging to some ingenious intellectual speculation which the experience of mankind is more and more clearly demonstrating to be practically worthless. To the Civilian who is determined to believe that all Jurisprudence relates either to Persons, to Things or to Actions, a volume of English Reports must no doubt be a severe trial. But to the Jurist who is content to analyse and classify facts as he finds them in existence, no reading will be more interesting or more instructive than that small portion of English Case-Law which really turns upon questions of pure Jurisprudence.

§ 318. To those minds which take this view of Precedent as compared with Dogma, no Legal change could well be more unwelcome than that which would imprison the free growth of Jural thought within the framework of a verbal Code. That Roman Dogma is usually a model of neat and accurate composition, and that English Precedent is often a prodigy of circumlocutory confusion, nobody pretends to deny. But no human stupidity can make Precedent ambiguous, and no human skill can prevent Dogma from being so. The intelligent Student finds it easy to condense the lengthy Case into a single clear and valuable idea. The pedantic Commentator finds it easy to dissolve the terse and pithy Text into a mist of unmeaning subtleties. Facts, however complicated, may always be brought to a point. Words, however perspicuous, never can. Let any one who doubts this take up an ancient and a modern volume of English Reports; and compare the keen dissection of recorded authority which now composes a legal argument, with the scholastic palaver about those odious stumbling-blocks known as Legal Maxims, which was so common among the pedants of a former generation.

§ 319. Upon these grounds, as well as upon others which I have elsewhere stated, I observe with much regret, I might almost say with much alarm, the enthusiastic admiration of Roman Jurisprudence which is becoming common among some of our most accomplished English Jurists. I am firmly convinced that the present anxiety of the English legal mind for a more scientific system of study may easily become a movement whose importance can scarcely be overrated. I am equally convinced that, if it is to end in nothing better than a more implicit adoption of the old Roman theories and a closer approach to the method of the continental Civilians, it will speedily be abandoned amid universal disappointment. That Roman Law is in its maturity and English Law in its infancy, I am perfectly willing to admit. That nothing can be more important to every English Jurist than a thorough acquaintance with Roman Law, necessarily follows from this admission. But the object for which that acquaintance ought to be used is a different question. I would treat the Imperial Codes as a store-house of materials, not as a model of architecture. In the former capacity they are confessedly invaluable, but in the latter they are depreciated by a pedantic slavery to words and by a thoroughly false principle of analysis.

## II. Municipal Allegiance

§ 320. The primary object for which every political community must be considered to exist is, as we have seen, the prevention of Injustice among the persons who compose it. Every Citizen is therefore bound, not merely by Natural Justice but by special Contract with the State to which he belongs, to respect what that State considers as the Rights of his fellow-Citizens; and any Citizen who wilfully and knowingly breaks this Obligation becomes liable to punishment, not merely by the act or authority of the injured party, but by the Jurisdiction of the State to which they both belong. It may therefore be reasonably maintained that, so far as the State offers a sufficient remedy for Wrong, the injured Citizen is bound to consider his right of Retaliation as withdrawn; and consequently that any violence which he may inflict upon the aggressor, beyond what is necessary for his own protection, becomes an offence, if not against the individual, at all events against the State.

§ 321. To what extent the State is morally justified in exercising its penal Jurisdiction, is a question of policy rather than of Jurisprudence. The offender himself cannot complain, so long as he undergoes no suffering which exceeds that inflicted by him. But it must never be forgotten that evil for evil is the limit, though not necessarily the measure, of criminal punishment. The argument, that experience has shown the insufficiency of equitable retaliation to suppress a particular offence, is one which, though long used with terrible effect by the men of blood who wore the English ermine in the last generation, will never be admitted by a conscientious Moralist. Lord Campbell's anecdote of the Judge who prayed that a convicted Forger might receive that mercy in Heaven which the safety of the paper currency made it necessary to deny him upon Earth, appears in these days no less ludicrous than shocking. But it may be feared that, in days still far from remote, the English Legislature seriously reasoned in the same unscrupulous spirit.

§ 322. Some Moralists have maintained the opinion, more specious but for that very reason more dangerous than the plea of Expediency, that the State is entitled to punish crimes, not through the medium of the natural right of Retaliation belonging to every injured party, but as the earthly representative of Divine authority and the earthly minister of Divine justice. Those who believe that one human being is morally justified in avenging whatever he chooses to think sin in another, are clearly consistent in ascribing the same prerogative to the State; and the question, whether anarchy or slavery is preferable, is altogether one of taste. But it would be difficult to maintain that a certain number of human beings acquire, by acting in concert, a power of detecting and a right of punishing moral evil which no individual among them singly possesses; or that they are able, by selecting a fellow-creature and styling him a King or a Judge, to confer upon him a jurisdiction which God has not conferred upon them.

§ 323. It is painful to recall the arguments by which some men of unquestionable piety and ability have endeavoured to support this extravagant doctrine. They lay down the principle that the world is God's world and that all who inhabit it are bound by God's Law; and from this they infer that human justice ought, so far as human fallibility will allow, to be a precise counterpart of God's justice. They do not advert to the obvious possibility, that there may be some of God's Laws which it is not His will to commit to human administration, and which human beings would therefore be guilty of a sin by attempting to enforce. But the truth is that a school of Moralists has lately arisen, who are in the habit of justifying their own feelings by gratuitously attributing them to the Deity; and in whose writings the use of the Divine Name only means that the writer entertains a strong consciousness of sympathy or antipathy for which he can give no intelligible reason.

§ 324. It ought moreover to be carefully borne in mind that, by admitting the principle of inflicting punishment as a retribution for moral evil, we introduce not only a new scale of penalties but a new list of offences. If we punish violence or fraud, not as a crime against man but as a sin against God, how can we refuse to punish those sins against God which are not crimes against man? And if we punish whatever we think a sin, how can we blame the most besotted fanatic for punishing whatever *he* thinks a sin? How can we complain of the Puritan for imprisoning the unwary Sabbath-breaker, or of the Abbess for immuring the fugitive Nun? How can we even condemn the Languedocian Crusades or the Spanish Inquisition? Justification by the necessity of self-defence is a plain question of fact, but there is no atrocity of persecution which may not be defended if we once permit human passion and folly to usurp the prerogative of perfect Wisdom and perfect Love.

§ 325. Appeals to unthinking superstition are commonly supported by appeals to childish sentiment. We are sometimes reminded that social security is a low and selfish motive, and that abhorrence of moral evil is a lofty and noble one. And this is unquestionably true. But we must not forget that a selfish action, though never meritorious, is often perfectly right; or that an unselfish action, though always respectable, may easily be altogether wrong. The passenger who knocks down a highwayman is probably acting from the mere instinct of self-preservation. The Inquisitor who burns a fellow-creature to ashes because they differ upon the terms of a metaphysical definition, may possibly be inspired by the purest and holiest zeal for theological truth. But this does not induce us to condemn self-defence or to approve of Autos-da-Fé. Experience proves that in this life duty and interest very often coincide, and that the ascetic who thinks self-indulgence a sin is constantly compelled to mortify inclination at the cost of disobeying conscience.

§ 326. But of all the delusions which have prevailed upon this subject, the strangest is perhaps that which discovers something grand and godlike in the vindictive requital of evil for evil, and which associates energetic strength of character with the obdurate infliction of unnecessary pain. Modern Sentiment whispers its awe-stricken admiration of the crazy rage and terror which induced a semi-barbarous Legislature to kill, by new and frightful agonies, a wretch who had committed a new and frightful crime. Modern Satire derides, with clamorous scorn, the scruples which condemn the cold-blooded murder of innocent men and the cowardly torture of innocent women. We might receive such a rebuke with patience, though assuredly not with acquiescence, if it proceeded from some stern Anglo-Indian proconsul, long tried and never found wanting in terrible danger and more terrible responsibility. But men of action know better than to talk lightly of human death or human misery. And sedentary men of genius cannot be too plainly informed that ferocity upon paper is not even a proof of that hateful and ignoble courage which consists in hardness of heart, and that there is no surer symptom of a servile and effeminate nature than the craven adoration of savage violence so common among the lower and feebler races of mankind.

§ 327. But the due observance of Private Rights forms only a part of the Social Obligation. Every Citizen must be held further bound to do everything which his fellow-

Citizens think necessary to the welfare of the State, and not to do anything which they think hurtful to the State. He will therefore be morally justified in resisting any constraint which they may attempt to impose, upon him, if he honestly believes that their true motive for doing so is not the public benefit. The chief practical consequence which follows from this distinction is the obligation of every State to divide the burthen of the public service as equally as possible among its Citizens. Whether this or that absurd command or prohibition is really dictated by public policy or not, is a question which must usually he left to the conscience of the community. But whether its execution is so contrived as to impose an unequal measure of inconvenience upon the members of the community, may easily be ascertained. And if so, the Citizens who suffer from the inequality may lawfully refuse to submit to it unless its necessity, or at least its *bona fides,* can be shown.

§ 328. Supposing that a Citizen is unable or unwilling to perform in his own person his share of the services required by the State, there can of course be no objection to his employment of an agent or substitute for the purpose. It may signify very much to Jones whether Brown or Robinson acts as his servant or partner; but, so long as the duty is effectually performed, it cannot signify to the State whether Brown or Robinson acts as soldier or policeman. Any Citizen may therefore, if he is willing to furnish the State with the means of providing a substitute in his room, justifiably decline to act personally in its service. And any Citizen who is personally unfit for the service of the State may justifiably be compelled, if he has the means of doing so, to furnish the means of providing a substitute. This is the principle of Taxation. Instead of calling upon every Citizen to join in protecting the State, we call upon every Citizen to contribute the means of hiring and maintaining a certain number of chosen men, whose business it thus becomes to devote their whole time to the public service.

§ 329. We now perceive the real simplicity of a question which some Moralists have pronounced to be, upon principles of Natural Justice, altogether insoluble. I mean the question, in what proportion the Citizens of a community ought to be taxed for its support. If we were to adopt the usual fallacy, that a man's taxes are the price which he pays for being protected by the State, we might well despair of fixing any scale of apportionment. Every man ought, upon that principle, to contribute according to the amount of protection which he requires; and who would undertake to estimate the precise risk of foreign or domestic violence which each man's mode of life incurs? But if we consider Taxation as the price which each Citizen pays for not personally protecting his neighbours, the conclusion becomes plain. There is no appreciable difference between the service which can be extorted by compulsion from one man and from another, and the price which each man is required to pay for liberty to withhold or to withdraw his services ought therefore *primâ facie* to be equal.

§ 330. But this general rule is clearly liable to be modified by the discretion of the State. The State, acting *bonâ fide* for the general welfare, may justifiably require services from one Citizen which it does not require from another. It may justifiably call upon an athletic stripling to act as a soldier, while it permits the sickly father of a family to stay at home and maintain his children. And it may, with equal justice, compel the rich man to pay the large contribution which he can comfortably afford, while it excuses the poor man from paying the trifle which would ruin him. In all civilized countries this principle of taxation is more or less adopted. Each Citizen is expected to contribute in proportion to the amount, however estimated, of his property. Whether the practice is justified by expediency this is not the place to consider; but, assuming it to be so justified, no Moralist who rightly comprehends the nature of Political Society will assert that it is prohibited by Justice.

§ 331. Still it must always be remembered that in Taxation, subject to the paramount consideration of the public safety, Equality is Equity. The State may justifiably sacrifice the convenience of individuals to its own welfare, but not to the selfishness or the prejudice of any portion of its members. The extraordinary contributions formerly imposed upon unpopular races, and the entire exemption allowed to peculiar families and professions, are familiar though obsolete examples of this kind of injustice. But there are still nations professing to be civilized, whose manufacturers are not ashamed to maintain, by appealing to the meanest national jealousies of an ignorant populace, the privilege of supplying their fellow-Citizens with bad goods at high prices. And even in countries where such barbarism is now unknown, bureaucratical pedantry is sometimes allowed to make an arbitrary distinction in favour of property acquired in a particular shape or under particular circumstances.

§ 332. The present form of the English Income -Tax is an instance of this kind. The advocates of that celebrated impost are accustomed to assert that its justice is one of the very few moral conclusions which are capable of arithmetical demonstration. And to a certain extent this is manifestly true. It is no doubt arithmetically demonstrable that, by making Brown and Jones pay an equal percentage upon equal receipts, we tax Brown and Jones equally; although Brown's receipts may be the produce of realized property and Jones's the remuneration of his personal labour. The true injustice lies in drawing an arbitrary line between property realized before and property realized after a certain date, and in calling the one Capital and the other Income. Whatever these two words may properly mean, they must surely be capable of some more rational definition than this. To tax all property now or hereafter in possession, whether expedient or not, would cleanly be equitable. But to tax me three or four shillings upon one sum of £100 because I received it in 1841, and three or four pounds upon another because I did not receive it until 1843, and then to talk of arithmetical demonstration, is reasoning worthy of that peculiar intellectual state winch is said to consist in the habit of drawing logical deductions from absurd premises.

§ 333. The Allegiance of a Citizen to his State is rather to be considered as a Status than as a Contract; at least it is a Contract of so public and notorious a character that it is difficult to conceive the *bonâ-fide* acquisition by a third person of a claim inconsistent with it.[39] But there seems to be no reason why it may not be renounced by the Citizen without the consent of the State. The contrary opinion, though long maintained and not yet wholly disowned by the best European Publicists, appears to rest entirely upon the barbarous theory which attributed to the Feudal superior a right of property in the Allegiance of his subject or vassal. But if we regard Allegiance merely as the equivalent of National Protection, we shall probably come to the conclusion that whoever is willing to abandon the one may be allowed, subject of course to whatever actual obligations he may already have incurred to his fellow-Citizens, to withdraw the other.

§ 334. This leads us to consider the effect which the commencement of Hostilities between two independent States will produce upon the Allegiance of their respective Citizens. If a State is an Association for mutual defence, there can be no doubt that a foreign attack upon or by the State to which I belong must impose upon me certain special obligations to my fellow-Citizens. I cannot, without breaking my faith and betraying my Allegiance, do anything to frustrate their efforts or to assist those of the enemy. I cannot even, so long as the War lasts, withdraw my Allegiance from my own State; and by attempting to become a Citizen of the hostile State I should undoubtedly commit a criminal offence. Every Belligerent State is moreover entitled to command the active assistance of its own Citizens according to its own discretion, but it is

---

[39] See § 34.

bound to do so upon strictly equitable terms. The burthen of compulsory service must be apportioned as equally as possible among the entire community, and no man must be required personally to undergo it without receiving due compensation for his time and trouble.

§ 335. Will the existence of War between two independent States invalidate a subsequent contract between a Citizen of the one and a Citizen of the other? and if so, upon what grounds? Not certainly for the absurd and barbarous reason formerly given, that by trading with the enemy we increase his wealth and thus enable him to persevere in his resistance. If this were all it might be answered that wealth, while it indirectly increases the power of the Delinquent, directly increases the funds available for the satisfaction of the Complainant; and that a politic Belligerent would wish his antagonist to be as rich and as defenceless as possible. But it may with better reason be contended that, by dealing with a Citizen of the hostile State, I assist to defraud the State to which I belong. For in so doing I both appropriate to my own private benefit property which already belongs to the enemy and is therefore liable to confiscation, and transfer to the enemy property of my own which thereby becomes similarly liable.

§ 336. From this it clearly follows that one independent State, having issued Reprisals against another, becomes entitled to arrest and confiscate whatever hostile property can be found in the hands of its own Citizens; that a Citizen who delivers hostile property to his own State cannot, after the conclusion of Peace, be held responsible to the spoliated proprietor for its confiscation; and that a Citizen who, with notice that Reprisals have been issued, delivers hostile property to its owner will be liable to his own State for its value. That one Belligerent must not, after concluding Peace with the other, confiscate property in the hands of his own Citizens which during the War he did nothing to appropriate, cannot of course be doubted. But it seems reasonable to consider a recognition by the Citizen of the

State's title to the property in his hands, or even an express personal order or notice from the State to the Citizen, as equivalent to an actual confiscation; and therefore as sufficient to prevent the title of the hostile proprietor from being revived by a subsequent Peace.

§ 337. There can be no doubt, that all private property captured by way of Reprisal ought, upon principles of natural equity, to be replaced by the State to which the spoliated proprietor belongs. By this rule the whole hardship of the International remedy would at once be removed.[40] The creditor takes his own wherever he can get it. It is not his business to apportion the respective liabilities of his debtors. It is their duty to make equitable contribution among themselves. It is in like manner the duty of a State to indemnify a private Citizen upon whom the burthen of an actual or alleged National obligation happens to be exclusively cast. This is clearly the case when private property is captured in satisfaction of a claim upon the State which the State has refused to allow. In such case the Captor has done right. It is the fellow-Citizens of the spoliated proprietor who, if they refuse to divide his loss among them, will do the Wrong.

§ 338. A Belligerent State is of course at liberty to conclude any Contract for the remuneration of its military Servants which may be thought advantageous to its service, and any unpunctuality in the observance of such an understanding is justly considered by all honourable men as disgraceful to a civilized Government. But no such transaction can possibly be thought to affect the rights of the adverse Belligerent. It is usual, for instance, to sell all movable property captured in War, and to divide the proceeds among the actual Captors, under the name of Booty or Prize-money; and this practice may, as between the State and the Soldier, be found both equitable and expedient. But there can be no doubt that all Prize-money ought, after de-

---

[40] See § 235.

ducting the necessary expenses of the capture, to be considered as laid out for the benefit, and therefore as chargeable to the account, of the State which distributes it. It is the impossibility of observing this rule which forms the true objection to the practice of issuing Letters of Marque. But, as the Laws of War unfortunately now stand, there is no conceivable reason why the capture of property by a Privateer should be less justifiable than by a National cruiser.

§ 339. Any independent State may of course forbid its Citizens to interfere in a foreign War. But a Neutral cannot be justly treated by a Belligerent State as responsible for the neutrality of its subjects. Strict impartiality is all that the Belligerent has any right to require, and strict impartiality is as clearly satisfied by permitting assistance to either party as by forbidding it to both. If therefore a Neutral State allows its Citizens to export Contraband of War for the benefit of the Belligerents, or even to enlist in their service, it adopts a policy which may or may not be wise and humane, but of which neither Belligerent has any right to complain. To such a complaint the answer might be given: We hold our authority for our own benefit and not for yours. So long as you are no worse off than you would be if it did not exist, how can you say that you are injured? If our Citizens choose to assist you, they are free to do so. If they choose to assist your enemy, you are free to treat them accordingly. But do not expect us to take the trouble of interfering with their choice.

§ 340. As Private Legislation is a declaration of the general rules upon which the State intends to administer Justice between its Citizens, so Public Legislation is a declaration of the general rules upon which the State intends to require Service from its Citizens to itself. But the validity of the two systems depends upon principles altogether different. What Private Law ought to be is a question of Justice, but what Public Law ought to be is principally and primarily a question of Expediency. If it can be shown that the safety of the State requires a particular regulation, not only is the State justified in enacting it, but every Citizen is bound in conscience to observe it. That the State is not morally justified in enacting Public Laws which are not necessary for the public welfare, and that whatever Public Laws are enacted must, subject to the public necessities, be strictly impartial in their operation, follows from what has already been said.[41] But still in prescribing Public Law the State acts, not as an impartial arbitrator, but as an interested party; and moreover as a party who has a right to consult his own interests to the exclusion of all others.

§ 341. The practical consequences of this distinction will be found very important. By the enactment of a Private Law the State becomes, as we have already seen, bound in justice to enforce it while it lasts, and not to repeal it without making due provision for whatever transactions may have taken place upon the faith of its validity.[42] But the enactment of a Public Law has no such effect. It is not the decision of a Judge but the command of a Master. It must therefore be considered, not as a Contract mutually binding, but as a Notice given by a superior for the direction of his inferior. By giving such a Notice, it is clear that the superior does not in any respect limit his own authority. If a Law is passed declaring a particular form of Testation valid, it would doubtless be unjust to treat it as invalid without due warning of the change. But it does not follow that, if a Law is passed defining the offence of Treason, an act which does not come within that definition may not in case of necessity be justly punishable. Acts of Attainder and Retrospective Penal Laws are wisely avoided by every civilized Legislature, but it would be absurd to deny that there may be cases in which they would be justifiable.

---

[41] See § 327.
[42] See § 310.

## III. Municipal Authority

§ 342. We have hitherto considered the authority of each independent State as identical with the collective will of the Citizens who compose it. In other words we have assumed, in defining the mutual Rights and Obligations of the State and the individual Citizen, that the one party is indisputably the State and the other indisputably a private individual. So long as this assumption holds good, the State and the Government are clearly one and the same thing. But we must now suppose that it proves false. The extent of the authority possessed by the State is now no longer disputed. The only question is, in whom does it reside? The Citizens have ceased to be unanimous. They are divided into two or more parties, each sincerely convinced that a different course of policy is necessary to the safety of the community, and each thinking itself entitled to repudiate the character of a body of private individuals and to claim the supreme authority of the State. Under such circumstances what is to be done? Are the opposite factions to fight it out? or is one of them, and if so which, to give way to the other?

§ 343. Those philosophers who have done so much to confound Political science by deducing its conclusions from abstract principle instead of practical experiment, can find only one answer to the question, where Civil Government ought to reside. They hold that the will of the numerical majority ought always to prevail. Why it ought always to prevail, I am not aware that they have ever satisfactorily explained. The almost insuperable practical absurdities which oppose the execution of their theory, they have shown considerable ingenuity in attempting to reconcile. But the theory itself seems to be assumed as self-evident. Such Publicists as have not the fear of democratic tyranny before their eyes may perhaps be inclined to dispute the maxim that, whenever three men agree to live together for mutual protection, any two of them may lawfully enslave the third. But if its justice be admitted, its consequences are no doubt irresistible. It leads directly to the conclusion, that the policy of a great nation ought to be regulated by a simple arithmetical computation and comparison of the various phases of idiocy which happen to constitute the opinion of its populace. And to this conclusion the sagacity of many foreign and of some few English politicians has implicitly assented.

§ 344. The contempt with which educated Englishmen usually regard this sort of pedantry is fortunately so intense as to make it almost unnecessary to examine the fallacy upon which the doctrine of Universal Suffrage rests. It is wholly founded upon a very obvious misapplication of the principle, that all men's rights are naturally equal. According to this principle, every beneficial enjoyment to which no man can establish an exclusive claim must of course be equally divided among the community. And from this it is inferred that justice requires the equal division of Political authority, and consequently that the Political authority of any two men ought to overrule that of any one. This inference contains a double mistake. In the first place, Political authority is not a beneficial enjoyment. It is a Trust to be exercised for the benefit of the State and not of the Citizen. In the second place, the despotism of the majority over the minority is not the equal division of Political authority. It is the annihilation of the political authority vested in a certain portion of the Citizens composing the State. An honest vote is worth nothing to the Voter, and an ineffectual vote is worth nothing at all.

§ 345. In what manner then is our question to be answered? It requires no answer whatever. It is one of those inquiries which, by what Publicists have recently been taught to call the Logic of Fact, always answer themselves. There is no use in considering what ought to happen, when we know that there is only one thing which possibly can happen. If the citizens of a State become divided into adverse parties, that which is inferior in physical force will infallibly end by giving way to the other. No declamations about the divine right of majorities will ever make a weak majority a match for a strong minority. All the mechanism of Universal Suffrage cannot make a shipload of Englishmen submit to be outvoted by a province of Bengalees, or a single Quinbus Flestrin by a nation of Lilliputians. The Moralist can only say that the strong ought to use their strength honestly and humanely. To say that when the strong and the weak differ the strong ought not to prevail, would be like saying that when a man steps out of the window he ought not to fall into the street.

§ 346. By the Authority of the State we therefore mean the will of any unanimous portion of its Citizens which whether by its number or by its character, is manifestly superior in physical force to the residue. To oppose that Authority is Rebellion; and there can be no doubt that every Rebel commits a most serious offence against his fellow-Citizens, or that when subdued he may justly be held liable to severe punishment. This liability does not depend upon the justice or injustice of his cause. A just cause may fairly be held to authorize violence, but only such violence as may reasonably be expected to end in success. Hopeless and useless violence, whatever may have been the provocation, must always be culpable. War for justice is a merit and may be a duty, but mere revenge for successful injustice is a crime. The most enthusiastic Jacobite, for instance, cannot reasonably deny that the Scottish insurrection of 1745 was a Rebellion; or that, if the brave men who attempted it did not deserve the severity with which they were treated, it was only because they acted under an honest delusion as to their chances of final victory.

§ 347. What then is to happen when the opposite parties are so equally divided, that their comparative strength cannot be ascertained without a trial? The only alternative is Compromise or Civil War. In such a country as England each party will yield something; and the State will proceed upon a course which neither thinks the best possible, but which both think better than standing still. In such a country as Mexico they will fight it out until one or both are exhausted. Which is the wiser alternative can scarcely be doubted, but which is the more morally laudable must be left to every man's conscience. If Miramon really believes that he will betray his country and peril his soul by yielding a single step to Juarez, who is to blame either Miramon or Juarez for leading their wretched followers to mutual slaughter? God alone knows whether such demagogues are hypocritical ruffians or deluded fanatics. Man must charitably presume their sincerity; and, when that presumption is admitted, the only remaining question is whether their forces are so equally balanced as to make the event, in a military point of view, the subject of reasonable doubt. The answer to that question will determine whether their strife is to be considered as the great social crime of Rebellion, or as the great national misfortune of Civil War.

§ 348. We now come to the important question of Foreign Intervention. Supposing that the Citizens of a State have taken up arms against each other, can the weaker faction justifiably invoke foreign assistance? In the case of a mere Rebellion, certainly not. Every Citizen has bound himself to obey the judgment of the State in whatever concerns the public welfare. He must know that the judgment of the State practically means the judgment of the strongest party in the State. He therefore, by calling in foreign assistance to overpower the strongest party in the State, breaks his obligations as a Citizen. Even in the case of a well-defined Civil War, the question is a very doubtful one. Here, it is true, we do not yet know which party represents the State. But how is that to be ascertained? By finding out which is the strongest. And how is it possible to find out which is the strongest, if foreigners are allowed to disturb the experiment by turning the scale according to their own opinion, not of what the State wishes, but of what the State ought to wish?

§ 349. It is scarcely worth while to notice the various

paltry excuses which have been invented to justify tyranny in extinguishing freedom. The vague phrases of intolerable oppression or excessive effusion of blood, so rashly adopted by the Publicists of former times, may mean anything or nothing at all. The favourite Austrian plea of invitation by a legitimate government involves, either the assumption of the whole question at issue, or the odious maxim that any villain who once gets uppermost ought to be kept so. The pretext of danger to one State from the continuance of internal disturbances in another, so fatal to the existence of Poland and to the liberties of Spain, amounts, either to the hypothesis that the disturbed State has actually given the intervenient State reason to declare War, or to the position that no weak State is entitled to manage its own affairs in a manner displeasing to its stronger neighbours. And the maxim, that identity of religious faith may entitle one State to exercise a qualified Protectorate on behalf of the oppressed subjects of another, is one of which it is sufficient to say that there is probably, at the present moment, no State in Europe between whom and some other it would not establish a standing Casus Belli.

§ 350. Attempts have been recently made to distinguish between foreign and *quasi*-compatriot Intervention. It has been contended that two politically independent States may be genealogically or geographically connected in such a manner as to give each a strong interest in the other's security, and that such a connection may, in cases of extreme mis-government by the one, justify forcible interference by the other. To this doctrine an English Government has, by declaring its opinion that Italians ought to be left to settle their own affairs among themselves, given a real or apparent sanction. A more groundless and dangerous principle was never laid down. It amounts to a distinct renunciation of the right to protect one kindred nation against another. There is scarcely a weak State in the world which it would not place at the mercy of some neighbour or relative. Far safer would it be to abolish the rule of non-Intervention altogether than to justify it thus. Better no door at all to the sheepfold, than one contrived to let in the wolf and keep out the watch-dog.

§ 351. But of course the principle of non-Intervention is one which must bind both parties in a State if it is to bind either. A Government which is maintained by foreign Intervention cannot complain if its opponents call in foreign Intervention to overthrow it. If a French army supports the Pope against the Romans, an Italian army may justifiably support the Romans against the Pope. If Austria replaces the King of Naples upon his throne, Sardinia may justifiably assist to remove him from it. The same distinction applies to the Intervention of foreigners as individuals. No foreigner can justifiably draw his sword in a Civil War, however strongly and rightly he may sympathize with the weaker party. But is that a Civil War which is carried on between natives on the one side and natives assisted by foreigners on the other? When a Government hires foreign mercenaries to keep down the people, why may not the people lawfully summon foreign volunteers to put down the Government? An Italian prince whose crown is protected by Irish or Swiss ought not to be scandalized if it is attacked by Tuscans and Piedmontese.

§ 352. We now understand what is properly meant by the Government of an independent State. In its strictest and at the same time its widest acceptation, it means any body of Citizens who have the power and the will to exercise irresistible control over the rest of the community. To many theorists this definition will appear, if true, a most painful and unwelcome truth, and in some cases it has no doubt been found so. But, as a general rule, its consequences are far less pernicious than those of any artificial system would be. The wholesome severity of Nature is infinitely preferable to the tender mercies of the ballot-box. Brute force may be a bad ruler, but even brute force is more respectable than mere number. Even Military Despotism, the worst and most hateful form of Government which appears capable of permanently existing in any human society, is better than the dead level of conventional tyranny which would, if it were practically attainable, form the ideal polity of the ultra-Democratic philosopher. Why this is so can easily be explained.

§ 353. In the first place, the fact of superior physical force presupposes a certain degree of moral and intellectual discipline. The fact of superior number has no connection with anything of the kind. A body of voters may be as incapable as so many swine of comprehending anything beyond the impulse of the moment. A body of soldiers, even if individually mere savages, have at least learnt to obey orders and to pull together for the common benefit. Even this low form of mental cultivation is a prodigious advantage. The connection between the welfare of the State and the welfare of the ruling class is so obvious, that nothing but the most childish incapability of self-control can prevent those who are interested in the latter from consulting in some degree the former. Even a military despot will therefore take care of his subjects, if not as a parent takes care of his children, at least as a grazier takes care of his oxen. And it is only when the mass of the community are no wiser than oxen, and would therefore be incapable of taking care of themselves, that a military despotism can long exist.

§ 354. In the second place, superior physical force is a very cumbrous and perilous, while superior number would be a most crushingly secure and perfect, instrument of tyranny. Under the former system, a strong and determined minority is pretty sure of a fair hearing and a reasonable compromise. Under the latter, the vote of a single fool would be sufficient to make one half of the community slaves to the other. Even in the worst ages of feudal anarchy, prudent and resolute men found it possible to create comparatively secure asylums against oppression. But in those immature and semi-barbarous modern communities where numerical and physical superiority are really almost the same thing, individual freedom can find no refuge whatever. There conventional prejudice reigns uncontrolled, and the man who dresses, dines, talks or thinks in a style which displeases his neighbours, becomes an outcast from society. In the particular cases of which I speak the inconvenience is perhaps unavoidable. But that any rational being should wish to create it by artificial cultivation, may well excite astonishment. A Cromwell or a Nicholas may be a necessary evil, but who that could help it would submit to Mrs. Grundy?

§ 355. But in maintaining that even Military Despotism is preferable to the pedantic tyranny of N + 1 over N, I have obviously selected the most unfavourable possible cases for my argument. The choice, in a community deserving to be termed civilized, is one of a very different kind. It there rests between Numerical and Intellectual Superiority. For upon intellectual superiority, as we all know, physical force in a great degree depends. The common aphorism, that Knowledge is Power, has been justly censured as ambiguous and inaccurate. Knowledge is no more Power than animal food is. muscular strength. Both substances may be swallowed, and in considerable quantities, by persons altogether incapable of assimilating or thriving upon them. But Intellect is unquestionably Power. Any portion of any human community which is superior to the residue in intellectual cultivation will infallibly acquire a collective power of causing physical welfare or suffering to its fellow-Citizens, proportionably greater than that exercised by any other equal number of them. The fact, if it be a fact, that every State is ultimately governed by Physical Force, leads therefore to the conclusion, that every civilized State must ultimately be governed by superiority of Intellect.

§ 356. That superiority of Intellect is sometimes combined with reckless selfishness of purpose, and that when so combined it may easily become a terrible scourge to mankind, cannot be disputed. But the existence of such cases has usually been. due, not so much to the height at which the intellectual tyrant soars, as to the lowness of the level over which he hovers. The ambition of one great genius may be gratified by leading to ruin a nation of deluded fanatics. Even the temporary policy of a dominant class, if very small in number, may to a certain extent be inconsistent with the prosperity of the State. But there is no more universal truth than this, that the permanent welfare of every large body of human beings depends upon the general welfare of their fellow-creatures. A State which contains a large class of Citizens intellectually capable of discerning what is for the public benefit, will therefore usually contain a large class of sincere patriots. And a Law of Providence which tends to place the supreme authority in the hands of such a class is consequently a wise and a merciful Law.

## IV. Municipal Government

§ 357. It is, as I have already noticed, just possible that there may be independent States whose whole discretionary authority is exercised by the collective body of their Citizens, or by that portion of them which has practically the power to control the rest. The simplest form of Delegated Government, if so it can be called, is therefore that which exists wherever the commands of the State are executed by a special class of persons selected and permanently embodied for the purpose. Every community not composed of absolute barbarians must, under some name or other, have something in the nature of a public armed force. It is unnecessary to say anything more concerning the peculiar rights and obligations of such persons. The Status of a Citizen temporarily employed in the external or internal protection of the State has been already discussed, and there is no difference except in point of duration between his duties and those of a regular soldier or policeman.

§ 358. The next step is naturally the Delegation of Judicial Authority. It is only in very small and very rude communities, that private questions of Right can be immediately decided by the whole body of the citizens. It therefore soon becomes necessary to intrust such questions to the discretion of Magistrates appointed for the purpose, subject of course to the superintendence of the State itself. A discretionary authority to decide private disputes carries with it, almost by logical necessity, an authority to determine their public consequences, or in other words to inflict punishment for such criminal offences as are not directly committed against the State. We thus arrive at the establishment of Civil and Criminal Courts of Justice. But that which, in the narrow and popular sense of the word, is termed a Government does not yet exist. The State retains in its own hands the exclusive power, not only of enacting permanent Laws, but of deciding all questions and issuing all commands which relate to its public policy; and the Magistrate is nothing but an Arbitrator between man and man.

§ 359. The institution of a Court of Justice necessarily implies the delegation to the presiding Magistrate of whatever authority may be required for the purpose of ascertaining the justice of the cases which he has to decide. He must therefore be empowered to summon before him, and if necessary to retain in custody, any Citizen against whom a civil or criminal process may have been commenced. He must also be empowered to command the presence and to punish the contumacy of any Citizen who may be required to give testimony as a Witness in any such process. And he must be intrusted with an ample discretion to repel what are termed Contempts of Court; or in other words to prevent or chastise the interference of any person who may attempt, whether by corruption or by intimidation, to interrupt the due prosecution and decision of a Suit. But the doctrine of some modern Publicists, that a Court of Justice may occasionally claim an International authority higher than that of the State by which it was created, seems to be founded, partly upon mere conventional Usage, and partly upon misapprehension of principle.

§ 360. It is the custom of belligerent States to appoint special tribunals, termed Prize-Courts, for the decision of cases in which property of a doubtful character has been seized by military force. In such Courts some of the greatest Jurists who ever lived have presided, and some of the most admirable judicial expositions upon record have been pronounced. But it is necessary to guard against the very common opinion, that such a Court occupies a position, as between the Belligerent and the Neutral, in any degree analogous to that of an independent tribunal. The Prize-Court is simply the legal adviser of the Belligerent, and nothing more or less. By employing a dignified Magistrate in that capacity, the Belligerent undoubtedly shows an intention of doing justice for which the Neutral, if disposed to act with moderation, will give him due credit. But the sentence of a Prize-Court can produce, except by virtue of some special International Usage or understanding, no change whatever in the rights of the parties concerned.

§ 361. There is consequently no foundation in Natural Justice for the doctrine, that a Belligerent incurs any additional responsibility by enforcing his strict rights without the intervention of a judicial proceeding. If the decision be just, it signifies nothing whether it was pronounced by a Judge or by a Commodore. The Belligerent is responsible for the result, and the Neutral has therefore no business to interfere with the process. If, on the other hand, the decision be unjust, it would be most dangerous to hold that the Belligerent is in any degree relieved from his responsibility by the forensic form in which the injustice has been committed. Such an excuse for Wrong would furnish all belligerent States with a most powerful motive for making their Prize-Courts as dependent as possible upon the pleasure of the Government or the caprice of the people. The man who acts without legal advice is justified if he acts rightly and the man who acts with legal advice, is responsible if he acts wrongly.

§ 362. These considerations show the fallacy of Hübner's proposal, that cases of capture by a Belligerent from a Neutral should be tried in the neutral Courts. If the contrary practice enabled the Belligerent to relieve himself from responsibility by the sentence of his own servants, the Neutral would have a clear right to complain. But this is not the case. The Belligerent is answerable for whatever he may eventually do, and for this very reason he is entitled to procure whatever advice he may think proper. He can no more he expected to sue in the neutral Prize-Court, than the plaintiff in a civil action can be expected to employ the defendant's attorney. Nor, if he were willing to do so, would the neutral State be well advised in entertaining the Suit. For, as the Belligerent is responsible if his Court unjustly condemns the prize, so the Neutral must be held responsible if his Court were unjustly to acquit her; and a new and formidable complication would thus he introduced into the mutual Status of belligerent and neutral States.

§ 363. The institution of that which is commonly understood by the word Government requires the delegation to some ascertainable person or persons of the entire Executive Authority possessed by the community. The whole visible action of the State is now carried on through the agency of individuals, and the main body of the citizens, whatever may be their real power, are apparently passive in its administration. The simplest form in which this case can be effected is of course that of a Monarchy, which consists in the appointment of a single individual as the supreme Representative of the State. Such an appointment clearly implies the possession by the Monarch of the entire Legislative as well as of the entire Executive power. For a person who is authorized by the State to do whatever he thinks proper is clearly at liberty to make a public declaration of any rule in conformity to which he may intend to exercise his authority, and likewise to annul or alter the rules so declared. And in this case the form of Government is said to be an Absolute Monarchy.

§ 364. But if by Absolute Monarchy is meant the irresponsible supremacy of a single individual, there can, except in mere outward form, be no such thing. No human being, whatever may be his natural faculties, can exert in his own person sufficient physical force to keep in subjection more than two or three of his fellow-creatures at once. And therefore every human being who exercises supreme authority over an independent State must do so, either by the voluntary consent of all the Citizens, or by the active support of a portion of them superior in physical force to the rest. Every Monarch is thus practically, whatever he may be theoretically, responsible to some portion or other of his subjects. In other words, every Monarch is in point of fact liable to be controlled, deposed or even punished, if a certain portion of his Subjects determine that he shall be so. But how far the Subjects of an Absolute Monarch will be morally justified in acting thus, has long been one of the most vehemently disputed questions in all Casuistry.

§ 365. In this place, however, the question must be considered as one simply of Jurisprudence, and from this point of view it admits of no doubt. The enlightened Patriot may think it his duty to bear much rather than risk a Civil War by resisting his Sovereign. The enthusiastic Loyalist may be ready to welcome any excess of tyranny rather than draw his sword against the Lord's Anointed. But neither the patriot nor the loyalist need deny that Monarchy is a Trust and not a Privilege. The one submits from anxiety for the safety of the State, and the other in obedience to the commands of God; but neither does so from regard for the personal rights of the Monarch. Neither therefore has anything in common with those Moralists who have shown themselves so infatuated as to maintain the possible existence of a Proprietary Monarchy, whose prerogatives ought in justice to be maintained for the exclusive benefit of the unfortunate wretch who presides over it. It is unnecessary to point out the inconsistency of this doctrine with the rule already laid down, that one human being can acquire no right of property in another. No such institution ever existed, except in the imagination of pedantic servility.

§ 366. From this it follows, not that a Monarch ought never to be entrusted with absolute power over his subjects, but that whatever power he possesses ought to be considered as placed in his hands for their benefit and not for his own. If a party among his subjects resists his authority he may be justified in maintaining it by physical force, but only so far as he thinks it necessary for the welfare of the community to do so. If this enemies succeed in deposing him he may lament the act for the sake of the community, but he has no right to complain of it as a personal injury to himself. The practical importance of this distinction can scarcely be overrated. It would, if clearly understood and recognized, put an end to those peculiarly inveterate civil dissensions which are caused by the assertion of Legitimacy, not as a principle but as a prerogative. Selfish Princes there will no doubt always be. But it is of immense consequence that they should conceal their selfishness. A decent pretence of patriotism makes little difference to the despotic Sovereign, and is an infinite relief to the exasperated Subject.

§ 367. In some countries these doctrines might be thought to have a Revolutionary tendency. In England they will be better understood. We know that it is because our Queen belongs to us, not we to her, that her position presents such a contrast to that of the Adored and Absolute Masters of whom Italy has recently got rid. We know that the difference between the Fiduciary and the Proprietary principles of Royalty is measured by the interval between the majestic ease with which England set her foot upon sedition in 1848, and the ignominious struggle and flight of the Neapolitan Bourbons in 1860. So thoroughly, in fact, do we know this, that the more loyal an Englishman is the less sympathy he usually feels for the loyalty of a foreign Absolutist. No two unselfish sentiments can be more directly opposed than the patriotism which regards the Sovereign as the living representative of the nation, and the canine fidelity which clings to a worthless person, or to a worthless family, under the vague impression that its object has by some mysterious process acquired a right of property in the obedience of a certain portion of the human race.

§ 368. The neglect of this plain distinction has been found no less inconvenient in speculation than mischievous in practice. It was the opinion that the Social Contract meant a Contract between the Sovereign and the Subject, which induced the utilitarian Moralists to dispute the simple and obvious truth, that a human community incurs, by the mere act of living together for mutual protection, certain mutual obligations of good faith. That blunder being once made and allowed to pass unrefused, the rest of their argument became easy. They were then enabled to show, not only that a Social Contract was impossible as a fact, but that it led to very dangerous consequences as a hypothesis. If, they contended, the whole structure of human Society is founded upon a Contract between the Government and the Nation, upon what principle can a bad Government, so long as it observes the Contract, be altered by the Nation without its own consent? Or upon what principle can a good Government, if it accidentally breaks the Contract, continue to claim the allegiance of a single contumacious Citizen?

§ 369. Not only are these objections unanswerable, but they are by no means the strongest which might be brought forward. The theory of a Social Contract between the Ruler and the Subject is not even a convenient form for the expression of Moral Truth. It is utterly irreconcilable with Moral Truth. It leads directly to the conclusion, not merely that one human being may become morally bound to obey another as his Slave, but that one human being may become morally entitled to command another as his Master. For a Contract, as we have seen, can only be said to exist when the Contractee acquires for his own benefit a personal Right of Control over the Contractor. If therefore I may bind myself to act as a Subject for the benefit of one man, why may I not bind myself to work gratuitously in a sugar plantation for the benefit of another? The answer must be left to those Moralists who believe that human beings can acquire, by getting together and calling themselves a State, any right of control over their fellow-Citizens which Natural Justice does not permit one individual to acquire over another.

§ 370. But all these difficulties will vanish at once if we adhere to the simple principles, that the only parties interested in the Social Contract are the Citizens who are bound by it, and that the Government is nothing but an agent or manager appointed to superintend its execution for the common benefit. We now perceive the absurdity of holding that the misconduct of a mere Trustee can possibly put an end to the Trust, or that his consent can possibly be necessary to an alteration of its terms. We may even go much further than this. We may appeal to evidence which shows that the Social Contract, be it convenient or otherwise as a hypothesis, does actually exist among us as a fact. It is really because he is conscious of having bound himself by a mutual understanding, not with Queen Victoria or with Lord Palmerston but with his own neighbours or townsmen, that an Englishman is ready to pay his money and to give his services. You might talk to him for ever about the greatest happiness of the greatest number, without inducing him to do as much for any country but his own. And this is because he is conscious, express it as we please, of having testified that Consent to a common purpose in which the essence of every valid Contract truly consists.

§ 371. The same distinction will enable us to perceive in what sense every Citizen may be said to have given his consent to the Law, however voluminous and complicated, of the State to which he belongs. The case is simply that of a number of contracting parties who employ an agent, or a body of agents, to draw up the terms of their Contract. The portion which each individual requires to understand is in most cases very small. It usually consists of a few general principles capable of being divined by instinct, and of a few petty regulations easily learnt by practice. But, were it otherwise, the nature of the obligation would continue the same. A Citizen is bound by the Law, not because it is the command of a master whom he has promised to obey, but because it is the decision of an arbitrator whom he has consented to appoint. And to say that he has not consented to it because he does not understand it, is as absurd as to argue that an. English soldier in the Crimea was not bound by the Peace of 1856 if he had not studied the Treaty of Paris.

§ 372. There can then, except in a State so small that its public action can be personally directed by a portion of its citizens superior in physical force to the rest, be no such thing as a practically irresponsible Government. It therefore becomes highly expedient to invent some machinery by which the ostensible Government can ascertain the will of that class in whom the supreme authority of the State really resides, without having recourse in doubtful cases to the actual experiment of Civil War. The expedient used for this purpose by the most civilized modern States is that of a Representative Constitution. A certain number of Delegates are elected by those classes of the people who, in the opinion, of the Legislator, are entitled to have a voice in the control of public affairs. And these Delegates form an Assembly or Senate, without whose express concurrence the legal power of the Government is restrained by the Constitution of the State within certain definite limits.

§ 373. It is clear from this explanation that a free political Constitution is in itself a thing of no value whatever. It is nothing but a machine contrived to indicate existing facts. So long as it does this with fidelity, it is a very convenient invention. When it ceases to do so, it becomes a dangerous delusion. And when it is used as an instrument for the purpose of rectifying what the Legislator must be supposed to consider as the mistakes of Providence, it is apt to be found the most exquisitely irritating provocative of civil dissension ever created by the folly of mankind. It is a common political aphorism, that good Constitutions grow and are not built. And this, in point of fact, is usually true. But there is no reason why a perfect Constitution should not be built, if the architect, instead of looking at facts as he thinks they ought to be, would resolutely look at them as they really are. It is because their inventors are too philosophical to adjust them according to the physical force of the Nation, that artificial Constitutions are usually such lamentable failures.

§ 374. The entire merit of a political Constitution depends upon its distribution of the Elective Franchise. In order to ascertain what a Representative Assembly is worth, the first question is, whom does it represent? If a knot of servile partisans, the Constitution is a fraudulent tyranny. If a mob of helpless serfs, the Constitution is a ridiculous nullity. In France, under the younger Bourbons, the Franchise was confined to a portion of the Citizens so small in number that the Government was able to secure a majority in the Chamber of Representatives by its personal influence over the Electors. In England, we have recently repelled a premature attempt to extend it to a class who have as yet very little real political influence in the community. But, had that attempt succeeded, its consequences might have proved much less important than both Democrats and Alarmists expected. It is highly probable that the middle classes, strong in union, in intelligence and in military discipline, would have quietly but distinctly shown that any violent practical change in our institutions was likely to prove a most dangerous and difficult undertaking.

§ 375. We thus perceive that the necessary elements of what is termed a Constitutional State are an Executive Government and a Representative Senate. But a further complication has been introduced by the practice of some modern communities. It has been their policy to make the possession of the supreme Executive authority as much as possible a passive Trust and as little as possible an active function. With this intention they have separated it from the ordinary administration of public affairs, and have confined its exercise to the decision of those great political questions upon which the national will seems equally divided. And they have at the same time surrounded the sovereign office with conspicuous wealth and splendour, and have made it, or permitted it to become, hereditary in some ancient and venerated family. There can be no reasonable doubt that their practical object has been fully attained. The establishment of a Hereditary Constitutional Monarchy is a most delicate and difficult task, but its benefits when fairly established have been found infinitely superior to those of any other form of Government.

§ 376. In the first place. Hereditary Monarchy has the great advantage of enlisting in the service of the State that powerful human instinct which modern Satire, always ready with a nickname instead of a reason, has baptized by the disrespectful name of Snobbishness; and which seems to consist in the inclination to regard with sympathy and admiration any person or family who may happen to occupy a high political or social position. It might not perhaps be difficult to show that this tendency, though often very irrational and therefore sometimes very ridiculous, is usually the result of generous and unselfish feelings, and therefore does not always deserve the scorn which has been thoughtlessly heaped upon it. But for this the Statesman cares as little as the humourist. The one wants something to use as the other wants something to laugh at, and it cannot be denied that the wants of both are supplied by the principle of Veneration for Rank. It would be difficult to overrate the impulse which patriotic ardour sometimes receives from the existence of a living symbol by whom the national mind and will appear to be represented.

§ 377. We need not, in order to prove the strength exerted by the sentiment of Personal Loyalty, go back to the times when honourable men thought it their duty to support bad Kings in breaking the Law. We have seen that sentiment cling desperately to patriotic courage, although perverted by the stubborn folly of insanity; to grace of manner, although disgraced by heartless profligacy; to simple kindness of heart, although embarrassed by helpless irresolution. It is easy to laugh at the best and noblest of subjects for preserving as a treasure the wine-glass in which he had seen the most frivolous of Sovereigns drink a toast, especially when we are told that the devotee terminated his pilgrimage by unwarily sitting down upon the relic. But the practical politician will acknowledge that the feeling which enabled a man like Walter Scott to pay, without thinking himself ridiculous, such homage to a man like George IV., must be a very genuine and a very strong one. Whatever he may think of its wisdom, he will recognize its existence as Power; and his object, let satirists say what they will, is to find Power and to use it.

§ 378. In the second place, every free Hereditary Monarchy secures a practical advantage of immense importance. It provides, in all cases of serious civil dissension, a thoroughly impartial and disinterested Umpire. It is evident that the person who is fit for this office must fulfil two conditions. He must be entirely free from all personal responsibility on account of the events which have caused the dispute, and he must from his situation be incapable of having any personal interest in its decision distinct from or inconsistent with that of the State. No brilliancy of genius, no elevation of character, can possibly inspire the confidence which is naturally felt in a Chief Magistrate who answers this description. For so simple is usually the subject of a great national dispute, that an impartial arbitrator requires no extraordinary intellect to decide it; and so exasperating and alarming are usually its circumstances and consequences, that no arbitrator can be relied upon as impartial who has any temptation to be otherwise. In such an emergency, therefore, no umpire can be so secure as a Hereditary Sovereign who has not been accustomed to take any personal share in the administration of public affairs.

§ 379. It is not too much to assert that to such an exercise of Royal authority England owes her present unity and prosperity. Thirty years ago, the nation was divided by a great political controversy. An important change in the Representative Laws was demanded by one party and refused by another. It was really in some degree doubtful whether the preponderance of physical force was on the side of multitude or on that of wealth and organization. Alarmists predicted a Civil War and a social Revolution. Even thoughtful and resolute men apprehended that the refusal of the national request would be the commencement of a long period of chronic discontent and disaffection. The King of England was at that time a man who, whatever were his personal virtues, certainly possessed no single qualification as a political leader, except the well-meaning honesty which only a lunatic could well in his position have been without. By his timely mediation the dispute was reconciled and the danger averted. Thankful as we all are for that great deliverance, it is strange how few of us seem to perceive that we owe it to Hereditary Monarchy.

§ 380. The style in which this invaluable institution has sometimes been depreciated will surprise no one who considers the excessive contempt in which thinking Englishmen hold political theory, and the portentous silliness of the political theories which unthinking Englishmen are consequently reduced to adopt. Those philosophers who call themselves practical men because they are accustomed to deny the existence of all facts which they do not comprehend, have often proved by arithmetical demonstration that Hereditary Monarchy is not worth what it costs. Those humourists who seem to consider political science as one of the fine arts, have found much to ridicule in the antiquated pageantry and the dignified inactivity of a Court. Very different is the manner in which the Statesman will form his judgment. To him the difference between a Royal Coronation and a Civic Procession is matter of fact, not matter of taste. He convinces himself that the one is still admired and that the other is beginning to he laughed at. He will therefore pronounce the one useful and the other absurd. And he will disregard, as of precisely equal value, the opinion of the cockney who stares at both with thoughtless delight and that of the satirist who sneers at both with fastidious derision.

## CHAPTER III
## TERRITORIAL RIGHTS AND OBLIGATIONS

In the preceding two chapters I have discussed the consequences which would be produced by the formation of independent States simply as personal Partnerships, and have carefully excluded the question of Territorial Dominion. It is no doubt difficult, in the present condition of the human race, to conceive the existence of the one element without the other. Even civilized communities are compelled, by the frequency of international disputes and the constant possibility of international hostility, to be scrupulously accurate in denning their frontiers; and in the case of uncivilized Tribes the necessity of precaution, and the danger of promiscuous dispersion, is of course still more obvious. In fact it will usually be found that, the more vagrant and savage are the habits of a Nation, the more compact and camp-like are its temporary occupations of the soil. But a different form of social life, though probably not a historical fact, is by no means either a physical or a moral impossibility.

It is not impossible, for instance, to imagine the colonization of an island or continent by two or more Nations which, although socially united by the closest ties, choose for some reason or other to continue politically distinct. In such a case the mutual confidence and goodwill of the Colonists might induce them to dispense with any international partition of the land. They might scatter over the country in single families, or live together in towns and villages, without thinking of or caring for any territorial rights except those acquired by private occupation. And yet the members of each fraternity might be effectually prevented, by the prejudices of race or by the scruples of superstition, from adopting the Laws or recognizing the authority of the other. Cases have often occurred? in which some such arrangement would unquestionably have been adopted, if mutual distrust and hatred had not made its due observance improbable.

It is clear that, under these circumstances, each of the two blended Associations (whom we will distinguish as the Houynhnms and the Yahoos) would retain its distinct International and Municipal Rights. They would be capable of waging War and of concluding Treaties with each other, and they would have authority to regulate the mutual dealings and to command the public services of their own Citizens. But they would be destitute of certain other prerogatives which we are accustomed to consider as equally inseparable from the Status of an independent Nation. Neither could under any circumstances claim any exclusive Jurisdiction over its own subjects. Every dispute between parties belonging to different Nations would thus be a subject for international negociation, if not for international War. If a Houynhnm, for instance, were to prefer a claim against a Yahoo, the Houynhnm Government could not be prevented from interfering to assist the complainant, nor the Yahoo Government from supporting the resistance of the defendant.

But we will now suppose that the two colonizing Societies have divided the colonized region between them, and have thus acquired Territorial as well as National Rights. It is obvious that several important questions, which under, the system of promiscuous colonization could not have arisen, will immediately present themselves. We have first to consider whether the fact of Territorial Occupation ought to confer upon the Occupant State any and what peculiar Rights within its own Territory as against mankind in general, and if so in what manner their existence ought to affect its personal authority over its own Citizens. And we have next to suppose the division or opposition of these two sources of Jurisdiction by the residence in one State of a Citizen belonging to another, and to inquire how far the consequences of such a residence may be altered by its special circumstances or character.

The present Chapter will thus be divided into the following four Sections: I. Territorial Dominion. II. Territorial Sovereignty. III. Territorial Residence. IV. Territorial Quasi-Residence.

## I. Territorial Dominion

§ 381. The Rights acquired by the Occupation of Territory in general have already been defined. They consist simply in the undisturbed enjoyment of the benefits which the Occupation is intended to secure. But the due application of this principle will evidently load to the conclusion, that there is a considerable difference between the Rights acquired by the Territorial Occupation of a number of independent Colonists and by the Territorial Occupation of a State or Nation. An individual who occupies land intends to secure nothing but residence and maintenance. A State or Nation which occupies land clearly intends to secure the further benefit of mutual protection in its enjoyment. It therefore follows that a State or Nation may possibly he justified in exercising over the Territory occupied by its Citizens a kind of Jurisdiction which a private Colonist would not be justified in attempting to exercise over his farm.

§ 382. We can scarcely refuse to admit that this Jurisdiction extends, if it should *bonâ fide* be thought necessary to insist upon its extension, to the entire exclusion of every Foreigner from the occupied Territory. It is impossible to deny that there are nations whose peculiar habits and institutions could scarcely be maintained if their Citizens were allowed free intercourse with the rest of mankind; and it is equally impossible to pronounce that such peculiar habits and institutions, however absurd they may appear to us, do not conduce to the happiness of those who maintain thorn. If therefore an independent State insists upon isolation, its will ought not to be resisted. Neither the subtleties of the medieval Publicists concerning the Right of Transit, nor the simpler American maxim that those who can trade and will not trade must be made to trade, can be allowed to limit its prerogative of uselessness. If the Chinese have occupied China for the express purpose of remaining infatuated barbarians, the European who endeavours to make them reasonable beings is clearly depriving them of the expected benefit of their labour.

§ 383. But this licence to folly must not be made a pretext for crime. Seclusion is one thing and hostility is another. The foreigner who is warned not to cross the Chinese frontier is not justified in attempting to do so, and if he makes such an attempt it may lawfully be resisted by force. But the foreigner who, without attempting or intending injury to any Chinese subject, has actually entered the Chinese territory must be compelled to withdraw from it, not only without unnecessary violence, but with reasonable care to avoid the infliction of suffering or hardship. He has a right to require protection until he reaches the nearest frontier, and to resist the privation of necessary repose or supplies on the way. Nor can his entrance, so far as it is absolutely necessary for his safety, be prohibited. The attempt to close a Chinese harbour against a foundering ship, or a Chinese market against a starving caravan, would undoubtedly be an outrage sufficient to justify the immediate employment of military force.

§ 384. The English Prize-Courts have, in connection with this subject, laid down the broad rule, that a Belligerent is entitled to prohibit during the War all Neutral trade with his enemy which was illegal before its commencement. But we cannot assent to this decision without letting in the vicious doctrine, that War justifies the wanton and unprofitable destruction of the enemy's resources.[43] To say that the enemy shall not, for his own convenience and to our prejudice, abandon in time of War any beneficial right which he has maintained in time of Peace, is simply to assert our claim upon whatever is his. But to say that we will enforce his Municipal Law, not only so far as it can be made profitable to us, but so far as it can be made inconvenient to him, is to assert a vested interest in the suffering of our fellow-creatures. Whether the Neutral can complain because he is not allowed to gain by the War, it is unnecessary to consider. It is the enemy himself who is injured, if the War is prosecuted so as to inflict upon him unnecessary annoyance.

§ 385. The right of excluding Foreigners from the National Territory obviously includes the right of enacting that no Foreigner shall become the proprietor of any part of that Territory. The Feudal Law, by connecting the duty of military service with the tenure of immoveable property, formerly made this restriction necessary in most European States; and in England, although now generally thought superfluous, it is still maintained. The ownership of a foreign landholder may, upon the same principle, be subjected by the Law of the Occupant State to any special restraints or burthens which may be thought expedient. And eve a supposing it to be unconditionally permitted, it is clear that it can only be exercised subject to the same restraints and deductions as if the landowner were a Citizen of the Occupant State. Not only therefore is the foreign landowner bound by the Territorial Rights of the State itself, but he can only assert his title, if interrupted, with its authority and by its assistance.

§ 386. This conclusion raises, in its simplest and most elementary form, the intricate question of Legislative Locality. Not only is it inconceivable that there should exist two independent States whose Private Law is precisely the

---

[43] See § 246.

same, but it is probable that there are very few individual States within whose Territory, if of any considerable extent, many local Statutes and Customs are not established. If therefore a Lilliputian Citizen can ever be compelled to prosecute a claim in the Blefuscudian Courts, it becomes highly probable that the Magistrate will have to decide whether the Law properly applicable to the case is that of Blefuscu or of Lilliput. For although the transaction by which the thing in question was originally appropriated must necessarily have taken place within the Blefuscudian Territory, yet the title of its Lilliputian owner may easily have been created or affected by acts done at his own place of abode; and in this case it may become necessary to decide whether the effect of such an act is to be determined by the Lilliputian or by the Blefuscudian Law.

§ 387. The medieval Civilians have enveloped the whole subject of Legislative Locality in one of those subtle yet complicated labyrinths of thought, the fatal secret of whose construction we are told that we owe to the great masters of Roman Jurisprudence. They begin by dividing the rules comprising any given system of Positive Law into two distinct classes, the first relating to Status and the second to Proprietary Rights, and these two classes they denominate the Personal and the Real Statute. They then lay down the general rule, that the applicable Personal Statute is determined by the Domicil of the Person and the applicable Real Statute by the Locality of the Thing. Having thus carefully separated Fact from Reason and involved it in Technicality, they proceed to dispute what rules of Law belong to the Personal and what to the Real Statute; until they succeed, incredible as it may appear, in persuading themselves that the whole question depends upon the verbal formula which the Legislator may chance to use. And finally they fix so many arbitrary exceptions to their own arbitrary rules, that the result of the whole is the possibility of drawing either conclusion from any conceivable state of facts.

§ 388. The best modern Jurists, justly indignant at the spectacle of so much perverted ingenuity, have altogether rejected, it may be too hastily, the division of Positive Law into Personal and Real Statutes. And yet it can easily be shown that common sense and practical utility authorize, if they do not require, some such distinction. Every question of Right must depend upon the effect of some visible transaction, and the Law which determines the effect of a visible transaction must be either the Law applicable to the Person who is its agent or the Law applicable to the Thing which is its subject. Now the Personal element of course exists in every case. Every legal transaction presupposes the agency of some human being or other. But the Real element may or may not exist. The act which has been done may be a purely personal one. We therefore simplify the question by separating the essential from the adventitious element, and by investigating, first the local operation of the Personal, and secondly the extent to which it may be overruled by the co-operation of the Real Statute.

§ 389. In the case which we are supposing the former question does not arise. The personal act whose effect is to be determined has been done within Lilliputian territory by a Lilliputian Citizen. If therefore any Personal Statute at all is applicable, it can only be that furnished by the Lilliputian Law. The present dispute is simply between the Personal and the Real Statutes. It is decided by the highest modern authorities in a manner with which no reflecting mind can possibly be satisfied. Almost all Jurists and Legislators agree that the validity of an act specifically affecting the title to immovable property must depend upon the Lex Loci Rei Sitæ, that is to say upon the Real Statute. But the best continental Civilians admit that the validity of an act which comprises the universal estate of the Agent ought, as regards any given portion of his immovable property, to depend upon the Personal Statute; and it is probable that the refusal of the English Courts to recognize this distinction is merely founded upon public policy.

§ 390. The decision of the English Courts may or may not be wrong, but that of the Civilians cannot possibly be right. If there is any difference between the acts which effect a specific change of title and those which modify a universal distribution, it is that the former arc usually much more solemn and significant than the latter. How can it be consistent with Natural Justice to hold that I am capable of disposing of my foreign estates by a hasty and clandestine marriage, yet incapable of altering thcir devolution by a formal prenuptial settlement? or that I am capable of binding them by contracting a book-debt in a shop, yet incapable of transferring them by a public and deliberate sale? Such a distinction can only be supported upon the principle, too familiar to the lax and rhetorical Publicists of a former age, that Justice must always be done except when it happens to be particularly troublesome to those who have to do it.

§ 391. It is possible that reflection may induce us to doubt whether the Jural effect of a Personal act ought not in *all* cases to depend upon the Law under which it is done; or in other words whether the Real Statute, merely as such, ought not to be entirely excluded from foreign application. The contrary opinion is no doubt supported by a formidable array of Roman technicality and German metaphysics, but it seems to have wonderfully little connection with common sense. It is admitted that every Citizen must, while resident at home, be considered as submitting himself to the Private Law of his own State. By that Law his Status among mankind must therefore be determined, and upon that Status must depend the extent of his responsibility to his fellow-creatures. How, under these circumstances, can the moral effect of an act done by him be altered by the accidental fact, that its ultimate consequences are intended to take place in another locality?

§ 392. Let us suppose, for example, that the Lilliputian Legislature has adopted the English, and the Blefuscudian the Roman Law of Personal Status. Every Lilliputian Citizen twenty-one years of age and resident at home must, upon this supposition, be considered as voluntarily and deliberately assuming the rights and obligations of a full-grown man.[44] Such a Citizen will therefore, by refusing to fulfil his Contracts upon the plea of immaturity, be guilty of gross injustice. It can make no difference that the subject-matter of the Contract happens to be Blefuscudian land. To such a plea the Blefuscudian Courts ought to reply: It is true that you are here an Infant, but it is also true that the act whose effect we are to determine was done in a place where you were an adult. That act is therefore sufficient to bind your beneficial rights all over the world. The contrary decision would enable you to exercise the rights of maturity by residing at home, and at the same time to retain the privileges of immaturity by investing your property abroad.

§ 393. Of course this reasoning is not applicable to those cases which depend upon considerations of public policy. I may justifiably enforce my Real Statute upon the ground that it is part of my Public Law, or exclude your Personal Statute upon the ground that it is part of yours. No French Court could be expected to hold that French lands may be effectually entailed upon the eldest son of an English proprietor at the present time, or might not have been effectually devised to an Irish Romanist a century ago. Nor can the Personal Statute he held applicable to a transaction in which the Real Statute has been intentionally invoked by the parties. It is, for instance, highly probable that, where Blefuscudian lands are sold by a Lilliputian owner, the terms of the Contract are meant to be regulated by the Blefuscudian and not by the Lilliputian Law. But this, as we have seen, is a question of Interpretation and not of Jurisprudence.[45]

§ 394. There is, as regards the application of the Real

---

[44] See § 177.
[45] Introd. IV.

Statute, one obvious difference between Immovable and Movable property. All Immovable property must necessarily continue subject to the Jurisdiction of the State of whose Territory it forms a part. But it is physically possible to transfer Movable property out of the Jurisdiction of one State into that of another. It is therefore morally possible that Movable property which ought to be at home may be abroad, and that Movable property which ought to be abroad may be at home. In such a case, assuming the Lex Loci Rei Sitæ to be applicable, Right ought clearly to prevail over Fact. The Courts of the State within whose Jurisdiction the property wrongfully or accidentally is, are bound in justice to regulate the Title by the Law of the State within whose Jurisdiction it would, but for the wrong or the accident, have been. It would be absurd to hold that the rightful authority of a proprietor can be affected by the unauthorized interference of another person.

## II. Territorial Sovereignty

§ 395. The primary purpose for which every independent State exists is, as we have seen, the enforcement of Justice between its own Citizens. An independent State occupies a distinct Territory must therefore be taken to do so for the purpose of enforcing Private Justice throughout that Territory, and all foreign States which recognize the independent Jurisdiction of the Occupant State must be held to have acquiesced in this undertaking. A personal claim preferred by a Lilliputian resident, in Lilliput against a Blefuscudian resident in Blefuscu will therefore belong to the exclusive Jurisdiction of the Blefuscudian State, because it can only be practically enforced within the Blefuscudian Territory. If the Blefuscudian Courts decide *bonâ fide* in favour of the Defendant, the Lilliputian State cannot justifiably interfere upon the ground that the merits of the case have been mistaken; and even if the adverse decision appears to be partial or corrupt, it is the Blefuscudian State and not the Defendant who is responsible to the Plaintiff.

§ 396. An Obligation arising between two Citizens of different States, each resident at home, must be considered, in the absence of express or tacit stipulation, as subject to the Law of the State in which the Obligor resides. The contrary doctrine would indirectly enable one independent State to impose its own Private Law, however unjust, upon the inhabitants of another; and the absurdity of a rule which would place the English press under the virtual control of M. de Persigny requires no demonstration. If therefore a Lilliputian Citizen, standing upon Lilliputian. ground, shoots at, or speaks disrespectfully of, a Blefuscudian Citizen across the frontier, the punishment of the assault, or the question whether the words are actionable, must be decided by the Lilliputian and not by the Blefuscudian Law. But the Blefuscudian Government, though it cannot in such a case insist upon the application of Blefuscudian Law, may justifiably hold the Lilliputian State responsible for the sufficiency of the reparation afforded by Lilliputian Law.

§ 397. But will the fact of Territorial Occupation necessarily confer upon the Occupant State any additional Sovereignty, or beneficial Right of Control, over its own Citizens resident within the occupied Territory? There are two cases in which it may reasonably be thought to do so. It is clear, in the first place, that no Citizen can effectually renounce his Allegiance while he continues to reside within the National dominions. It is, or according to the principles of Natural Justice it ought to be, competent to every man to make himself a Citizen of any State which will accept his Allegiance.[46] It may even be thought competent to every man to make himself a homleess outcast, bound by no political ties to any of his fellow-creatures. But it is not competent to any man to enjoy the security and comfort of civilized life without taking upon himself the duties of a citizen, nor even to do so indirectly by becoming the nomi-

---

[46] See § 333.

nal subject of one State while passing his life under the protection of another.

§ 398. In the second place, the Occupant State may equitably constitute itself, as against its own Citizens, the legal owner of all property which may be found unappropriated within the occupied Territory. If a State were nothing but a fraternity of scattered individuals, no such claim could be supported. It would be absurd to hold that the Jewish Nation, or the Society of Freemasons, has any title to the property of such of their members as may die intestate and without natural heirs. But a community which has bound itself to do justice and maintain peace within a certain boundary, has acquired the right to say that there shall, within that boundary, be no scrambling for waste lands or mislaid goods. The paramount title of the State may of course, like any other title, be defeated by adverse possession or even by *bonâ-fide* occupation and improvement.[47] But there is no injustice in holding that mere physical Possession, or even mere beneficial Enjoyment, ought not to prevail against it.

§ 399. The next step is to suppose the fact of Emigration. If two Citizens of different States meet upon extra-National ground, and the one incurs an Obligation to the other, there can be no doubt that the Obligee may justifiably enforce his Right by any means which would have been justifiable if the parties were living in a state of Nature. The only question is, whether the measure of the Obligation is to be the Law of the State to which the Obligor belongs; or, in other words, whether the Personal Statute is Local or Domiciliary. Either answer may no doubt be intelligibly given and consistently maintained. In primitive times, when there was little intercourse between the different races of mankind, every Citizen was held to carry with him the Law of his own State. In modern times, the English and Anglo-American Courts have established the more liberal and

---

[47] See § 100.

simple doctrine, that wherever a Foreigner goes he must take the Law as he finds it. But the absurdity of intermingling the two principles is surely self-evident.

§ 400. The answer which Natural Justice gives to the question can scarcely be doubtful. It would be difficult to conceive a more absurd or inequitable rule than that which would compel or permit a human being to go about the world, trailing after him all the ridiculous disabilities and restrictions which the superstitious folly of his own Legislature may have fastened upon him. Imagine a dozen travellers quarrelling at an inn, each of whom incurs a different measure of liability if he knocks down his neighbour. Or imagine a group of pedlars bargaining at a fair, each of whom must be understood to make his proposals subject to a different Law of Contract. Since all mankind cannot agree to adopt the same system of Jurisprudence, the next best expedient is clear. Let the Jurisdiction of each independent community define the territory throughout which its own Civil Law is to be enforced, and let it be distinctly understood that the effect of every act done within that territory will be determined, whatever may be the national character of the agent, by the Local Law.

§ 401. The continental Civilians admit that the existence and effect of an Obligation must be regulated by the Law of its Locality. But, true to their fatal habit of substituting words for things, they unanimously maintain that the Law of Status belongs to the Personal Statute, and that the Personal Statute must depend upon the Domicil of the Person. I do not hesitate to pronounce that upon this point, as upon many others, the practical good sense of the English Courts has achieved a signal victory over their philosophical rivals. Upon what possible principle can the distinction be supported, that a Lilliputian Citizen who goes abroad leaves behind him so much of the Lilliputian Law as is common to all his countrymen alike, but takes with him so much of it as is peculiar to the class to which he belongs? The fact is that no such doctrine could have continued to exist, if the close resemblance between the Statual Law of all civilized nations had not rendered the question practically unimportant. It is impossible to believe that, if the Law of China fixed the period of maturity at forty years of age, a Chinese merchant of thirty-nine would be allowed to repudiate a Contract made in Europe.

§ 402. Upon the same principle, the effect of an act whose Locality is extra-National must be regulated, not by the Civil Law of any particular State, but by those principles of Natural Justice which are common to all. In what books of reference, it has been derisively asked, are such principles to be found? It seems strange that so shallow a sarcasm should ever have proceeded from such a Jurist as the accomplished Savigny. It is perfectly easy, in every civilized system of Private Law, to distinguish those rules which have been dictated by the Legislator's general views of equity from those which have been rendered necessary by national Custom or by Remedial Expediency. Suppose, for instance, that an English Magistrate is required to decide the effect of a transaction which took place at sea between an English and a Dutch merchant-captain. It is evident that he would act most absurdly and unjustly by permitting the Defendant to plead the Statute of Frauds or of Limitations. The weight due to parol evidence, or the effect produced by lapse of time, would in such a case be a question for the Jury. But the Judge ought to be familiar with many precedents equally applicable to an act done in Westminster Hall and to an act done in the centre of the Atlantic Ocean, and upon these precedents he might reasonably form his opinion.

§ 403. But the rule, that the Law of an Obligation depends upon its Locality, must of course, when the question to be decided is the Interpretation of a Contract, be applied subject to the Intention of the parties. An express stipulation, that a Contract concluded abroad shall be construed according to the Law of the Contractor's Domicil, would clearly be binding. And such a stipulation might perhaps be taken as tacitly made, if it could be proved that the Contractor, although actually abroad, believed himself to be within the Jurisdiction of his own country. Such a stipulation may also be considered as implied when the performance of a Contract concluded abroad is expressly fixed at home. And the same principle will of course apply to those numerous Contracts which, although they do not expressly fix any place of performance, must be interpreted as properly and principally performable at the place of the Contractor's Domicil. In all these easels the Law of the Domicil must be adopted, not because the Personal Statute is Domiciliary, but because the Obligor's Domicil is the Constructive Locality of the Obligation.

§ 404. To all this reasoning there is one comprehensive exception. No State can be expected to enforce any rule, whether of Foreign Law or of Natural Justice, which contradicts its own Public Policy. The Private Law of a State is nothing but the rule which it adopts in doing justice between individuals; and, if the parties to a certain transaction have agreed to dispense with that rule and to adopt another, there is no reason why they should not be held bound by their agreement. But the Public Law of a State is the rule which it adopts for the protection of its own interest, and no private individual can be allowed to say that such a rule ought to be waived because it prevents full justice from being done to him. In such a case the answer would be: Our first duty, and the first object of our Law, is to protect the public safety. If your private rights are inconsistent with that object, they must to that extent, however indisputable in themselves, be overruled. We cannot justifiably do what we think injurious to the community, because it may happen that fraud or accident has made it necessary to you. If your country requires it you must submit to be cheated, just as, if your country required it, you would submit to be shot at.

§ 405. This distinction will be found to explain most, if not all, of those English decisions upon Private International Law which have been thought irreconcilable with the general principles established upon the subject. Thus it is clear that freehold property in England is invariably held bound by the Law of Primogeniture, not because the English Courts deny the general rule that Successions *ab Intestato* are regulated by the Law of the Intestate's Domicil, but because they consider the Law of primogeniture as an essential part of the policy of the State. It is equally clear that children born before marriage are in England always held illegitimate, not because the English Courts deny the general rule that the operation of a Contract is to be regulated by the Law of its Locality, but because they consider any relaxation of the English Law of Marriage as au evil to society. And there is no doubt that, if these conclusions can reasonably be disputed, they must be so by denying, not the applicability of the English Law in the particular case, but its utility in all cases.

§ 406. We will next assume that, of the two Foreigners whom we are supposing to encounter upon the High Seas, the one has already a claim against the other; and that this claim has been prosecuted in, and rejected by, the Courts of the State to which the Defendant belongs. In this case it is clear that, as against the Defendant personally, the claim is extinct; and consequently that, whatever may have been its original merits, the Plaintiff will be guilty of a piratical offence if he now asserts it by force. For an appeal by a Citizen of one State to the Courts of another can only be considered as a submission to Arbitration, and therefore as a conditional Release to the party sued. And even when property belonging to a Lilliputian has been *bonâ fide* adjudged by the Blefuscudian Courts to a Blefuscudian Citizen, the rightful owner cannot afterwards reclaim it from the adverse possessor, although their place of meeting is not within the Blefuscudian Territory; because he is bound by his own State's recognition of the independent Jurisdiction exercised by that of Blefuscu.

§ 407. From this it follows that, when property captured by way of Reprisal has been carried by the Captor into his own Territory, the proprietor's right of Recapture is at an end.[48] It can now no longer be enforced without committing violence within the Territory of a Foreign State, and such violence no private individual can justifiably commit. The proprietor's remedy is now an appeal, in the first place to the justice of the State by whose authority his property has been seized, and in the second to that of the State to which he belongs. Nor, if he should hereafter be able to identify the captured property upon the High Seas, or in any other extra-National locality, will he be justified in forcibly reclaiming it if it has been condemned by the Captor's Prize-Court. For the hostile State has now, by confirming the Capture, substituted its own responsibility for that of the person in whose hands the property may be; and the proprietor can therefore no longer reassert his title except by the authority of his own State.

§ 408. But a State which issues Counter-Reprisals is of course entitled to capture all property which it would have been justified in capturing as a Complainant, and it may therefore easily happen that property captured by way of Counter-Reprisal can be identified as having been previously captured by way of Reprisal from the present Captor. Is such a Capture a Recapture or not? In other words, is the captured property to be confiscated for the benefit of the State, or is it to revert, subject to the Recaptor's claim for Salvage, to its original owner? If the capturing State acted, as all civilized States ought to act, upon the equitable principle of General Average, this question would become unimportant; since in this case the ultimate loss of the proprietor would in any event be distributed among the community.[49] But in the contrary case the inquiry ought to be, whether, when the Capture took place, the owner's private right of Recapture had expired or not. For if the property,

---

[48] See § 236.
[49] See § 337.

during the interval between the two Captures, was carried within the territorial jurisdiction of the first Captor, it has lost its identity, and the specific title of its original owner is extinguished.

§ 409. This same principle is applicable where property captured by one hostile State from another has been sold to a Neutral purchaser. The Captor can of course confer upon the purchaser no title superior to his own, and the purchaser therefore takes the property subject to the original owner's right of recapture during the interval between its capture and its arrival within the Captor's Jurisdiction. But when that interval expires the title of the purchaser becomes indefeasible; and the hostile State cannot justifiably recapture the purchased property, although afterwards found upon the High Seas or even within its own Jurisdiction. For the original ownership of the property has now been destroyed; and, although of course liable to capture in the hands of a Citizen of the capturing State, it is, as we have seen, in the character of property belonging to that State, and not of property wrongfully appropriated by it, that it is so liable. If therefore it becomes the *bonâ-fide* property of a Neutral purchaser, it is no more subject to the claims of the hostile State than if it had originally belonged to the vendor. And consequently a Captor, if he succeeds in carrying his prize into his own Territory, can clearly confer a valid title upon a subsequent Neutral purchaser.

§ 410. To this general rule there is an obvious exception. It is manifest that a Neutral cannot be allowed, by purchasing captured property from one Belligerent, to make the situation of the other less favourable than it would otherwise have been. If therefore it clearly appears that the captured property, notwithstanding its arrival within the Captor's Jurisdiction, was still, owing to the fact of its capture, in such a physical situation as to be more exposed to attack than it would have been if it had originally belonged to the Captor, the neutral Purchaser must take his title subject to this risk. How long it will so continue is of course a question of Fact, and the conventional forms and arbitrary periods of time by which International Usage has defined it are mere expedients for evading the difficulty of a correct decision. But no Jurist will maintain that the Captor ought to be enabled, by the intervention of the Neutral, to transfer his enemy's chance of recapture from a ship in an exposed roadstead to a sum of money in the national Treasury.

§ 411. As between the Occupant State and its own Emigrant Citizens, the fact of Territorial Occupation need make no difference whatever. A Citizen who goes abroad without renouncing his Allegiance will continue subject to the authority of his Government so long as he is not within the Territorial Jurisdiction of any foreign State, and will be punishable upon his return home for whatever offences he may in the meantime have committed against it. But the National Occupation of Territory may, in the absence of any contrary declaration by the Legislature, be fairly interpreted as releasing the emigrant Citizen from the obligation of submitting his claims to the arbitration of the State. If therefore two Citizens quarrel in, the street they must settle their dispute before the Magistrate, but if they quarrel upon a desert island they are *primâ facie* guilty of no offence by fighting it out. The State to which they belong, although undoubtedly bound to enforce its own Private Law between them upon their return, has no apparent interest in forbidding them to enforce it between themselves during their absence.

## III. Territorial Residence

§ 412. We have next to suppose the case, no longer of a State exercising Jurisdiction over its own Citizens within its own Territory, but of a Citizen belonging to one State who is permitted to reside within the Territory of another. There can be no doubt that whoever enters a Territory which has been occupied by an independent Community for the express purpose of executing Justice within it, must *primâ facie* be taken to have submitted himself to the Jurisdiction of that Community. If therefore a Lilliputian Resident in Blefuscu incurs an Obligation to a Blefuscudian Citizen, it is the Blefuscudian and not the Lilliputian Magistrate by whom the question of his liability must he decided; nor, so long as this Jurisdiction is *bonâ fide* exercised, has the Blefuscudian State any right to interfere in his favour. And even if an adverse decision is fraudulently pronounced by the Blefuscudian Court, it is the Blefuscudian State and not the Plaintiff who will be responsible to the Lilliputian State for the consequences.

§ 413. The next question is, what degree of Sovereignty the Occupant State has acquired over the Resident Foreigner. The answer must clearly depend upon the amount of protection which he receives from the Occupant State. If a Lilliputian Resident in Blefuscu is treated by the Blefuscudian Government, during his Residence, as a Lilliputian Citizen, he may fairly be expected, during his residence, to obey and to support the social system whose benefit he is receiving. In other words he is compellable to serve personally, and to pay taxes upon his Blefuscudian property, for the maintenance of the domestic institutions of the Blefuscudian State, and will be liable to punishment if he transgresses the Blefuscudian Public Law. But he is not compelled to serve the Blefuscudian State in a foreign War, or to pay taxes for the prosecution of such a War; because he is exempt as a Neutral from Reprisals by a foreign enemy, and would be entitled to the protection of his own Government if this right were infringed.

§ 414. But there is, as regards the enactment of Public Law, one obvious distinction between the case of a native and that of a foreign offender. As between the State and the Citizen, Public Law is merely a Command; but, as between the State and the rest of mankind, it may fairly be considered as an Undertaking. The Government may be entitled to say to the Citizen: We punish you because you have broken, not this or that specific Statute, but the general Allegiance which you owe to your country. But the Foreigner is entitled to say to the State: I came here because I believed your assurance that my life and property would not be at the mercy of arbitrary violence, and that I should be safe so long as I did not break certain known regulations. You were at liberty to exclude me, and you were at liberty to admit me upon different terms. But you are not at liberty to hold out an inducement to foreign Immigrants, and afterwards to disregard it upon the plea of your own interest; and, if you do so in my case, I have a right to invoke the protection of my own Government.

§ 415. The same principle will furnish us with an answer to the question, how far a foreign Resident is subject to the arbitrary authority of an absolute Monarch. The Foreigner has of course submitted to be bound for the time being by the social understanding, whatever it may be, which he finds established in his place of Residence. In the present case this understanding must be taken to be, that the Sovereign may act according to his own discretion provided he acts *bonâ fide* for the good of the State. To that extent therefore, but no further, the State to which the Foreigner belongs is precluded from interfering for his protection. If for instance Paul of Russia had fined an Englishman for wearing a round hat in the streets of St. Petersburg, the English Government ought not to have required restitution; because that celebrated Edict was really intended by its crazy author for the public benefit. But if Louis XV. of France had sent an Englishman to the Bastile for speaking disrespectfully of Madame de Pompadour, the English Government might justifiably have insisted upon his liberation; because in this case the act would clearly have been a fraudulent abuse of public authority for the gratification of private malice.

§ 416. This brings us to the question, how far an independent State can be justified upon grounds of public policy in making an express distinction by Law between its own Citizens and Foreigners resident within its territory, to the disadvantage of the latter. The principle upon which the answer must be given seems sufficiently clear. Every independent State has, as we have seen, a right to exclude Foreigners from its dominions;[50] and consequently every State which admits Foreigners into its dominions has a right to deprive them of all or any of the advantages of such admission. If therefore the Blefuscudian Legislature were to enact that no Foreigner shall be capable of acquiring property within the Blefuscudian Territory, or that no Contract between a foreign Resident and a Blefuscudian Citizen shall be held valid in the Blefuscudian Courts, the enactment, absurd and iniquitous as it would be, could not be considered by the Lilliputian Government as a *Casus Belli.* The right to say, You shall not come here, includes the right to say, You shall acquire no benefit by coming here.

§ 417. But no State has a right to deprive a Foreigner entering its dominions of the natural rights which he previously possessed, except so far as such rights are of a kind which it does not recognize in its own Citizens. Nor has any State a right to deprive the foreign Resident, by a new and unforeseen enactment, of rights which he has already acquired upon the faith of their validity by the Law of the land. An enactment that all Foreigners who may hereafter enter the Blefuscudian territory shall be sold as slaves, or even that the property which such Foreigners may bring with them shall be doubly taxed, would justify the Lilliputian Government in resisting its execution by force of arms. And so would an enactment that all property acquired by foreign Residents in Blefuscu shall be confiscated, or that all Contracts between foreign Residents and Blefuscudian Citizens shall be annulled. Exclusion is a right, but punishment for intrusion is an injury; and admission for the purpose of robbery is a breach of faith as well as a breach of justice.

---

[50] See § 382.

§ 418. We are now able to comprehend the true principle of that famous doctrine of International Law which is known as the Rule of 1756.[51] Supposing that the Lilliputian and Blefuscudian States are at War, and that a Lilliputian cruiser intercepts a Neutral trader in the act of carrying on a species of commerce forbidden to Foreigners by the Blefuscudian Law, to what extent can the Captor enforce this Law against the Neutral? The correct answer seems to be, that the liability of the Neutral to the Captor must be measured by that which he has actually incurred to the adverse Belligerent. To that extent he may fairly be considered to hold property belonging to the hostile Government, and this property may lawfully be seized and confiscated by the Captor. Whatever fine, forfeiture, or extraordinary duty the Blefuscudian State might justifiably have exacted from the Neutral may therefore be enforced for the benefit of the Lilliputian State. Nor can the Blefuscudian Legislature prevent the exercise of this right by repealing the prohibitory Law during or in contemplation of the War, since this would be the abandonment of a prerogative upon which the enemy has already acquired a claim.

§ 419. The next step is to suppose that the Lilliputian Immigrant returns home after committing an offence or incurring an Obligation within the Blefuscudian Territory. His person is now within the exclusive Jurisdiction of his own. State, and with that Jurisdiction the foreign State has of course no right to interfere. Nor, if he is *bonâ fide* tried and acquitted by the Lilliputian Courts, can the Blefuscudian State complain of the decision upon the ground of error. But there can be no doubt, whatever may be the present usage upon the subject, that every independent State is bound in justice not to annul the foreign obligations of its Citizens. If therefore the Lilliputian State refuses to take cognizance of the Blefuscudian claim, the Blefuscudian Government will be justified in taking means to enforce it

---

[51] See § 334.

within the Lilliputian Territory; and if such enforcement is resisted by the Lilliputian Government, the Blefuscudian Government will have a sufficient ground for the issue of Reprisals.

§ 420. But suppose that the foreign Resident returns home after a Decree against him has been pronounced, but before it can be executed. The Court which pronounced the Decree has of course no Jurisdiction to execute it within the Territory of a foreign State. But upon what principle ought the domestic Court to act, if called upon to do so? It is universally acknowledged that the Decree may fairly be received as *primâ-facie* evidence of the Obligation which it recognizes. It is also acknowledged that its validity must be disallowed if it can be proved to have been procured by fraudulent means, or to have been pronounced by a Court which had not Jurisdiction over the cause. But can the Defendant be permitted to overrule it by evidence of its inconsistency with the true merits of the dispute? It seems very difficult to hold that he cannot. There is surely no reasonable principle which binds one independent State to make a person under its protection comply with the commands of another, without listening to his offer of proof that they are unjust.

§ 421. The situation of a Plaintiff who seeks to reverse in the Courts of a foreign State an unfavourable Decree pronounced by those of his own is certainly less favourable. In this case the unsuccessful Claimant has himself chosen the tribunal by which his claim has been rejected. If he can prove that his confidence was betrayed, he is at liberty to complain of the rejection. Even if he can procure an acknowledgment that the Decree was questionable, and that the Defendant has unfairly avoided a renewed discussion of the case, he may fairly appeal to the one State for the recon-sideration which the other has been prevented from granting. But it does not lie in his mouth to denounce the Jurisdiction which was selected by himself, as either intellectually or authoritatively incompetent. And therefore a suit may fairly be considered as barred by the adverse judgment of a foreign Court, unless the Plaintiff can prove, either that the judgment was procured by fraud, or that the Court which pronounced it is dissatisfied with it.

§ 422. It now only remains to consider the relative Status of two or more Foreigners resident within the Territory of the same State. That the Occupant State has Jurisdiction to determine and enforce their mutual rights cannot be doubted, but it does not follow that they are entitled to require its exercise. The State would have a right to answer: We occupy our Territory for our own exclusive convenience. You have entered it of your own free will, and you are welcome to stay there. But you must not expect us to interfere in your private disputes. From our own Citizens we will see that you sustain no wrong; but, if you quarrel among yourselves, you will have to fight it out just as if you had landed upon a desert island. That such principles of government are equally inhuman and impolitic, and that the few civilized States which profess them have found it necessary to qualify them until they have become no less intellectually absurd, than morally odious, is no doubt true. But it is equally true that any independent State which chooses to practise such barbarous inhospitality may do so without becoming responsible to any human authority.

§ 423. Unfortunately, the rule ascertained by modern International Usage goes much further than this. It is held that every independent State is entitled, not only to refuse all interference in questions of Right arising between Foreigners resident within its dominions, but at the same time to restrain or punish the forcible assertion of such claims by the parties themselves. However firmly the practice may be established, the absurdity of the principle is self-evident. It enables every Nation, if foolish and wicked enough to do so, to use its territory as an inviolable sanctuary for foreign malefactors. It is true that no Nation can be compelled so make its Territorial Occupation a public benefit, but it is equally clear that no Nation can justifiably make it a public nuisance. There are only two allowable courses. The State which protects the Foreigner is doing its duty. The State which leaves the Foreigner to protect himself is exercising its right. But the State which neither protects the Foreigner nor allows him to protect himself is committing a Wrong.

§ 424. From this it follows that one Belligerent cannot exercise his right of Capture over property belonging to the other within the Territory of a Neutral State, and that if he does so the Neutral may justifiably compel him either to make restitution or to submit to arbitration. But it also follows that the spoliated Belligerent is not entitled to require the interference of the Neutral in his favour. It is clear that, if an independent State chooses to permit either private or public War between Foreigners within its Jurisdiction, no human being except its own unfortunate Citizens has any right to complain. But it is equally clear that a State which is not prepared to go this extravagant length has no choice but resolutely to assert its Neutral rights. The slightest partiality will amount to a *Casus Belli.* If you allow my enemy to capture my property upon your coast, you must not complain if I waylay him upon your high road, or in the streets of your metropolis, to fight the matter out. And if you forcibly prevent me from doing so, you make yourself my enemy and justify me in treating you as such.

## IV. Territorial Quasi-Residence

§ 425. In what cases the Status of a resident Foreigner ought to be affected by the peculiarities of his Domiciliary Private Law, is a question which has already been virtually discussed; since it is clear that the Lilliputian Magistrate is bound in equity to apply the Blefuscudian Law to an act done by a Blefuscudian, and the Lilliputian Law to an act done by a Lilliputian, upon precisely the same principles. If the Courts of every Locality which has any Laws peculiar to itself were to insist upon ap- plying those Laws to every question of Right within then Jurisdiction, it is evident that the same dispute would often be liable to several different decisions, as this or that Court chanced to acquire personal authority over the parties concerned. A practice so arbitrary and so favourable to fraud would of course soon become intolerable, and the principle of deciding points of pure Jurisprudence according to the Law of the Forum has therefore been rejected by all civilized Legislatures. In all such cases the only question ought to be, Under what Law did the transaction whose effect is to be determined take place?

§ 426 But it must be remembered, although the exception does not fall within the purpose of the present Work that this rule is only applicable to points of pure Jurisprudence. In ascertaining the facts of a case, every Court must of course be permitted to use those means which it considers the most likely to be successful; and the applicable Law of Procedure and Evidence is therefore that of the Forum in which the proceedings chance to take place. It may however be doubted whether this distinction applies to those arbitrary Laws of Evidence whose object is, not the verification of actual Fact but the substitution of general Probability for special Conjecture. In deciding whether a claim is barred by lapse of time, or whether it can be established by parol evidence or by an unattested instrument, the Law of the Locality and not that of the Forum ought to be the test; since the same transaction would otherwise be valid or invalid according to the place where it happened to be called in question. The reasoning of the best foreign Civilians is upon this point unanswerable, and that of the English Courts has been by no means satisfactory.

§ 427. It is acknowledged that these are questions which the Legislature of every independent State must decide for itself. A State which is at liberty to make its own Law is of course at liberty to adopt or exclude the Law of other States according to its own discretion, and the absurd application of foreign Law is no more a ground for foreign intervention than the absurd enactment of domestic Law. Even to enforce the Law of the Forum would not be a breach of International Justice. An independent State may justifiably say to mankind, Whatever questions of Right are decided here will be decided without reference to any opinions except our own. Such a rule would be harsh and absurd, but if consistently enforced it would be indisputably valid. The whole question is one of private Justice between man and man, and it is only upon the ground of partiality or corruption that one independent State can justifiably complain of its determination by another.

§ 428. Unfortunately, the Publicists of modern Europe have not been consistent in taking this simple view of the subject. They have adopted the opinion, that the dignity of every independent State is indirectly concerned in the due application of its Laws by foreign Courts; and consequently that the decision of such cases is a question, not indeed of International Justice, but of International Comity or courtesy. Unmeaning as this doctrine may appear in theory, it has led to very mischievous consequences in practice. It has given rise to the odious usage of Retorsion, according to which the Lilliputian Legislature, having taken offence because the Lilliputian Law is misapplied by the Blefuscudian Courts, retaliates by directing the Lilliputian Courts to misapply the Blefuscudian Law in precisely the same manner; a cause of resentment, and a mode of displaying it, about as dignified as an enactment that bad French shall be taught at English schools as long as bad English is spoken at Paris. The distinction is altogether absurd, and the phrase of International Comity means considerably worse than nothing.

§ 429. So far as the Personal Allegiance which a Foreigner owes to his own State is consistent with the Territorial Allegiance which he owes to that in which he resides, it will of course continue to bind him; and if he breaks it he may be punished when he returns home. But it does not follow that the foreign State can be required or expected to enforce this Allegiance while he remains abroad. There is an obvious distinction, which all civilized States rightly observe, between those foreign refugees who are private Delinquents and those who are Political offenders. Both are, or may be, equally guilty and justly liable to equal punishment. But the adverse Decree of the State to which they belong is in the former case the decision of a disinterested arbitrator, which ought to be respected until it is proved erroneous. In the other it is the assertion of an interested party, which ought not to be considered as of any weight until it is proved true. The extradition without trial of a political refugee is therefore a wrongful act, and the only civilized State which has recently committed it is justly regarded by all Europe as a dishonoured nation.

§ 430. Strictly speaking, this principle would no doubt apply to all Criminal Judgments. Whatever the original offence of the criminal may have been, the intention of the sentence is, or ought to be, the security of the community from the public consequences of his act. The State which condemns the Delinquent is thus in one sense a party to the Delict, and the uniform refusal of all independent States to execute foreign Criminal Sentences is therefore justifiable. Still there is an obvious distinction between an ordinary Criminal Judgment and a purely Political Command. In the latter case the State has, or may easily have, an adverse interest of its own sufficient to tempt it to an unjust decision. In the former it has no conceivable motive for condemning the culprit, except upon the supposition of his guilt. And therefore a State within whose territory a condemned criminal has taken refuge may fairly consider itself justified in delivering him over for punishment without further trial; provided of course that his offence is one which would have been held justly punishable if he had committed it at his present place of abode, and that there is no evidence of any corruption or partiality in the proceedings against him.

§ 431. The same distinction leads to the conclusion that the Courts of one independent State cannot be required to enforce the Public Law of another, as against a Citizen of the latter resident within the Territory of the former, except so far as they consider it consistent with Natural Justice. We have seen that, in administering justice between individuals, the effect of a given transaction cannot be fairly determined without referring to the Law under which it took place; because, absurd as that Law may be in itself, the parties must be supposed to have acted upon the faith of its existence.[52] But, in administering justice between a foreign State and one of its Citizens, a different principle must be adopted. We are now deciding, not between two independent parties who have entered into certain relations subject to certain antecedent conditions, but between a Superior who has issued a command and an Inferior who has submitted to it. The command of course may be perfectly justifiable, and the disobedience a manifest breach of faith. But a third party who is required to interfere may reasonably insist upon satisfactory proof that this is so.

§ 432. There are unfortunately but too many examples of Public Laws which the State by whom they were enacted has considered necessary to its safety, but which have been regarded with just abhorrence by the rest of mankind. The worst surviving examples are perhaps the Spanish Law of Heresy and the Anglo-American Law of Negro Slavery, but the absurd and odious restrictions which most civilized Nations have imposed upon foreign commerce deserve as little respect from those which understand the truths of Political Economy. Unfortunately, the English authorities have in this direction proceeded to an unjustifiable length. They have decided that a Contract to join in defrauding the revenue of a foreign State is valid in England, and may be the subject of an action in an English Court. Whatever may have been the true ground of this decision, it seems altogether indefensible. There can scarcely be any doubt that an independent State is justified in raising the contributions necessary for its service out of foreign exports and imports; or that the Citizen who evades, or who seeks to procure the evasion of, such a regulation is committing a breach of

---

[52] See § 400.

Natural Justice.

§ 433. The right of every independent State to command the military services of its Citizens will necessarily make some difference in the Status of a Citizen of one Belligerent State resident within the Territory of the other. Thus if Lilliput and Blefuscu are at War, a Blefuscudian Citizen who is found within the Lilliputian Territory may justifiably be detained as a public enemy unless he can prove that his presence there was compulsory or accidental; and, if it appears that his intentions were hostile to the Lilliputian State, he will be liable to criminal punishment as a Spy. But all Blefuscudian Citizens resident within the Lilliputian dominions at the commencement of the War are entitled to a free passage to their own country, unless they can be shown to have used their residence for some hostile purpose. It was by breaking this rule that the greatest Prince and Conqueror of modern times committed his worst offence, and may perhaps have incurred his most irreparable misfortune.

§ 434. To what extent will a resident Foreigner alter his Status by becoming Domiciled in his place of residence? that is to say, by remaining there without the intention to depart at the end of any fixed time or upon the occurrence of any particular event? That the fact of Domicil may easily be of the greatest importance in the interpretation of transactions whose effect depends upon Intention, is of course unquestionable; but with this subject we have at present no concern. The English and Anglo-American Prize-Courts have established the rule, that one Belligerent State is entitled to seize and confiscate the property of a neutral Citizen domiciled in the other. But it is difficult to give full assent to so sweeping a maxim. That the Public Law of the domiciliary State, or its special understanding with the domiciled person, might easily be such as to justify it, may be conceded. But it would be monstrous to hold that, by the simple act of fixing my permanent abode at Naples, I necessarily make myself responsible to all the world for the conduct of the Neapolitan Government.

§ 435. To the entire doctrine of Territorial Jurisdiction over Aliens there are some few obvious exceptions. We have seen that the Citizens of one State, committing acts of hostile violence against those of another, do not become personally responsible if they had the authority of their own Government for the aggression.[53] This rule is clearly applicable to the violation of foreign Territory, and to all acts of lawful hostility committed within it. Supposing then that a Lilliputian army invades the Blefuscudian Territory, and that it is defeated and compelled to surrender, it follows that the prisoners ought to be considered as having only come within the Blefuscudian Jurisdiction at the moment when their capture became complete. In other words, they will be responsible to the Blefuscudian State for their conduct during captivity, and likewise for so much of their previous conduct, whether as against their enemies or as between themselves, as may have been wrongful or criminal in itself; but not for any part of their previous conduct which would have been justifiable if it had not taken place within the Blefuscudian Territory.

§ 436. But an individual cannot of course be exempted from the Jurisdiction of one State by the *clandestine* commands of another. If I enter the territory of a foreign State without showing that I do so otherwise than as an ordinary traveller, I place myself under that State's protection; and by doing so I forfeit my claim to be regarded in any other character. Thus a Lilliputian officer who in time of war enters the Blefuscudian camp in disguise is criminally punishable as a Spy if he did so to procure information, and as a Traitor if he did so to encourage mutiny or desertion. And such was the crime of those ingenious Jacobites who laid a plot to shoot William III. on the road from Kensington to London, and called it attacking the enemy in his winter quarters. Nor will the case be altered when the object of the crime is himself a Citizen of the State which commands it,

---

[53] See § 252.

or even when he went abroad in company with and subject to the secret authority of the offender. For an independent State cannot be deprived of its Jurisdiction, without its own consent, by the voluntary submission of one individual to another.

§ 437. What then will be the consequence if a Foreigner is admitted within the Territory of one State, after fair notice that he is employed in the public service of another? Naturally that he will be exempted from the Jurisdiction of the foreign State so far as, and no farther than, his public character requires him to be so. Suppose for instance that a Lilliputian regiment is permitted to traverse the Blefuscudian Territory, or a Lilliputian ship of war to anchor in a Blefuscudian harbour. It is clear that the Lilliputian soldiers or sailors do not thereby become amenable, as between themselves, to the Jurisdiction of the Blefuscudian State. Nor, supposing Lilliput to be a Belligerent and Blefuscu a Neutral, does the Blefuscudian Government acquire a right to interfere for the liberation of any prisoners of war or captured property which the Lilliputian forces may carry with them. But any act of violence by a Lilliputian soldier or sailor against a Blefuscudian Citizen will be punishable by the Blefuscudian Courts according to Blefuscudian Law. And any act of treacherous hostility by the Lilliputian commander against the Blefuscudian State, although authorized by the secret commands of the Lilliputian Government, will expose the whole party to he treated as pirates and assassins.

§ 438. This reasoning enables us to understand the Status of a foreign Ambassador. An Ambassador is a person employed by one independent State, and received by another, as the agent and representative of the first in transacting international business with the second. And the inconvenience of considering the same person as the representative of one party and the subject of the other is so obvious, that the foreign State which has admitted him in the former character is bound not to treat him in the latter. An Ambassador is therefore exempt from the Jurisdiction of the

State in which he resides; nor can he, without the consent of the Government which he represents, bind himself not to insist upon this privilege. If he incurs an Obligation his own Government must discharge it, and if he commits a crime his own Government must punish it. The utmost which the foreign Government can do is to send him home under arrest, and to insist upon the due performance of justice when he arrives there.

§ 439. Ought an Ambassador's Right of Inviolability to include any and what person besides himself? Whatever the usages of diplomatic courtesy may prescribe, the answer of Natural Justice must be determined by the consideration whether the person in question is one who has the power of exercising, whether directly or indirectly, any influence over the Ambassador's discretion. A subordinate official, if empowered to take, however secretly or sparingly, an independent part in the business of the Embassy, is of course exempt. The same principle applies to all persons whose personal connection with the Ambassador, whether by kindred or by affection, is such as could possibly be used by an unscrupulous Government for the purpose of affecting his conduct by indirect intimidation. And, considered in this point of view, the rule which extends the privilege of the Ambassador to such of his fellow-Citizens as have accompanied him from home seems scarcely too comprehensive. But the immunity usually allowed to his servants hired abroad seems unnecessary, and the protection which the Right of Asylum formerly enabled him to extend to every temporary or casual inmate of his residence was of course a manifest absurdity.

§ 440. There can be no doubt that the Government which employs an Ambassador may allow him to submit to the Jurisdiction of the State which has received him, or even that it may authorize the State which has received him to exercise Jurisdiction over him without his submission. And from this it seems to follow that, when an Ambassador, by the command or with the consent of his own Government, commits an offence against the Law of the State which has received him, he may justly be treated as amenable to the Jurisdiction of that State. If therefore a foreign Ambassador were, in compliance with the secret instructions of his employers, to engage in a conspiracy or rebellion against the State in whose dominions he is resident, he might in my opinion be most justly tried and executed as a Traitor. For in such a case, not only is the representative character of the criminal tainted with fraud and therefore insufficient to protect him, but the State which he represents is itself guilty of an international offence, and can therefore confer no privilege upon its agent in the Wrong.

§ 441. Every individual who is *de facto* the supreme Executive Magistrate of an independent State is considered to be in his own person the International Representative of that State; and therefore, if permitted by a foreign Government to enter its dominions, will not by doing so become subject to the Jurisdiction of the foreign State. The Status of such a foreign Resident is precisely that of an Ambassador, and his constitutional prerogative must be taken as the measure of his representative authority. He may consequently submit to the jurisdiction of the Municipal Courts, provided he has power to permit his own Ambassador to do so. And when, as sometimes happens, a petty Prince is not forbidden by his domestic Status to enter the military service of a foreign Sovereign, it is clear that by doing so he gives full Jurisdiction over his person to the Government whose hired officer he becomes. If for instance the subjects of an Italian Grand-Duke had no right to complain of his acceptance of a commission in the Austrian service, they clearly had no right, as they would probably have had no inclination, to complain of his execution for neglect of duty by sentence of an Austrian Court-martial.

§ 442. What then is the Status of a Foreigner who, though not *de facto* capable of exercising any political authority, is recognized by the Government within whose Territory he resides as the Sovereign *de jure* of an independent State? That of a private individual and nothing more. The peculiar privileges of Sovereigns resident abroad arise, not from any indelible character of personal sanctity which they are considered to possess, but from the nature of the office which they actually discharge. In the case supposed, the exiled Sovereign has no duties whose performance is inconsistent with his subjection to the Jurisdiction of any State within whose Territory he may happen to be. To that Jurisdiction, both civil and criminal, he ought therefore to be held amenable. And if a dethroned King of Lilliput, having taken refuge at the Court of Blefuscu, were by his agents to incite disturbances in the Lilliputian realm, the Lilliputian Government would be justly entitled to insist upon his trial and punishment according to the Blefuscudian Law.

## CHAPTER IV
## EXTRA-TERRITORIAL RIGHTS AND OBLIGATIONS

I have assumed, throughout the preceding Chapter, that the Territory occupied by a State as such is necessarily identical with that occupied by its Citizens as individuals. But it may easily become questionable whether this is so. It is questionable whether the peculiar purposes of National Occupation may not possibly confer upon the Occupant State an exclusive Jurisdiction over Territory which, as regards its Citizens individually, must be considered as unappropriated. It is also questionable whether an independent State may not possibly acquire a certain right of Sovereignty over Territory occupied by persons who are not its Citizens. These questions I shall endeavour to answer in the present Chapter, which will consequently be divided into the two following Sections: I. Extra-Territorial Appropriation. II. Extra-Territorial Sovereignty.

## I. Extra-Territorial Appropriation

§ 443. We begin by assuming the simple fact, that certain Citizens have, by the command or with the authority of the State to which they belong, appropriated certain unoccupied Territory. This fact is sufficient to raise the question, whether the same considerations which have been shown to confer upon the Occupant State a peculiar authority over the occupied Territory may not also be thought to have conferred upon it the same authority over a margin of Territory which has not been individually occupied. It is a question exceedingly simple in itself, but there is no subject upon which the opinions of the speculative Jurist are likely to differ more widely from the actual practice of mankind. The jealous rapacity of despots and democracies has demanded, and the pedantic ingenuity of Civilians has supplied, a theory of National Occupation such as the untutored reason of the emigrant peasant rejects with derision. There is in fact a very striking contrast between the subtle absurdity of the system adopted by European Statesmen, and the equitable wisdom of the customs observed by Canadian lumberers and Australian graziers. No honest man would think of claiming a farm or a pasture, if his title were no better than those upon which great nations are accustomed to claim islands and continents.

§ 444. It is commonly said, and in a certain sense with truth, that the uninhabitable spaces by which the surface of the Earth is intersected are the natural boundaries of independent States. There can be no doubt that, if the political distribution of the human race were to be arranged by general agreement for their common convenience, the Jurisdiction of each distinct Government ought to comprise a distinct tract of habitable land. Every frontier ought to be terminated by a sea, a desert, or a range of mountains. The vast basins of the Amazon and the Hoangho would naturally become mighty Empires, the valleys of the Alps and the Andes would be occupied by groups of confederate Republics, and the Territory of each supreme or subordinate community would be commensurate with the soil drained by some central or tributary river. But the Publicist must not, like the prince in the fable, deduce compulsory obligations from the possible advantages of an imaginary compromise. The theory of Natural Boundaries has been made the foundation of so much sophistry and so much tyranny, that, just and ingenious as in itself it is, its name has become not undeservedly odious to every honest politician.

§ 445. It is to this theory that we owe the monstrous doctrine which recently prevailed, and which the highest authorities consider still to prevail, upon the subject of National Occupation of Territory. It is held that an independent State, by taking possession of an uninhabited tract of seacoast, acquires an exclusive title to all the uninhabited territory which is drained by any river, or by the tributaries of any river, whose mouth is comprehended within the occupied district. From this dogma it follows that, supposing the continent of North America to be uninhabited, a boat's crew of buccaneers would, by occupying a few acres of soil on each side of the mouth of the Mississippi, acquire the right of for ever excluding the rest of mankind from the whole vast region which lies between the Alleghanies and the Rocky Mountains. It also follows that, as between two contiguous colonies belonging to different Nations, the rights acquired by their Occupation will depend, not upon their respective numbers or industry, but upon the geological formation of some unknown wilderness two or three thousand miles inland. The statement of such conclusions is a sufficient refutation of their premises.

§ 446. The true rule is perfectly obvious. Every State or Nation which occupies land becomes entitled to claim Jurisdiction, not only over the territory actually occupied, but over so much of the adjacent territory as may be required for its defence. What extent of territory this definition will include, is of course a question of fact which must depend upon the existing state of military science. But the general principles upon which it is to be answered are sufficiently clear. A Colony acquires, by the occupation of land. Jurisdiction over all contiguous territory whose possession by foreigners would enable them, by any means of warfare known to either party, to render the enjoyment of the colonial Territory impossible or insecure. It is evident that this rule will comprise, not only all inhabitable territory which intersects or immediately surrounds the colonial Territory, but also all uninhabitable territory from which the colonial Territory can be commanded by any manner of military annoyance. Thus the Colonists have a right to say that no Foreigner shall occupy a mountain range, or a tract of desert or seacoast, whose occupation would enable him to attack them with advantage. The physical possibility of receiving injury is the natural measure of the elbow-room required by every national occupation of land.

§ 447. The same principle clearly entitles every State to claim Jurisdiction over any portion of the Sea, or of any inland lake or navigable river, from which its Territory might be commanded or annoyed. But modern International Usage has tacitly, perhaps unwarily, adopted the distance at which the State can *inflict* injury as the measure of its maritime Jurisdiction; and has therefore fixed the limit, not at a cannon-shot from the nearest inhabited or inhabitable coast, but at a cannon-shot from the nearest mud-bank or sand-spit upon which artillery could possibly be planted. The difference is in this case trifling enough, but if the same principle were applied to terrestrial Jurisdiction its consequences might be very serious. The occupation of the valley confers a title to the impending mountain ridge, the title to the ridge would confer a title to the valley which it commands on the other side; and thus, from valley to ridge and from ridge to valley, the actual cultivation of a dozen fields might, in some regions of the Earth, carry with it the constructive possession of a kingdom.

§ 448. It often happens that the mouth of a navigable river is subject to the Jurisdiction of one independent State, and its upper waters to that of another; and there are instances in which one State has Jurisdiction over the mouth of a strait or inlet, and another over the waters of the bay or inland sea to which it leads. In such a case, is the State which holds the communication entitled to obstruct it? Can Turkey at her own caprice exclude Europe from the Euxine Sea, or can Canada and the Southern Confederacy close the St. Lawrence and the Mississippi against the North-Western States? It is a question which has been the subject of many long negotiations and complicated treaties, but which seems capable of being solved by a very simple test. Can any substantial motive be shown for prohibiting the navigation, except the wish to inflict injury upon the States whose subjects would otherwise use it? If so, the prohibition, whether reasonable or not, ought to be respected. If not, it becomes an act of direct hostility, and as such can only be justified by evidence of sufficient provocation.

§ 449. Where the territory of one independent State is separated from that of another by a strait, estuary or navigable river whose centre is within cannon-shot of each shore, the obvious expedient is to divide the presidiary margin equally between the two Jurisdictions. But there seems to be no reasonable foundation for the converse doctrine, that the whole of a strait or river, though more than two cannon-shots in breadth, is subject to the Jurisdiction of the State or States to which its opposite shores belong. Not only can no obvious necessity be shown for such a rule, but its admission would lead to the most perplexing consequences. How is it possible to draw the line between a Strait and an Ocean? And if England is entitled to Jurisdiction over the Bristol Channel and the King's Chambers, why was not Denmark justified in maintaining the same claim over the North Sea between Norway and Iceland, or Portugal over the Atlantic Ocean between Lisbon and Brazil?

§ 450. By many maritime Nations, and by none more pertinaciously than our own, Jurisdiction over certain special tracts of open Sea has been actually claimed. Every English Jurist remembers with regret that the Mare Liberum of the illustrious Grotius called forth a tissue of barbarous sophisms lamentably unworthy of a Selden, and provoked a spiteful attempt at persecution thoroughly worthy of a Stuart. Even Bynkershoek is content to vindicate the freedom of the Seas by alleging the physical impossibility of their permanent occupation; and seems to admit the ridiculous doctrine, that the ships of one Nation might, by incessantly traversing a particular tract of Ocean with the intention of making it their own, acquire the temporary right of prohibiting its navigation by those of any other. But all these tyrannical pretensions have long been at an end; and the few and trifling traces of them which remain are to be justified, not upon the ground of International Law, but upon that of special Treaty or immemorial Usage.

§ 451. We have hitherto supposed the territorial occupation of an independent State to be an unequivocal physical fact, but there are some cases in which it is doubtful or transitory. Every Community of human beings must necessarily, in some shape or other, depend for subsistence upon the produce of the soil. But in some regions of the Earth there exist national Communities which do not occupy for this purpose any fixed portion of territory. The more savage of these migratory Tribes wander from place to place in search of game and natural produce; the more civilized in search of pasture for their sheep or cattle. In either case their migrations usually include an immense tract of country, and it frequently happens that in these tracts are comprised districts admirably adapted for cultivation. These facts bring us to the examination of that peculiar form of Territorial Right which is known to Anglo-American Jurists as the Indian Title. Are a few hundred families of hunters or shepherds to monopolize for ever the valleys of a mighty continent? or are they to be deliberately trampled into annihilation by the irresistible influx of some great agricultural people?

§ 452. The solution of this question has involved much guilt and much misery, but it would be far from difficult if mankind were really anxious to comprehend and to respect each other's rights. The migratory Tribe has already acquired, by the fact of its prior enjoyment, a title to the undisturbed derivation of subsistence from the natural resources of an ascertainable portion of the Earth. This title the agricultural Immigrant is bound in justice not to violate. He is at liberty to cultivate so much of the soil as can be spared, and he may of course select whatever locality he pleases for this purpose. But he is guilty of unjustifiable intrusion if he does not leave sufficient space for the hunting-grounds or pastures of the aboriginal inhabitants. And if it should appear that he has transgressed this limit, he becomes bound to make good to his wandering neighbours the subsistence which he has wrongfully withdrawn from them.

§ 453. But can a right of exclusive Jurisdiction be conferred upon a State by an act which is insufficient to confer *any* right of property upon an individual? It is usually maintained that the Discovery of an uninhabited territory, by a person commissioned to take possession of such territories on behalf of an independent State, will vest in that State an inchoate right of Dominion which may be converted into a complete right by the colonization of the discovered territory within a reasonable space of time. And this may be pronounced an admissible doctrine, if it is understood as confined to those cases where the Discoverer is sent out with the *bonâ-fide* intention of finding a location for the immediate settlement of a Colony. For in such a case the Discoverer, or the State whose agent he is, has clearly incurred risk and toil with the result of increasing the material resources of the human race, and the benefit of that result is primarily due, so long as it is not forfeited by neglect, to those by whose exertions it was obtained.

§ 454. But the Right of Discovery has been practically asserted in a very different shape. It has been contended that a public officer properly authorized may, by landing upon a previously undiscovered coast and declaring his intention of taking possession, confer upon the State by which he is employed a right of Dominion, which will authorize that State to exclude all foreign settlers from the discovered territory so long as the intention of ultimately occupying it shall continue. And this doctrine, monstrous as it is, has recently been exaggerated by a great Transatlantic Commonwealth; which seriously claimed exclusive Dominion over the whole territory drained by a first-rate river, upon the pretext that, many years before, an American merchant-ship had accidentally discovered its mouth. Not more absurd, and far less dangerous, was the dogma of the Canonists, that the Pope, as Lord Paramount of the whole Earth, is authorized to distribute its uninhabited territory at his own discretion.

§ 455. The same distinction will be found applicable to the temporary occupation of extra-National territory by a party of emigrant Citizens. It may be conceded that such a party, leaving home by the order and in the service of their Government, will carry about with it, so long as it does not enter the Territory of any other State, the exclusive Jurisdiction of its own. For the external acts of a national expedition the State which sends it forth is clearly responsible, and as between themselves its members are of course bound to submit to the discipline imposed by their employers. But there seems to be no good reason for extending the rule to a party of Citizens who leave home together for the purpose of attempting a private enterprise. Such a company of adventurers may no doubt be restrained by the Public Law of the State to which they belong from invoking or submitting to foreign interference. But who is to tell me that I must stand by and see murder committed, because some Legislature at the Antipodes has forbidden me to prevent it?

§ 456. The decisions of modern International Law upon this subject are totally irreconcileable with each other.

It is settled that any independent State may punish an act of piracy upon the High Seas, without the consent of the State to which the pirate belongs. It is also settled that the Courts of one independent State have no jurisdiction to punish a crime committed upon the High Seas on board a private ship belonging to another. But between these two established rules there are several intermediate questions which are still in dispute. The right of a Belligerent State to compel the services of its own Citizens, if found on board a Neutral vessel at sea, has been steadily maintained by one great maritime nation and resolutely denied by another. And the right of a Belligerent cruiser to seize hostile property under the same circumstances, though long successfully asserted, seems now likely to be abandoned as a concession to the general convenience of a commercial age.

§ 457. The distinction, that a private ship at sea is liable to foreign Jurisdiction as regards her dealings with other ships but not as regards the dealings of her crew with each other, is certainly by no means satisfactory; but still, if clearly established by International Usage, it would be perfectly intelligible. We can understand, though we may not approve, a Law which permits a British cruiser to enforce British rights against an American merchantman, but which forbids her to prevent the captain of an American merchantman from slaughtering his own crew. But the distinction, that a private ship at sea may be punished by foreign interference for piracy but not prevented from otherwise infringing foreign rights, is undeniably self-contradictory. If the deck and ribs of a floating vessel have really the magical property of excluding Natural Justice from the space within, why can they not protect a pirate? If they have not, upon what conceivable principle can they protect a deserter?

§ 458. It is scarcely worth while to notice the absurd opinion, that an independent State can, by permitting private to sail under the Convoy or protection of public ships, communicate to the former the peculiar privileges of the latter. A public ship at sea is exempt from foreign Jurisdiction because, however wrongful her proceedings may be, she cannot be searched or detained without obvious risk of injury to the State in whose service she is. But how can this reasoning be applied to a merchantman under her Convoy? If we have no right to prevent an English trader from being searched by a Federal cruiser, how can we acquire such a right by the mere form of commissioning an English man-of-war for the purpose? That act will not give us any interest in the convoyed ship which we had not before. But the truth is that the doctrine has never been seriously asserted, except by rivals prepared to commit, or by theorists resolved to maintain, any injustice which could possibly interfere with the naval superiority of the English nation.

## II. Extra-Territorial Sovereignty

§ 459. There can be no doubt that one Belligerent will be justified in confiscating all moveable property, unless proved to belong to a Neutral, which he can succeed in capturing within the Territory of the other. But mere predatory incursions, though not forbidden by Natural Justice, are a savage and miserable mode of exacting Satisfaction. The only form of Territorial Reprisal which a civilized Government can worthily adopt, is the permanent military Occupation of the whole, or of some sufficiently valuable portion, of the enemy's Territory. By such a measure the Occupant acquires a temporary Sovereignty over the occupied Territory, and therefore becomes bound in justice to treat it during the Occupation as if it were his own. He must not impose any form or amount of contribution upon the inhabitants which the hostile Government itself, supposing it willing to discharge his claim of its own accord, would not have been justified in imposing; and he must support by his authority the due administration, according to the Law of the hostile State, of private Justice.

§ 460. But the military Occupant, although bound to

treat the occupied Territory as in other respects his own, is not precluded from continuing to exercise his right of Reprisals against the residuary population of the hostile State. He may therefore confiscate all movable property, found within the occupied province, which belongs to any Citizen of the hostile State resident elsewhere. He may also compel for his own benefit the payment or performance of all Debts or obligations, due from any person resident within the occupied province to any Citizen of the hostile State resident elsewhere; and the hostile State will be bound, upon recovering possession of the occupied province, to allow such payment or performance as a valid discharge. And he may confiscate the produce of all immovable property situate within the occupied province, but belonging to Citizens of the hostile State resident elsewhere. But of course he cannot confer a valid title, beyond the term of his own occupation, upon a purchaser of such property; because his Sovereignty, not being recognized by the enemy, can only be regarded as commensurate with his physical power.

§ 461. Does a military Occupant acquire any and what claim upon property situate within the Jurisdiction of a neutral State, but belonging to a Citizen of the occupied Territory? That he can relinquish the title so as to bind the proprietor, or that his neglect to enforce it can bar the proprietor by Prescription, is only to be maintained upon the principle that War justifies wanton destruction; and is therefore an opinion utterly unworthy of a civilized Publicist. Nor can it be thought that a partial or precarious Occupation will justify the Occupant in requiring delivery of the hostile property by the Neutral, or even the Neutral in making it to the Occupant; since in this case the general event of the struggle is still undecided, and to concede its fruits is to prejudge its merits. But it may fairly be contended that, where the entire Territory of one State is *de facto* subjugated by the irresistible power of another, the Conqueror has become entitled, not to destroy his opponent's foreign rights, but to appropriate them by way of Satisfaction; and consequently that payment to him may be required from, and will discharge, his opponent's foreign Obligors.

§ 462. But in no case and upon no pretence whatever can a successful Belligerent claim the right of appropriating, by way of Satisfaction, a territory which he has occupied for that purpose. If titles by conquest have ever been treated as valid, it has been in semi-barbarous times or by lax and unscrupulous Publicists. No principle of Natural Justice is more clearly established than that an Obligee, not being a purchaser, cannot by any act of his own make himself so. Now a Complainant who occupies the territory of the Delinquent is, to all intents and purposes, an Obligee taking the property of his obligor in execution. When the amount due is satisfied, he is bound to make restitution. Until it is satisfied, he is entitled to retain possession. But he cannot substitute a perpetual right of Dominion for a definite claim to compensation. In such cases the question is, not whether the existence of Hostilities will enable the Obligee to acquire a title which would in time of peace have been invalid, but whether it will not invalidate, upon the ground of undue pressure, a cession by the Obligor which might in time of peace have been effectual.

§ 463. Still it does not follow from this, that the Status of a Conqueror is one which Natural Justice cannot recognize. The State which destroys the independence of another cannot be said to have acquired a title, but it has undoubtedly incurred a most serious obligation. It is bound in justice to protect the conquered population, so long as they require and desire its protection, in the same manner as it protects its own Citizens. Such is clearly the position of the English Government in India. We have acquired there, for the most part by very unjustifiable means, an Empire which we now find at least as troublesome as it is profitable. But it does not follow that we are justified in relinquishing it. The man who has kidnapped a child cannot make reparation by turning it out of doors. Recent events have proved that our Indian subjects generally regard us, not certainly with affection and perhaps scarcely with respect, but still as for the present their only accessible protectors. It is upon this ground that we are for the present bound to protect them.

§ 464. The Law of War, as at present defined by International Usage, permits a Belligerent, by the formal establishment of a Blockade for that purpose, to exclude Neutral commerce from any territory in the occupation of his enemy. It is universally allowed that a Blockade is valid, not only when established for some distinct and ulterior military object, but when intended for the sole purpose of injuring the enemy by destroying his foreign trade. Nor is this, like some belligerent practices not yet formally abandoned, a mere obsolete relic of medieval violence. The best modern authorities have declared that the principle of Commercial Blockade is lust and necessary, and one great North-American power is at the present moment maintaining such a Blockade along the entire coast of another. But it is my firm conviction that a better age than the present will look back with astonishment, not merely at the injustice and inexpediency of the doctrine, but at its entire want of logical perspicuity and precision.

§ 465. It is conceded, as we have already seen, that one Belligerent has no right to prohibit Neutrals from trading with the other.[54] But it is maintained that, by stationing a certain force at a certain place for that express purpose and by giving notice to the Neutral State that he has done so, he acquires such a right. Suppose for example that France and England are at war. An English frigate, cruising in the Bay of Biscay in order to stop American merchantmen bound to Bordeaux, is committing a breach of International Law. But an English fleet, anchoring off the Garonne with the selfsame intention, is acting quite justifiably. Surely such a

---

[54] See § 248.

distinction is utterly absurd. There is, upon the face of the hypothesis, no justification whatever in the one case which does not exist in the other. The only real difference is, that the fleet suppresses Neutral commerce much more effectually and extensively than the frigate. But if the suppression is unjustifiable, so much the worse. Completeness and deliberation cannot make a wrong act right, though they may make a wrong act more wrong.

§ 466. It is acknowledged that a Commercial Blockade, in order to be valid, must be physically effective. The strict conclusion from this admission seems to be, that the Blockade is ineffective if a single ship can be shown to have evaded it. But such a rule would put an end to the whole practice. The professors of International Jurisprudence are therefore compelled to establish some test of the effective character of a Blockade, other than the plain question whether it has really proved effective or not. The result of this singular necessity has been that utter confusion which must always arise when Description is substituted for Definition. We are told that a Blockade is not effective unless the risk of an attempt to enter the place is manifest and great; unless an adequate blockading force is actually present; unless the blockading ships form an arc of circumvallation round the entrance of the port. In other words, we get two or three unknown quantities in exchange for one, and are then expected to solve the equation. It is lamentable to find the most accomplished of English Jurists reduced, by the absurdity of International Law, to the expedient of thus answering one enigma by proposing another.

§ 467. The truth is, that the phrase Effective Blockade is one of those which are from their nature incapable of definition. It has, in the language of metaphysicians, no objective meaning whatever. In other words it is capable, according to the circumstances of the case, of many different meanings. In order to determine whether a given Blockade is effective, we must first answer the question, Effective for what purpose? For the purpose of excluding Neutral commerce? For that purpose no Blockade is either thoroughly effective or wholly ineffective. A Blockade by a single gunboat is quite enough to make the approach of a commercial harbour insecure. A Blockade by a hundred sail of the line is not enough to make its entrance physically impossible. Even if we admit the possibility of an effective Commercial Blockade, we find ourselves unable to fix the test of its existence. Strictly speaking, there is no such thing. Popularly speaking, there is nothing of the kind which may not be termed so.

§ 468. But of course it must often happen that the commerce of a Neutral within the Territory of one Belligerent finds itself in conflict with the military operations of the other. In such a case which is to give way? There can be only one answer. The maxim, that Belligerent operations must be subject to the freedom of Neutral commerce, would give every nation which is commercial irresponsible power over every nation which is not. It would be utterly impossible to attack with effect such a city as London is, or as Venice was; and any great trading community might therefore insult the whole world without serious danger. The sound rule obviously is, that whoever trades with foreigners must do so subject to the chance of War, and to the consequent necessity of doing nothing to impede the proceedings of the hostile Belligerent. If he attempts such an act inadvertently, he may justifiably lie prevented, at whatever loss or inconvenience to himself, from completing it. But if he attempts it intentionally, he may justifiably be treated as a Citizen, combatant or non-combatant according to circumstances, of the State whose cause he has adopted.

§ 469. Upon this principle is founded the Right of Military Blockade. It is justly held that any Belligerent State, being engaged in an operation whose success requires the absence of external communication with a locality occupied by its enemy, may lawfully forbid all persons whatever to attempt such communication. In such a case the prohibited attempt becomes a Breach of Blockade. If it is made in ignorance of the Blockade, the Neutral can only be prevented from entering the blockaded place; but if it is made with notice it becomes an act of hostility, and the property carried by the Neutral is therefore liable to capture and confiscation as that of an enemy. The English Prize-Courts have even decided that a Neutral ship which puts to sea with the intention of breaking a Blockade is thereby guilty of breaking it, and is consequently liable to capture until her intention has been clearly abandoned. The doctrine has been thought harsh, but apparently without reason. The intention being admitted, any visible act which conduces to the fulfilment of that intention, and which has no other apparent or conceivable motive, must be considered as an attempt to fulfil it; and the attempt to fulfil a wrongful intention is of coarse a Wrong.

§ 470. The simple rule, that a Blockade is only justifiable so far as it is necessary for the success of some independent military operation, would exclude all moral injustice and all practical inconvenience. The Neutral cannot complain of a Belligerent who merely says: Trade as you will with the other side, hut trade so as not to impede my operations; it is my business to attack my enemy, and yours to keep out of my way. Nor can he reasonably dispute the effective character of a Blockade which is practically recognized by the enemy himself. If an English fleet is blockading a French squadron in Brest, the question is whether the blockaded ships have actually been prevented from putting to sea. If the Allied forces are besieging Sebastopol, the question is whether there is a reasonable prospect of taking the place, and whether the Blockade of the harbour is necessary for the purpose. In either case it is easy to distinguish an effective from a colourable Military Blockade.

§ 471. There can be no doubt that one independent State may, by a Treaty of Union, abdicate its independence and place its Territory under the Sovereignty of another; or that such a Treaty, although it cannot transfer the personal Allegiance of a Citizen who has not assented to it, will bind him so long as he resides within the united territory. And the same purpose may be effected upon equal terms by the conclusion of a Federal Union between two independent States, by which each of the contracting parties vests a certain portion of its Sovereign authority in a central Government appointed for the common benefit. So one independent State may, either by an express Treaty of Cession or by a tacit act of acquiescence, transfer to another its Sovereignty over a certain part of its Territory; provided that the inhabitants of the ceded province, or that portion of them in which the supreme Authority would reside if it were an independent State, consent to the transfer. Nor, upon the principles already laid down, can such a Cession, be considered as rescinded, except during the continuance of hostilities, by a subsequent War between the parties.[55]

§ 472. Can one independent State justifiably oppose, or justifiably require indemnification for, a Treaty of Union or of Cession between two others, upon the pretext that it will alter the Balance of Power to their advantage? Just as much as one independent State can justifiably complain, upon the same ground, of the internal peace and prosperity of another. The present generation of Englishmen has seen, with disdainful astonishment, the avowal of this hateful doctrine by foreign statesmen professing Liberal principles of government. Let us be thankful that our own rulers have long ago learnt, not perhaps the disinterested generosity which rejoices when others thrive at its own expense, but at least the manly and enlightened policy which teaches that the welfare of the customer is the welfare of the trader, and that the strength which consists in the weakness of others is a contemptible imposture. England is said to be selfish, and there is a sense in which the accusation may possibly be true; but the difference is infinite between the selfishness of a worldly man and the selfishness of a greedy child.

§ 473. The only motive which will justify the interfer-

---

[55] See § 265.

ence of one independent State for the purpose of preventing a Treaty between two others, is the belief that one of the contracting parties is acting under compulsion. A Treaty of Union between a strong and a weak State, or even a gratuitous Cession of Territory by a weak State to a strong one, may be a valid, but is undoubtedly a suspicious transaction. In such cases it is the right of all independent States, and it may become the duty of all independent States whose interests are affected by the change, to offer their mediation to the weaker party; and not to withdraw it until they are satisfied that no undue influence has been, or can be, exercised by the stronger. Motives of policy may of course excuse their non-interference, just as motives of policy might excuse one State for looking on while another is openly robbed by a third. But the cases are precisely parallel, and no apprehended scarcity of cotton which would not justify neutrality in the one case can justify it in the other.

§ 474. It is possible that the mutual relations of two independent, or nominally independent. States may he such as to disable them from. concluding a valid Treaty. Such is the situation of two Belligerents, one of whom has by his superior military force subjugated the entire Territory of the other. And such, to a certain degree, is that of an agricultural Colony and a migratory Tribe, whose settlements and hunting-grounds intersect each other. But even in such cases as these the subject population may do by their individual conduct what they have lost the power of doing by a corporate act. If they, or that portion of them which has power to bind the whole, accept the benefits and claim the rights which are offered them by the dominant State, they cannot afterwards treat its authority as that of a usurper. And even when this has not taken place, their subjection is undoubtedly sufficient to prevent them from conferring, as against the dominant State, any Territorial Sovereignty upon a third party.

§ 475. We will take the example which naturally occurs to every English reader. Seven centuries ago, Ireland was unjustly invaded and subjugated by England. It may be conceded that nothing deserving the title of an Irish State, or of an Irish Government, has during that time existed. But no impartial Moralist will deny that the Irish Nation has, not as an independent State but as a collection of human beings, voluntarily and deliberately recognized the authority of the British Government Again and again they have publicly and solemnly claimed and exercised the rights of British subjects. They have met by millions to vote, or to influence the votes of others, at elections for the British Parliament. They have met by millions to petition the British Crown, and to threaten secession from the British Empire in case of refusal. The significance of such acts cannot be mistaken. Those who have done them may complain of domestic misgovernment, but they must not talk of foreign Conquest. If Ireland separates from England it must be as Virginia separated from Massachusetts, not as Poland might separate from Russia.

§ 476. This brings us to a question, recently the subject of eager discussion throughout the civilized world, and still the source of terrible misfortune to a great Empire. Suppose that the inhabitants of a province or district, comprised within the Territory of an independent State, unanimously determine, whether for the purpose of forming an independent State of their own or of annexing themselves to another already in existence, to secede from the community. How far, in the absence of positive Constitutional Law, is such a Secession authorized by Natural Justice?. Put in this simple form, the question is one which no Moralist will hesitate to answer. The formation of a State is not a mere partnership for a temporary purpose, but a solemn social compact intended to last for ever. If a certain number of the parties desire to put an end to its existence so far as they are concerned, they can only do so by removing themselves from its operation or by procuring the consent of their fellow-Citizens to its dissolution. The national Territory cannot be dismembered except by the act of the Nation.

§ 477. But in this simple form, I need scarcely add, the question is never likely to be put. No body of rational beings will ever forfeit the sympathy of mankind by openly acknowledging that they wish to renounce their Allegiance from motives of mere caprice. Every Secessionist party will naturally take care to bring forward grave accusations of wilful and fraudulent misgovernment against the State from which it wishes to secede; and there can be no doubt that such misgovernment, if admitted or proved, would be fully sufficient to justify the attempt of Secession. But that such misgovernment will never be admitted, and can seldom be indisputably proved, is as certain as that it will always be alleged. The question therefore depends upon the principles already laid down concerning other internal dissensions.[56] If the Secessionists have a reasonable prospect of effecting their object by military force, their attempt to do so will be Civil War. If not, it will be Rebellion.

§ 478. But it is impossible to pass from the subject without remarking that, whatever may be the strict Justice of the case as between the parties concerned, a peculiarly heavy moral responsibility will always be assumed by a State which attempts to prevent Secession by force of arms. A nation hard pressed by external assailants may of course be compelled to cling desperately to a disaffected province, not as a territory which she wishes to subdue, but as an outwork which she dares not surrender. But excluding, as we have hitherto excluded, the element of foreign hostility, it is difficult to suggest any justifiable motive for the reconquest of a dependency which has unanimously revolted. The conversion of Citizens into rivals is an evil, but the conversion of Citizens into slaves would be a far greater evil. And such an attempt, if unnecessary, would be among the greatest crimes which a State can commit. It could spring from nothing but national pride and passion, and

[56] See § 346, 347.

could end in nothing but national disgrace and ruin.

§ 479. But there is, or at least there easily may be, a very important difference between the international consequences of a Secession and that of an ordinary Revolution. A strictly domestic Revolution may conceivably occur, and indeed often has occurred, without causing the slightest alteration in the relations previously existing between the revolutionized State and the rest of mankind. The substitution by military force of one Government for another, though it must always be a subject of some anxiety to the weaker neighbours of the State in which it takes place, may not require, or even justify, any change in their external policy. But in the case of a Civil War for the purpose of Secession, the question is whether a certain territory is to be considered as belonging to one, or to more than one, independent State. This question is one which directly affects the policy of every foreign State whose Citizens have any intercourse with the inhabitants of the disputed province, and which therefore every such State must sooner or later answer.

§ 480. In the first place, it will become necessary to decide whether the seceding province is to be recognized as a Belligerent or not. This is, as we have already seen, a question of fact which must depend upon the military possibilities of the case. But its affirmative decision, whether right or wrong, is far from possessing the significance which has sometimes been absurdly attributed to it. It binds the recognizing State to nothing whatever. It is in fact, considered as an international transaction, a mere nullity. Correctly understood, it is nothing but a public notice that the recognizing State has formed a certain judgment concerning certain facts, and that its public servants are therefore to be held exempt from personal responsibility in acting accordingly. It means no more than this: These men are at War for a purpose with whose justice we have nothing to do; but we are of opinion that they have shown a strength and a determination which entitle them to be treated as a

Belligerent power, or in other words as a combatant body whose chance of success is so good that they may fairly call upon all men who are not their enemies to stand aside and let them fight it out.

§ 481. In the second place, the success of a Secessionist War will make it necessary to decide how soon the seceding province is to be recognized as an Independent State. This is of course a question which every foreign State must decide upon the evidence before it. The rights of an independent State arise from the fact of its independence, and not from the formal Recognition of that fact by its neighbours If the foreigner believes that there is, or that there is not, a chance of subduing the seceding province, nobody can blame him for not professing to believe otherwise. But in either case he acts at his peril. The seceding province may possibly find itself able to say, as the French Republic said to Austria, that those who deny its existence are ridiculous, and that those who dare to act upon the denial will be insane. Or the dominant State may succeed in convincing the world, as England convinced the American sympathizers with the Canadian insurrection, that in acknowledging the Secession it has mistaken a vision for a reality. In either case the mere fact of Recognition or non-Recognition will of course, except as regards the individuals who may have acted upon it, become utterly insignificant.

Made in United States
Troutdale, OR
11/03/2026

56844514R00193